the lila guide

by PARENTS *for* PARENTS

baby-friendly atlanta area

NEW PARENT SURVIVAL GUIDE TO SHOPPING, ACTIVITIES, RESTAURANTS AND MORE...

2ND EDITION

LOCAL EDITOR: LISSA POIROT

PUBLISHED BY THE LILAGUIDE/OAM SOLUTIONS, INC.
SAN FRANCISCO, CA WWW.LILAGUIDE.COM

Published by:
OAM Solutions, Inc.
139 Saturn Street
San Francisco, CA 94114, USA
415.252.1300
orders@lilaguide.com
www.lilaguide.com

ISBN. 1-932847-11-1
First Printing: 2005
Printed in the USA

table of contents

No, for the last time, the baby does not come with a handbook. And even if there were a handbook, you wouldn't read it. You'd fill out the warranty card, throw out the box, and start playing right away. Until a few hours passed and you were hit with the epiphany of, "Gee whiz honey, what in the wide, wide world of childcare are we doing here?"

Relax. We had that panicked thought when we had our daughter Delilah. And so did **all the parents** we talked to when they had their children. And while we all knew there was no handbook, there was, we found, a whole lot of **word-of-mouth information**. Everyone we talked to had some bit of child rearing advice about what baby gear store is the most helpful. Some **nugget of parenting wisdom** about which restaurant tolerates strained carrots on the floor. It all really seemed to help. Someone, we thought, should write this down.

And that's when, please pardon the pun, the lilaguide was born. The book you're now holding is a guide **written by local parents for local parents**. It's what happens when someone actually does write it down (and organizes it, calculates it, and presents it in an easy-to-use format).

Nearly 7,500 surveys have produced this first edition of **the lilaguide: Baby-Friendly Atlanta Area**. It provides a truly unique insider's view of over 1,100 "parent-friendly" stores, activities, restaurants, and service providers that are about to become a very big part of your life. And while this guide won't tell you how to change a diaper or how to get by on little or no sleep (that's what grandparents are for), it will tell you what other **local parents have learned** about the amazing things your city and neighborhood have to offer.

As you peruse these reviews, please remember that this guide is **not intended to be a comprehensive directory** since it does not contain every baby store or activity in the area. Rather, it is intended to provide a short-list of places that your neighbors and friends **deemed exciting and noteworthy**. If a place or business is not listed, it simply means that nobody (or not enough people) rated or submitted information about it to us. **Please let us know** about your favorite parent and baby-friendly businesses and service providers by participating in our online survey at **www.lilaguide.com**. We always want your opinions!

So there you have it. Now go make some phone calls, clean up the house, take a nap, or do something on your list before the baby arrives.

Enjoy!

Oli & Elysa

Oli Mittermaier & Elysa Marco, MD

PS

We love getting feedback (good and bad) so don't be bashful. Email us at **lila@lilaguide.com** with your thoughts, comments and suggestions. We'll be sure to try to include them in next year's edition!

We'd like to take a moment to offer a heart-felt thank you to all the **parents who participated in our survey** and took the time to share their thoughts and opinions. Without your participation, we would never have been able to create this unique guide.

Thanks to our extra helpful Atlanta area contributors **Elizabeth Compton**, and **Beth Lawton** for going above and beyond in the quest for hip tot spots.

Thanks also to **Lisa Barnes**, **Nora Borowsky**, **Todd Cooper**, **Amy Iannone**, **Katy Jacobson**, **Felicity John Odell**, **Shira Johnson**, **Kasia Kappes**, **Jen Krug**, **Dana Kulvin**, **Deborah Schneider**, **Kevin Schwall**, **April Stewart**, and **Nina Thompson** for their tireless editorial eyes, **Satoko Furuta** and **Paul D. Smith** for their beautiful sense of design, and **Lane Foard** for making the words yell.

Special thanks to **Paul D. Smith**, **Ken Miles**, and **Ali Wing** for their consistent support and overall encouragement in all things lilaguide, and of course **our parents** for their unconditional support in this and all our other endeavors.

And last, but certainly not least, thanks to **little Delilah** for inspiring us to embark on this challenging, yet incredibly fulfilling project.

disclaimer

This book is designed to share parents' opinions regarding baby-related products, services and activities. It is sold with the understanding that the information contained in the book **does not represent the publisher's opinion** or recommendations.

The reviews contained in this guide are based on **public opinion surveys** and are therefore subjective in nature. The publisher shall have neither liability nor responsibility to any person or entity with respect to any loss or damage caused, or alleged to have been caused, directly or indirectly, by the information contained in this book.

ratings

Most listings have stars and numbers as part of their write-up. These symbols mean the following:

❺ / ★★★★★	extraordinary
❹ / ★★★★☆	very good
❸ / ★★★☆☆	good
❷ / ★★☆☆☆	fair
❶ / ★☆☆☆☆	poor
✓	available
✗	not available/relevant

If a ☆ is listed instead of ★, it means that the rating is less reliable because a small number of parents surveyed the listing. Furthermore, if a listing has **no stars** or **criteria ratings**, it means that although the listing was rated, the number of surveys submitted was so low that we did not feel it justified an actual rating.

quotes & reviews

The quotes/reviews are taken directly from surveys submitted to us via our website (**www.lilaguide.com**). Other than spelling and minor grammatical changes, they come to you as they came to us. Quotes were selected based on how well they appeared to represent the collective opinions of the surveys submitted.

fact checking

We have contacted all of the businesses listed to verify their address and phone number, as well as to inquire about their hours, class schedules and web site information. Since some of this information may change after this guide has been printed, we appreciate you letting us know of any errors by notifying us via email at **lila@lilaguide.com**.

baby basics & accessories

City of Atlanta

★★★★★

"lila picks"

- ★Baby Cakes Children's Decor 'n More
- ★Bellini
- ★Chickenlips
- ★Chocolate Soup
- ★Crib-it
- ★Kangaroo Pouch
- ★New Baby Products
- ★Oilily
- ★Punkin Patch

April Cornell ★★★½☆

"...beautiful, classic dresses and accessories for special occasions... I love the matching 'mommy and me' outfits... lots of fun knickknacks for sale... great selection of baby wear on their web site... rest assured your baby won't look like every other child in these adorable outfits... very frilly and girlie—beautiful..."

Furniture, Bedding & Decor	✗	$$$	Prices
Gear & Equipment	✗	❸	Product availability
Nursing & Feeding	✗	❹	Staff knowledge
Safety & Babycare	✗	❹	Customer service
Clothing, Shoes & Accessories	✓	❹	Decor
Books, Toys & Entertainment	✗		

WWW.APRILCORNELL.COM

ATLANTA—3500 PEACHTREE RD NE (AT PHIPPS PLZ); 404.848.9195; M-SA 10-9, SU 12-5:30

Babies R Us ★★★★☆

"...everything baby under one roof... they have a wide selection and carry most 'mainstream' items such as Graco, Fisher-Price, Avent and Britax... great customer service—given how big the stores are, I was pleasantly surprised at how attentive the staff was... easy return policy... super busy on weekends so try to visit on a weekday for the best service... keep an eye out for great coupons, deals and frequent sales... easy and comprehensive registry... shopping here is so easy—you've got to check it out..."

Furniture, Bedding & Decor	✓	$$$	Prices
Gear & Equipment	✓	❹	Product availability
Nursing & Feeding	✓	❹	Staff knowledge
Safety & Babycare	✓	❹	Customer service
Clothing, Shoes & Accessories	✓	❹	Decor
Books, Toys & Entertainment	✓		

WWW.BABIESRUS.COM

ATLANTA—1155 MOUNT VERNON HWY (AT PERIMETER MALL); 770.913.0222; M-SA 9:30-9:30, SU 11-7; PARKING IN FRONT OF BLDG

Baby Cakes Children's Decor 'n More ★★★★★

"...the perfect store for finding a nice baby gift... cute clothes, bedding and accessories—perfect for finding a special shower gift... very nice customer service... always offering to help before you have to ask!.. easy delivery... a comprehensive line of baby gear and accessories... a beautiful store with lots of wonderful furniture and custom bedding... you're going to want to buy something here, so plan on spending some money..."

Furniture, Bedding & Decor .... ✓
Gear & Equipment .... ✓
Nursing & Feeding .... ✗
Safety & Babycare .... ✗
Clothing, Shoes & Accessories....... ✗
Books, Toys & Entertainment .... ✓

$$$$ .... Prices
❹ .... Product availability
❹ .... Staff knowledge
❹ .... Customer service
❹ .... Decor

WWW.EBABYCAKES.COM

ATLANTA—1833 PEACHTREE RD NE (AT 28TH ST NW); 404.367.8772; M-SA 10-6; PARKING BEHIND BLDG

Baby Depot At Burlington Coat Factory ★★★½☆

"...a large, 'super store' layout with a ton of baby gear... wide aisles, packed shelves, barely existent customer service and awesome prices... everything from bottles, car seats and strollers to gliders, cribs and clothes... I always find something worth getting... a little disorganized and hard to locate items you're looking for... the staff is not always knowledgeable about their merchandise... return policy is store credit only..."

Furniture, Bedding & Decor .... ✓
Gear & Equipment .... ✓
Nursing & Feeding .... ✓
Safety & Babycare .... ✓
Clothing, Shoes & Accessories....... ✓
Books, Toys & Entertainment .... ✓

$$ .... Prices
❸ .... Product availability
❸ .... Staff knowledge
❸ .... Customer service
❸ .... Decor

WWW.BABYDEPOT.COM

ATLANTA—2841 GREENBRIAR PKWY SW (AT HEADLAND DR SW); 404.349.6300; M-SA 10-9, SU 11-6; PARKING LOT

ATLANTA—4166 BUFORD HWY NE (AT OAK SHADOW DR NE); 404.634.5566; M-SA 10-9, SU 10-6 ; PARKING LOT

BabyGap/GapKids ★★★★☆

"...colorful baby and toddler clothing in clean, well-lit stores... great return policy... it's the Gap, so you know what you're getting—colorful, cute and well-made clothing... best place for baby hats... prices are reasonable especially since there's always a sale of some sort going on... sales, sales, sales—frequent and fantastic... everything I'm looking for in infant clothing—snap crotches, snaps up the front, all natural fabrics and great styling... fun seasonal selections—a great place to shop for gifts as well as for your own kids... although it can get busy, staff generally seem accommodating and helpful..."

Furniture, Bedding & Decor .... ✗
Gear & Equipment .... ✗
Nursing & Feeding .... ✗
Safety & Babycare .... ✗
Clothing, Shoes & Accessories....... ✓
Books, Toys & Entertainment .... ✓

$$$ .... Prices
❹ .... Product availability
❹ .... Staff knowledge
❹ .... Customer service
❹ .... Decor

WWW.GAP.COM

ATLANTA—3393 PEACHTREE RD NE (AT LENOX SQUARE MALL); 404.261.0395; M-SA 10-9, SU 12-6; PARKING IN FRONT OF BLDG

ATLANTA—4400 ASHFORD DUNWOODY RD NE (AT PERIMETER MALL); 770.392.9155; M-SA 10-9, SU 12-6; PARKING IN FRONT OF BLDG

Bellini ★★★★★

"...high-end furniture for a gorgeous nursery... if you're looking for the kind of furniture you see in magazines then this is the place to go... excellent quality... yes, it's pricey, but the quality is impeccable... free delivery and setup... their furniture is built to withstand the abuse my tots dish out... they sell very unique merchandise, ranging from cribs to bedding and even some clothes... our nursery design was inspired by their store decor... I wish they had more frequent sales..."

Furniture, Bedding & Decor	✓	$$$$	Prices
Gear & Equipment	✗	❹	Product availability
Nursing & Feeding	✗	❹	Staff knowledge
Safety & Babycare	✗	❹	Customer service
Clothing, Shoes & Accessories	✗	❹	Decor
Books, Toys & Entertainment	✓		

WWW.BELLINI.COM

ATLANTA—5285 ROSWELL RD NE (AT MARYEANNA DR NE); 404.851.1588; M-SA 10-6 ; PARKING LOT

Buckles ★★★★☆

"...one of the best places to find cool European footwear... wonderful service, quick and accurate with sizing... if you don't mind paying a little more for high-quality shoes for your kids, then this is the store for you... best to go during a sale or when you need something for a special occasion... they do have a frequent buyer program and a twins discounts... the staff is really sweet and helpful..."

Furniture, Bedding & Decor	✗	$$$$	Prices
Gear & Equipment	✗	❹	Product availability
Nursing & Feeding	✗	❹	Staff knowledge
Safety & Babycare	✗	❹	Customer service
Clothing, Shoes & Accessories	✓	❸	Decor
Books, Toys & Entertainment	✗		

ATLANTA—3145 PEACHTREE RD NE (AT MATHIESON RD NE); 404.365.0746; M-SA 10-5; PARKING LOT

Buster Brown Shoes ★★★☆☆

"...they do a superb job at sizing, especially if your kid needs extra-wide or extra-narrow shoes... the selection is definitely better for girls than for boys... kind of expensive, but they do have well-manufactured shoes... good customer service and helpful staff..."

Furniture, Bedding & Decor	✗	$$$	Prices
Gear & Equipment	✗	❸	Product availability
Nursing & Feeding	✗	❸	Staff knowledge
Safety & Babycare	✗	❸	Customer service
Clothing, Shoes & Accessories	✓	❸	Decor
Books, Toys & Entertainment	✗		

WWW.BUSTERBROWNSHOES.COM

ATLANTA—1000 CUMBERLAND MALL (AT RT 407); 770.436.8099; M-SA 10-9, SU12-6

ATLANTA—2003 NORTH LAKE MALL (AT BRIARCLIFF RD); 770.939.9589; M-F 10-9, SU 12-6; PARKING LOT

ATLANTA—2841 GREENBRIAR PKWY SW (AT GREENBRIAR MALL); 404.349.4252; M-SA 10-9, SU12-6

ATLANTA—3393 PEACHTREE RD (AT LENOX RD); 404.237.4967; M-SA 10-9, SU12-6; PARKING LOT

Chickenlips ★★★★★

"...great little shop for unique clothes, toys, and gifts you won't find in department stores... hand-painted furniture, handmade clothing, etc... the customer service is fabulous... pricey, but worth it... friendly atmosphere and beautiful gifts... specialty decor items help individualize kids room... little picket fence area where your child can play while you shop..."

Furniture, Bedding & Decor	✓	$$$	Prices
Gear & Equipment	✗	❹	Product availability
Nursing & Feeding	✗	❹	Staff knowledge
Safety & Babycare	✗	❹	Customer service
Clothing, Shoes & Accessories	✓	❹	Decor
Books, Toys & Entertainment	✓		

ATLANTA—5484 CHAMBLEE DUNWOODY RD (AT THE SHOPS OF DUNWOODY); 770.395.1234; M-F 10-6, SA 10-5

Children's Place, The ★★★½☆

"...great bargains on cute clothing... shoes, socks, swimsuits, sunglasses and everything in between... lots of '3 for $20' type deals on sleepers, pants and mix-and-match separates... so much more affordable than the other 'big chains'... don't expect the most unique stuff here, but it wears and washes well... cheap clothing for cheap prices... you can leave the store with bags full of clothes without putting a huge dent in your wallet..."

Furniture, Bedding & Decor	✗	$$	Prices
Gear & Equipment	✗	❹	Product availability
Nursing & Feeding	✗	❹	Staff knowledge
Safety & Babycare	✗	❹	Customer service
Clothing, Shoes & Accessories	✓	❹	Decor
Books, Toys & Entertainment	✓		

WWW.CHILDRENSPLACE.COM

ATLANTA—1230 CUMBERLAND MALL (AT RT 407); 770.435.6112; M-SA 10-9, SU 12-6; MALL PARKING

ATLANTA—2100 PLEASANT HILL RD NW (AT ORLY TER); 678.584.0030; M-SA 10-9, SU 11-7; PARKING LOT

ATLANTA—4400 ASHFORD DUNWOODY RD NE (AT PERIMETER MALL); 770.671.8675; M-SA 10-9, SU 12-6; MALL PARKING

Children's Shop, The ★★★★☆

"...a place for special and unique items, outfits and gifts... beautiful christening clothes... cute play clothes and you can order a wide variety of monogrammed items (diaper covers, bibs, pillows, etc.)... excellent selection of dresses and shoes... helpful staff... top brands... great selection for boys, better than most... personalized waterproof bibs are very cool..."

Furniture, Bedding & Decor	✗	$$$$	Prices
Gear & Equipment	✗	❹	Product availability
Nursing & Feeding	✗	❹	Staff knowledge
Safety & Babycare	✗	❹	Customer service
Clothing, Shoes & Accessories	✓	❹	Decor
Books, Toys & Entertainment	✓		

ATLANTA—2385 PEACHTREE RD NE (AT JUNCTION AVE NE); 404.365.8496; M-SA 9:30-5:30; PARKING LOT

Chocolate Soup ★★★★★

"...a great place to go and find out-of-the-ordinary items for your kids... the hippest clothes including my favorite brands like Baby Lulu and Le Top... very helpful staff... well worth the visit—their sales are awesome... tons of great merchandise at good prices... unique items—especially for girls... they have great sales, so be sure to sign up for

mailing list... I'm never disappointed and always find something cute... a great variety of designer duds... ”

Furniture, Bedding & Decor	✗	$$$	Prices
Gear & Equipment	✗	❹	Product availability
Nursing & Feeding	✗	❹	Staff knowledge
Safety & Babycare	✗	❹	Customer service
Clothing, Shoes & Accessories	✓	❸	Decor
Books, Toys & Entertainment	✗		

ATLANTA—6681 ROSWELL RD NE (AT ABERNATHY RD NW); 404.303.9047; M W 10-6, T TH 10-8, F-SA 10-6, SU 1-5; PARKING LOT

Consignkidz ★★★½☆

“*...terrific shop whether you want to buy or sell... the staff is wonderful to work with... deals to be had for all things baby or maternity... there is a lot of stuff to fish through to find the right stuff for your child...*”

Furniture, Bedding & Decor	✓	$$	Prices
Gear & Equipment	✓	❸	Product availability
Nursing & Feeding	✓	❸	Staff knowledge
Safety & Babycare	✓	❸	Customer service
Clothing, Shoes & Accessories	✓	❷	Decor
Books, Toys & Entertainment	✓		

ATLANTA—2205 LAVISTA RD NE (AT N DRUID HILLS); 404.929.0222; M-SA 10-5:45; PARKING LOT

Crib-it ★★★★★

“*...fantastic consignment shop for baby gear, crib bedding, nursery furniture and decor... great source for a wide selection of cheap baby equipment... upscale boutique items at reasonable prices... they also carry new merchandise like wooden toys, puzzles and other gift items... great for gently used toys, especially ride-ons... check in regularly for new arrivals... the owners are very friendly and will call you if you are searching for a particular product...*”

Furniture, Bedding & Decor	✓	$$	Prices
Gear & Equipment	✗	❸	Product availability
Nursing & Feeding	✗	❹	Staff knowledge
Safety & Babycare	✗	❹	Customer service
Clothing, Shoes & Accessories	✗	❸	Decor
Books, Toys & Entertainment	✓		

WWW.CRIB-IT.COM

ATLANTA—433 BISHOP ST NW (AT NORTHSIDE DR NW/24TH ST); 404.817.0905; M-SA 10-5; PARKING LOT

Diaper Depot ★★★★☆

“*...absolutely amazing—they have every kind of diaper that you can imagine (for all ages)... they sell diapers and wipes by the case... discounted prices... amazing diapering products that would be hard to find anywhere else... a must see if you want to get a sense of all the diaper-related stuff out there...*”

Furniture, Bedding & Decor	✗	$	Prices
Gear & Equipment	✗	❹	Product availability
Nursing & Feeding	✗	❸	Staff knowledge
Safety & Babycare	✓	❸	Customer service
Clothing, Shoes & Accessories	✗	❸	Decor
Books, Toys & Entertainment	✗		

ATLANTA—2080 PEACHTREE INDUSTRIAL CT (AT PEACHTREE INDUSTRIAL BLVD); 770.986.8928; M-SA 10:30-7; PARKING LOT

Dillard's ★★★★☆

“*...this store has beautiful clothes, and if you catch a sale, you can get great quality clothes at super bargain prices... good customer service* *and helpful staff... a huge selection of merchandise for boys and girls... nice layette department... some furnishings like little tables and chairs... beautiful displays... the best part is that in addition to shopping for your kids, you can also shop for yourself...* ”

Furniture, Bedding & Decor	✓	$$$	Prices
Gear & Equipment	✗	4	Product availability
Nursing & Feeding	✗	3	Staff knowledge
Safety & Babycare	✗	4	Customer service
Clothing, Shoes & Accessories	✓	4	Decor
Books, Toys & Entertainment	✓		

WWW.DILLARDS.COM

ATLANTA—4500 ASHFORD DUNWOODY RD (AT PERIMETER MALL); 678.320.9140; M-SA 10-9, SU 12-6

Disney Store, The ★★★½☆

“*...everything Disney you could possibly want—toys, books, videos, clothes, lithographs and loud Disney music as you shop through the store with your ecstatic tot... giant movie screens show classic Disney movies... perky, friendly staff... can be really busy during weekends and holidays... the best selection of Halloween costumes...* ”

Furniture, Bedding & Decor	✗	$$$	Prices
Gear & Equipment	✗	4	Product availability
Nursing & Feeding	✗	4	Staff knowledge
Safety & Babycare	✗	4	Customer service
Clothing, Shoes & Accessories	✓	4	Decor
Books, Toys & Entertainment	✓		

WWW.DISNEYSTORE.COM

ATLANTA—4800 BRIARCLIFF RD (AT NORTHLAKE MALL); 770.414.5033; M-SA 10-9, SU 12-6; FREE PARKING

Gretchen's Children's Shop ★★★½☆

“*...a sweet 'old-school' store filled with adorable items for tots... Lily Pulitzer, Florence Eisman and other fabulous designers... from nursery gear to dresses and shoes... very cute shop... timeless clothing with available monogramming... beautiful, unique birth announcements... the perfect place to find something for that special occasion... large selection and great customer service... free wrapping...* ”

Furniture, Bedding & Decor	✓	$$$$	Prices
Gear & Equipment	✗	4	Product availability
Nursing & Feeding	✗	4	Staff knowledge
Safety & Babycare	✗	4	Customer service
Clothing, Shoes & Accessories	✓	4	Decor
Books, Toys & Entertainment	✗		

WWW.GRETCHENSONLINE.COM

ATLANTA—1246 W PACES FERRY RD NW (AT NORTHSIDE PKWY NW); 404.237.8020; M-SA 9:30-5:30; PARKING LOT

Gymboree ★★★★☆

“*...beautiful clothing and great quality... colorful and stylish baby and kids wear... lots of fun birthday gift ideas... easy exchange and return policy... items usually go on sale pretty quickly... save money with Gymbucks... many stores have a play area which makes shopping with my kids fun (let alone feasible)...* ”

Furniture, Bedding & Decor	✗	$$$	Prices
Gear & Equipment	✗	4	Product availability
Nursing & Feeding	✗	4	Staff knowledge
Safety & Babycare	✗	4	Customer service
Clothing, Shoes & Accessories	✓	4	Decor
Books, Toys & Entertainment	✓		

WWW.GYMBOREE.COM

ATLANTA—1331 CUMBERLAND MALL (AT RT 407); 770.319.7007; M-SA 10-9, SU 12-6; MALL PARKING

ATLANTA—3393 PEACHTREE RD NE (AT LENOX SQUARE MALL); 404.841.6422; M-SA 10-9, SU 12-6; MALL PARKING

ATLANTA—4400 ASHFORD DUNWOODY RD NE (AT PERIMETER MALL); 770.551.0070; M-SA 10-9, SU 12-6; MALL PARKING

Hanger-roo For Moms And Tots ★★★½☆

"...new and used clothing and gear... babies, kids and maternity wear, too... it's crowded, but the staff really knows what they've got and can help you find what you need... equipment, baby gear, toys, name bracelets... I keep returning and always find a must-have at a price I can afford..."

Furniture, Bedding & Decor	✓	$$$	Prices
Gear & Equipment	✓	4	Product availability
Nursing & Feeding	✓	4	Staff knowledge
Safety & Babycare	✓	4	Customer service
Clothing, Shoes & Accessories	✓	4	Decor
Books, Toys & Entertainment	✓		

WWW.HANGER-ROO.COM

ATLANTA—5352 PEACHTREE RD (AT PIERCE DR NE); 770.451.8911; T-SA 10-4

IKEA ★★★★½

"...the coolest-looking and best-priced bedding, bibs and eating utensils in town... fun, practical style and the prices are definitely right... one of the few stores around that lets kids climb and crawl on furniture... the kids' area has a slide, tunnels, tents... is it an indoor playground or a store?.. unending decorating ideas for families on a budget (lamps, rugs, beds, bedding)... it's all about organization—cubbies, drawers, shelves, seats that double as a trunk and step stool... arts and crafts galore... free childcare while you shop... cheap eats if you get hungry..."

Furniture, Bedding & Decor	✓	$$	Prices
Gear & Equipment	✗	4	Product availability
Nursing & Feeding	✓	4	Staff knowledge
Safety & Babycare	✓	4	Customer service
Clothing, Shoes & Accessories	✗	4	Decor
Books, Toys & Entertainment	✓		

WWW.IKEA.COM

ATLANTA—441 16TH ST (OFF MECASLIN ST); 404.745.4532; DAILY 10-9

Jacadi ★★★★☆

"...beautiful French clothes, baby bumpers and quilts... elegant and perfect for special occasions... quite expensive, but the clothing is hip and the quality really good... many handmade clothing and bedding items... take advantage of their sales... more of a store to buy gifts than practical, everyday clothes... beautiful, special clothing—especially for newborns and toddlers... velvet pajamas, coordinated nursery items... stores are as pretty as the clothes... they have a huge (half-off everything) sale twice a year that makes it very affordable..."

Furniture, Bedding & Decor	✓	$$$$	Prices
Gear & Equipment	✗	4	Product availability
Nursing & Feeding	✗	4	Staff knowledge
Safety & Babycare	✗	4	Customer service
Clothing, Shoes & Accessories	✓	4	Decor
Books, Toys & Entertainment	✓		

WWW.JACADIUSA.COM

ATLANTA—3393 PEACHTREE RD NE (AT LENOX SQUARE MALL); 404.848.0202; M-SA 10-9, SU 12-6; MALL PARKING

JCPenney ★★★½☆

"...always a good place to find clothes and other baby basics... the registry process was seamless... staff is generally friendly but the lines always seem long and slow... they don't have the greatest selection of toddler clothes, but their baby section is great... we had some damaged furniture delivered but customer service was easy and accommodating... a pretty limited selection of gear, but what they have is priced right..."

Furniture, Bedding & Decor	✓	$$	Prices
Gear & Equipment	✓	❸	Product availability
Nursing & Feeding	✓	❸	Staff knowledge
Safety & Babycare	✓	❸	Customer service
Clothing, Shoes & Accessories	✓	❸	Decor
Books, Toys & Entertainment	✓		

WWW.JCPENNEY.COM

ATLANTA—2100 PLEASANT HILL RD NW (AT N CASTLEGATE DR); 770.476.3220; M-SA 10-9, SU 12-6; MALL PARKING

Kangaroo Pouch ★★★★★

"...furniture and clothing store all in one... awesome clothes with a good selection for boys and girls... the best place for hair bows... watch for 'dollar days' sale for good deals... helpful customer service... expensive, but a good place to find a unique baby gift or upscale clothing line... high-end shop with a range of prices... gift wrapping is free..."

Furniture, Bedding & Decor	✓	$$$$	Prices
Gear & Equipment	✗	❹	Product availability
Nursing & Feeding	✗	❹	Staff knowledge
Safety & Babycare	✗	❹	Customer service
Clothing, Shoes & Accessories	✓	❹	Decor
Books, Toys & Entertainment	✗		

WWW.KANGAROOPOUCHATLANTA.COM

ATLANTA—56 E ANDREWS DR NW (AT CAINS HILL PL NW); 404.231.1616; M-SA 10-5; PARKING LOT

KB Toys ★★★☆☆

"...hectic and always buzzing... wall-to-wall plastic and blinking lights... more Fisher-Price, Elmo and Sponge Bob than the eye can handle... a toy super store with discounted prices... they always have some kind of special sale going on... if you're looking for the latest and greatest popular toy, then look no further—not the place for unique or unusual toys... perfect for bulk toy shopping—especially around the holidays..."

Furniture, Bedding & Decor	✗	$$	Prices
Gear & Equipment	✗	❸	Product availability
Nursing & Feeding	✗	❸	Staff knowledge
Safety & Babycare	✗	❸	Customer service
Clothing, Shoes & Accessories	✗	❸	Decor
Books, Toys & Entertainment	✓		

WWW.KBTOYS.COM

ATLANTA—HWY 41 & I-285 (AT CUMBERLAND MALL); 770.434.1805; M-SA 10-9, SU 12-6; MALL PARKING

Kid's Foot Locker ★★★½☆

"...Nike, Reebok and Adidas for your little ones... hip, trendy and quite pricey... perfect for the sports addict dad who wants his kid sporting the latest NFL duds... shoes cost close to what the adult variety costs... generally good quality... they carry infant and toddler sizes..."

Furniture, Bedding & Decor .... ✗
Gear & Equipment .... ✗
Nursing & Feeding .... ✗
Safety & Babycare .... ✗
Clothing, Shoes & Accessories .... ✓
Books, Toys & Entertainment .... ✗

$$$ .... Prices
❸ .... Product availability
❸ .... Staff knowledge
❸ .... Customer service
❸ .... Decor

WWW.KIDSFOOTLOCKER.COM

ATLANTA—1341 CUMBERLAND MALL (AT RT 407); 770.319.1940; M-SA 10-9, SU 12-6

ATLANTA—2841 GREENBRIAR PKWY SW (AT GREENBRIAR MALL); 404.349.9161; M-SA 10-9, SU 12-6

ATLANTA—3383 PEACHTREE RD NE (AT STRATFORD RD NE); 404.237.4950; M-SA 10-9, SU 12-6

Macy's ★★★½☆

"...Macy's has it all and I never leave empty-handed... if you time your visit right you can find some great deals... go during the week so you don't get overwhelmed with the weekend crowd... good for staples as well as beautiful party dresses for girls... lots of brand-names like Carter's, Guess, and Ralph Lauren... not much in terms of assistance... newspaper coupons and sales help keep the cost down... some stores are better organized and maintained than others... if you're going to shop at a department store for your baby, then Macy's is a safe bet..."

Furniture, Bedding & Decor .... ✓
Gear & Equipment .... ✗
Nursing & Feeding .... ✗
Safety & Babycare .... ✗
Clothing, Shoes & Accessories .... ✓
Books, Toys & Entertainment .... ✓

$$$ .... Prices
❸ .... Product availability
❸ .... Staff knowledge
❸ .... Customer service
❸ .... Decor

WWW.MACYS.COM

ATLANTA—1300 CUMBERLAND MALL (AT RT 407); 770.434.2611; M-SA 10-9, SU 12-7; MALL PARKING

ATLANTA—2841 GREENBRIAR PKWY (AT GREENBRIAR MALL); 404.346.2690; M-SA 10-9, SU 12-7; MALL PARKING

ATLANTA—3393 PEACHTREE RD NE (AT LENOX SQ MALL); 404.231.2800; M-SA 10-9, SU 12-7; MALL PARKING

ATLANTA—4300 ASHFORD DUNWOODY RD (AT PERIMETER MALL); 770.396.2800; M-SA 10-9, SU 12-7; MALL PARKING

ATLANTA—4800 BRIARCLIFF RD (AT NORTHLAKE SHOPPING MALL); 770.491.2800; M-SA 10-9, SU 12-7; MALL PARKING

Mad Bug Clothing Co ★★★☆☆

"...great place for hip moms and well-dressed tots... they have lots of girl items, but I wish they had a bigger selection of boys' clothing... fabulous, unique gifts... big-city attitude with big-city prices..."

Furniture, Bedding & Decor .... ✗
Gear & Equipment .... ✗
Nursing & Feeding .... ✗
Safety & Babycare .... ✗
Clothing, Shoes & Accessories .... ✓
Books, Toys & Entertainment .... ✓

$$$$ .... Prices
❸ .... Product availability
❹ .... Staff knowledge
❸ .... Customer service
❹ .... Decor

ATLANTA—6297 ROSWELL RD NE (AT SANDY SPRINGS RD); 404.250.1151; M-SA 10-6; PARKING LOT

Marshalls ★★½☆☆

"...the ultimate hit or miss... you can generally find all the basics—pajamas, onesies, and booties for a fraction of the regular price... I love to browse the toy aisle for inexpensive shower and birthday gifts... I only go when I am feeling patient and persistent... the aisles are crammed with goods..."

Furniture, Bedding & Decor ✗	$$ Prices
Gear & Equipment ✗	❸ Product availability
Nursing & Feeding ✗	❷ Staff knowledge
Safety & Babycare ✗	❷ Customer service
Clothing, Shoes & Accessories ✓	❸ Decor
Books, Toys & Entertainment ✓	

WWW.MARSHALLSONLINE.COM

ATLANTA—1131 HAMMOND DR; 770.396.8623; M-SA 9:30-9:30, SU 11-7

New Baby Products ★★★★★

"...great to have an in-town specialty store that offers everything your baby needs... best for looking at gear and nursery bedding... I shop here regularly because they pretty much have it all... they have been around for years and are a staple for new parents... a big selection of nursery furnishings packed into a pretty tight space... the service is friendly and fast... it's tough to navigate their aisles so leave your stroller in the car... they carry many popular brands and products at much more reasonable prices than other stores..."

Furniture, Bedding & Decor ✓	$$$ Prices
Gear & Equipment ✓	❹ Product availability
Nursing & Feeding ✓	❹ Staff knowledge
Safety & Babycare ✓	❹ Customer service
Clothing, Shoes & Accessories ✓	❸ Decor
Books, Toys & Entertainment ✓	

WWW.NEWBABYPRODUCTS.COM

ATLANTA—2200 CHESHIRE BRIDGE RD NE (AT WOODLAND AVE NE); 404.321.3874; M 10-8, T-SA 10-6; PARKING LOT

Nordstrom ★★★★☆

"...quality service and quality clothes... awesome kids shoe department—almost as good as the one for adults... free balloons in the children's shoe area as well as drawing tables... in addition to their own brand, they carry a very nice selection of other high-end baby clothing including Ralph Lauren, Robeez, etc... adorable baby clothes—they make great shower gifts... such a wonderful shopping experience—their lounge is perfect for breastfeeding and for changing diapers... well-rounded selection of baby basics as well as fancy clothes for special events..."

Furniture, Bedding & Decor ✓	$$$$ Prices
Gear & Equipment ✓	❹ Product availability
Nursing & Feeding ✗	❹ Staff knowledge
Safety & Babycare ✗	❹ Customer service
Clothing, Shoes & Accessories ✓	❹ Decor
Books, Toys & Entertainment ✓	

WWW.NORDSTROM.COM

ATLANTA—3500 PEACHTREE RD NE (OFF ROXFORD RD); 404.442.3000; M-SA 10-9, SU 12-6

ATLANTA—4390 ASHFORD DUNWOODY RD NE (AT HAMMOND DR); 770.394.1141; M-TH 10-9, F-SA 10-9:30, SU 12-6:30; PARKING LOT

Oilily ★★★★★

"...exclusive shop with fun, colorful clothing... prices are a bit steep, but if you value unique, well-designed clothes, this is the place... better selection for girls than boys but there are special items for either sex... your tot will definitely stand out from the crowd in these unique pieces... my kids love wearing their 'cool' clothes... whimsical items for mom, too..."

Furniture, Bedding & Decor ✗	$$$$ Prices
Gear & Equipment ✗	❹ Product availability
Nursing & Feeding ✗	❹ Staff knowledge

Safety & Babycare	✗	❹	Customer service
Clothing, Shoes & Accessories	✓	❹	Decor
Books, Toys & Entertainment	✗		

WWW.OILILYUSA.COM

ATLANTA—3393 PEACHTREE RD NE (AT LENOX SQUARE MALL); 404.816.6556; M-SA 10-9, SU 12-6

Old Navy ★★★★☆

"...hip and 'in' clothes for infants and tots... plenty of steals on clearance items... T-shirts and pants for $10 or less... busy, busy, busy—long lines, especially on weekends... nothing fancy and you won't mind when your kids get down and dirty in these clothes... easy to wash, decent quality... you can shop for your baby, your toddler, your teen and yourself all at the same time... clothes are especially affordable when you hit their sales (post-holiday sales are amazing!)..."

Furniture, Bedding & Decor	✗	$$	Prices
Gear & Equipment	✗	❹	Product availability
Nursing & Feeding	✗	❸	Staff knowledge
Safety & Babycare	✗	❸	Customer service
Clothing, Shoes & Accessories	✓	❸	Decor
Books, Toys & Entertainment	✗		

WWW.OLDNAVY.COM

ATLANTA—1 BUCKHEAD LOOP NE (AT TURNER MCDONALD PKWY); 404.467.0670; M-SA 9-9, SU 11-7; PARKING LOT

ATLANTA—1161 HAMMOND DR NE (NEAR PERIMETER MALL); 770.522.8444; M-SA 9-9, SU 11-7; PARKING LOT

ATLANTA—3101 COBB PKWY (AT CUMBERLAND BLVD SE); 770.952.9899; M-SA 9-9, SU 11-7; PARKING LOT

ATLANTA—4800 BRIARCLIFF RD NE (AT NORTHLAKE SHOPPING MALL); 770.270.0131; M-SA 10-9, SU 12-6; MALL PARKING

Payless Shoe Source ★★★☆☆

"...a good place for deals on children's shoes... staff is helpful with sizing... the selection and prices for kids' shoes can't be beat, but the quality isn't always spectacular... good leather shoes for cheap... great variety of all sizes and widths... I get my son's shoes here and don't feel like I'm wasting my money since he'll outgrow them in 3 months anyway..."

Furniture, Bedding & Decor	✗	$$	Prices
Gear & Equipment	✗	❸	Product availability
Nursing & Feeding	✗	❸	Staff knowledge
Safety & Babycare	✗	❸	Customer service
Clothing, Shoes & Accessories	✓	❸	Decor
Books, Toys & Entertainment	✗		

WWW.PAYLESS.COM

ATLANTA—2489 VILLAGE CREEK LODGE SE (AT BOULDERCREST BLVD SE); 404.624.7707; M-SA 9:30-8, SU 12-6

ATLANTA—2640 METROPOLITAN PKWY SW (AT CLEVELAND AVE SW); 404.766.9995; M-SA 10-8, SU 12-6

ATLANTA—2841 GREENBRIAR PKWY SW (AT GREENBRIAR MALL); 404.349.6919; M-SA 10-9, SU 12-6

ATLANTA—55 PEACHTREE ST SW (AT ALABAMA ST SW); 404.659.5200

ATLANTA—850 OAK ST NW (AT W END MALL); 404.753.1225; M-SA 10-9, SU 12-6

ATLANTA—WESTRIDGE SHOPPING CTR (AT WILLIS MILL RD SW); 404.696.7779; M-SA 10-8, SU 12-6

Pottery Barn Kids ★★★★½

“...stylish furniture, rugs, rockers and much more... they've found the right mix between quality and price... finally a company that stands behind what they sell—their customer service is great... gorgeous baby decor and furniture that will make your nursery to-die-for... the play area is so much fun—my daughter never wants to leave... a beautiful store with tons of ideas for setting up your nursery or kid's room... bright colors and cute patterns with basics to mix and match... if you see something in the catalog, but not in the store, just ask because they often have it in the back... ”

Furniture, Bedding & Decor	✓	$$$$	Prices
Gear & Equipment	✗	❹	Product availability
Nursing & Feeding	✗	❹	Staff knowledge
Safety & Babycare	✗	❹	Customer service
Clothing, Shoes & Accessories	✗	❺	Decor
Books, Toys & Entertainment	✓		

WWW.POTTERYBARNKIDS.COM

ATLANTA—3393 PEACHTREE RD NE (AT LENOX RD NE); 404.442.9122; M-SA 10-9, SU 12-6; PARKING LOT

ATLANTA—5145 PEACHTREE PKWY NW (AT CHAMBLEE TUCKER RD); 770.840.9640; M-SA 10-9, SU 12-6; PARKING LOT

Punkin Patch ★★★★★

“...a must see for hip new parents... a pleasure to browse throughout this store... most adorable nursery and juvenile furnishings in Atlanta... absolutely the best for nursery decor... beautiful high-end linens and furniture... a great selection of baby gifts and wonderful clothing... the staff is pleasant and provides excellent customer service... a fabulous store where you can get wonderful ideas for your own nursery... ”

Furniture, Bedding & Decor	✓	$$$$	Prices
Gear & Equipment	✗	❹	Product availability
Nursing & Feeding	✗	❶	Staff knowledge
Safety & Babycare	✗	❹	Customer service
Clothing, Shoes & Accessories	✓	❺	Decor
Books, Toys & Entertainment	✗		

WWW.PUNKIN-PATCH.COM

ATLANTA—2140 PEACHTREE RD NW (AT PEACHTREE PARK RD NE); 404.350.2454; T-SA 10-5; PARKING LOT

Rainbow Kids ★★½☆☆

“...fun clothing styles for infants and tots at low prices... the quality isn't the same as the more expensive brands, but the sleepers and play outfits always hold up well... great place for basics... cute trendy shoe selection for your little walker... we love the prices... up-to-date selection... ”

Furniture, Bedding & Decor	✗	$$	Prices
Gear & Equipment	✓	❸	Product availability
Nursing & Feeding	✗	❸	Staff knowledge
Safety & Babycare	✗	❸	Customer service
Clothing, Shoes & Accessories	✓	❸	Decor
Books, Toys & Entertainment	✓		

WWW.RAINBOWSHOPS.COM

ATLANTA—1000 NORTHLAKE MALL (AT NORTHLAKE PKWY NE); 770.491.7700; DAILY 10-9

ATLANTA—2064 CAMPBELL RD (AT CAMPBELLTOWN PLACE); 404.753.4103; M-SA 10-8, SU 11-6

ATLANTA—3050 MARTIN LUTHER KING DR SW (AT LYNHURST DR SW); 404.699.9981; M-SA 10-7, SU 12-6

ATLANTA—62 PEACHTREE ST SW (AT MARTIN LUTHER KIND JR DR SW); 404.521.2234; M-SA 9-7, SU 12-6

ATLANTA—833 RALPH AVERNATHIE BLVD SW (AT LEE ST SW); 404.753.2282; M-SA 10-9, SU 11-6

Ross Dress For Less ★★★☆☆

"...if you're in the mood for bargain hunting and are okay with potentially coming up empty-handed, then Ross is for you... don't expect to get educated about baby products here... go early on a week day and you'll find an organized store and staff that is helpful and available—forget weekends... their selection is pretty inconsistent, but I have found some incredible bargains... a great place to stock up on birthday presents or stocking stuffers..."

Furniture, Bedding & Decor	✗	$$	Prices
Gear & Equipment	✗	❸	Product availability
Nursing & Feeding	✗	❸	Staff knowledge
Safety & Babycare	✗	❸	Customer service
Clothing, Shoes & Accessories	✓	❸	Decor
Books, Toys & Entertainment	✓		

WWW.ROSSSTORES.COM

ATLANTA—5932 ROSWELL RD NE (AT CLIFTWOOD DR NE); 404.843.1474; M-SA 9:30-9:30, SU 11-7; PARKING LOT

Sears ★★★☆☆

"...a decent selection of clothes and basic baby equipment... check out the Kids Club program—it's a great way to save money... you go to Sears to save money, not to be pampered... the quality of their merchandise is better than Wal-Mart, but don't expect anything too special or different... not much in terms of gear, but tons of well-priced baby and toddler clothing..."

Furniture, Bedding & Decor	✓	$$	Prices
Gear & Equipment	✓	❸	Product availability
Nursing & Feeding	✓	❸	Staff knowledge
Safety & Babycare	✓	❸	Customer service
Clothing, Shoes & Accessories	✓	❸	Decor
Books, Toys & Entertainment	✓		

WWW.SEARS.COM

ATLANTA—1500 CUMBERLAND MALL (AT RT 407); 770.433.7400; M-F 10-9, SA 10-6, SU 11-5; MALL PARKING

ATLANTA—2201 HENDERSON MILL RD NE (AT NORTHLAKE SHOPPING MALL); 770.493.3210; M-SA 10-9, SU 11-7

Sprout ★★★★☆

"...a great in-town shop for baby accessories... I have received many gifts from Sprout and have purchased unique one-of-a-kind shower and birthday gifts for my friends and their kids... gorgeous merchandise... very cute and pricey... easy place to park and just stop in... a must-see for Atlanta moms..."

Furniture, Bedding & Decor	✗	$$$$	Prices
Gear & Equipment	✓	❹	Product availability
Nursing & Feeding	✗	❹	Staff knowledge
Safety & Babycare	✗	❹	Customer service
Clothing, Shoes & Accessories	✓	❺	Decor
Books, Toys & Entertainment	✓		

ATLANTA—1198 HOWELL MILL RD NW (AT 14TH ST NW); 404.352.0864; M-SA 11-6

Strasburg Children ★★★★☆

"...totally adorable special occasion outfits for babies and kids... classic baby, toddler, and kids clothes... dress-up clothes for kids... if

you are looking for a flower girl or ring bearer outfit, look no further... handmade clothes that will last through multiple kids or generations... it's not cheap, but you can find great sales if you are patient... ”

Furniture, Bedding & Decor ✗	$$$$ Prices
Gear & Equipment ✗	❹ Product availability
Nursing & Feeding ✗	❹ Staff knowledge
Safety & Babycare ✗	❹ Customer service
Clothing, Shoes & Accessories ✓	❹ Decor
Books, Toys & Entertainment ✗	

WWW.STRASBURGCHILDREN.COM

ATLANTA—3500 PEACHTREE RD NE (AT PHIPPS PLAZA); 404.816.4042; M-SA 10-9, SU 12-5:30

ATLANTA—3625 DALLAS HWY (AT THE AVES); 770.428.5455; M-SA 10-9 SU 12-6

Stride Rite Shoes ★★★½☆

“...wonderful selection of baby and toddler shoes... sandals, sneakers, and even special-occasion shoes... decent quality shoes that last... they know a lot about kids' shoes and take the time to get it right—they always measure my son's feet before fittings... store sizes vary, but they always have something in stock that works... they've even special ordered shoes for my daughter... a fun 'first shoe' buying experience... ”

Furniture, Bedding & Decor ✗	$$$ Prices
Gear & Equipment ✗	❹ Product availability
Nursing & Feeding ✗	❹ Staff knowledge
Safety & Babycare ✗	❹ Customer service
Clothing, Shoes & Accessories ✓	❹ Decor
Books, Toys & Entertainment ✗	

WWW.STRIDERITE.COM

ATLANTA—4400 ASHFORD DUNWOODY (AT PERIMETER MALL); 770.394.3537; M-SA 10-9, SU 12-6; PARKING LOT

Sweet Repeats ★★★½☆

“...they usually have a nice selection of kids' clothes... cute, upscale consignment store... not the best selection of toddler shoes... hit or miss... worth checking back often... clothes are always in really great shape... I have bought some cute smocked outfits at reasonable prices... ”

Furniture, Bedding & Decor ✗	$$ Prices
Gear & Equipment ✗	❹ Product availability
Nursing & Feeding ✗	❹ Staff knowledge
Safety & Babycare ✗	❹ Customer service
Clothing, Shoes & Accessories ✓	❸ Decor
Books, Toys & Entertainment ✗	

ATLANTA—321 PHARR RD (AT FULTON DR); 404.261.7519; M-SA 10-5 ; PARKING LOT

Talbots Kids ★★★½☆

“...a nice alternative to the typical department store experience... expensive, but fantastic quality... great for holiday and special occasion outfits including christening outfits... well-priced, conservative children's clothing... cute selections for infants, toddlers and kids... sales are fantastic—up to half off at least a couple times a year... the best part is, you can also shop for yourself while shopping for baby... ”

Furniture, Bedding & Decor ✗	$$$$ Prices
Gear & Equipment ✗	❹ Product availability
Nursing & Feeding ✗	❹ Staff knowledge
Safety & Babycare ✗	❹ Customer service
Clothing, Shoes & Accessories ✓	❹ Decor

Books, Toys & Entertainment......... ✗

WWW.TALBOTS.COM

ATLANTA—2391 PEACHTREE RD NE (AT PEACHTREE BATTLE PROMENADE); 404.261.9222; M-F 10-7, SA 10-6, SU 12-5

Target ★★★★☆

"...our favorite place to shop for kids' stuff—good selection and very affordable... guilt-free shopping—kids grow so fast so I don't want to pay high department-store prices... everything from diapers and sippy cups to car seats and strollers... easy return policy... generally helpful staff, but you don't go for the service—you go for the prices... decent registry that won't freak your friends out with outrageous prices... easy, convenient shopping for well-priced items... all the big-box brands available—Graco, Evenflo, Eddie Bauer, etc...."

Furniture, Bedding & Decor	✓	$$	Prices
Gear & Equipment	✓	❹	Product availability
Nursing & Feeding	✓	❸	Staff knowledge
Safety & Babycare	✓	❸	Customer service
Clothing, Shoes & Accessories	✓	❸	Decor
Books, Toys & Entertainment	✓		

WWW.TARGET.COM

ATLANTA—235 JOHNSON FERRY RD NW (AT ABERNATHY RD NW); 404.256.4600; M-SA 8-10, SU 8-9; PARKING IN FRONT OF BLDG

ATLANTA—2400 N DRUID HILLS RD NE (AT WOODCLIFF DR NE); 404.267.0060; M-SA 8-10, SU 8-9; PARKING IN FRONT OF BLDG

ATLANTA—3535 PEACHTREE RD NE (AT PHIPPS PLAZA); 404.237.9494; M-SA 8-10, SU 8-9; PARKING IN FRONT OF BLDG

Toys R Us ★★★½☆

"...not just toys, but also tons of gear and supplies including diapers and formula... a hectic shopping experience but the prices make it all worthwhile... I've experienced good and bad service at the same store on the same day... the stores are huge and can be overwhelming... most big brand-names available... leave the kids at home unless you want to end up with a cart full of toys..."

Furniture, Bedding & Decor	✓	$$$	Prices
Gear & Equipment	✓	❹	Product availability
Nursing & Feeding	✓	❸	Staff knowledge
Safety & Babycare	✓	❸	Customer service
Clothing, Shoes & Accessories	✓	❸	Decor
Books, Toys & Entertainment	✓		

WWW.TOYSRUS.COM

ATLANTA—1 BUCKHEAD LOOP DR NE (AT MAPLE DR NE); 404.467.8697; M-SA 9-9, SU 11-7; PARKING LOT

ATLANTA—2997 COBB PKWY S (AT PROFESSIONAL PKY SE); 770.951.8052; M-SA 9:30-9:30, SU 11-7; PARKING LOT

North Fulton

★★★★★

"lila picks"

- ★Babies R Us
- ★Kid's Room Stuff
- ★Jack & Jill Children's Boutique

Babies R Us ★★★★★

"...everything baby under one roof... they have a wide selection and carry most 'mainstream' items such as Graco, Fisher-Price, Avent and Britax... great customer service—given how big the stores are, I was pleasantly surprised at how attentive the staff was... easy return policy... super busy on weekends so try to visit on a weekday for the best service... keep an eye out for great coupons, deals and frequent sales... easy and comprehensive registry... shopping here is so easy—you've got to check it out..."

Furniture, Bedding & Decor .... ✓
Gear & Equipment .... ✓
Nursing & Feeding .... ✓
Safety & Babycare .... ✓
Clothing, Shoes & Accessories .... ✓
Books, Toys & Entertainment .... ✓

$$$ .... Prices
❹ .... Product availability
❹ .... Staff knowledge
❹ .... Customer service
❹ .... Decor

WWW.BABIESRUS.COM

ALPHARETTA—6380 NORTH POINT PKWY (AT NORTH POINT MALL); 770.752.9000; M-SA 9:30-9:30, SU 11-7; PARKING IN FRONT OF BLDG

Baby Depot At Burlington Coat Factory ★★★½☆

"...a large, 'super store' layout with a ton of baby gear... wide aisles, packed shelves, barely existent customer service and awesome prices... everything from bottles, car seats and strollers to gliders, cribs and clothes... I always find something worth getting... a little disorganized and hard to locate items you're looking for... the staff is not always knowledgeable about their merchandise... return policy is store credit only..."

Furniture, Bedding & Decor .... ✓
Gear & Equipment .... ✓
Nursing & Feeding .... ✓
Safety & Babycare .... ✓
Clothing, Shoes & Accessories .... ✓
Books, Toys & Entertainment .... ✓

$$ .... Prices
❸ .... Product availability
❸ .... Staff knowledge
❸ .... Customer service
❸ .... Decor

WWW.BABYDEPOT.COM

ROSWELL—608 HOLCOMB BRIDGE RD (AT ROSWELL MALL); 770.518.9800; M-SA 10-9, SU 11-6; MALL PARKING

BabyGap/GapKids ★★★★☆

"...colorful baby and toddler clothing in clean, well-lit stores... great return policy... it's the Gap, so you know what you're getting—colorful,

cute and well-made clothing... best place for baby hats... prices are reasonable especially since there's always a sale of some sort going on... sales, sales, sales—frequent and fantastic... everything I'm looking for in infant clothing—snap crotches, snaps up the front, all natural fabrics and great styling... fun seasonal selections—a great place to shop for gifts as well as for your own kids... although it can get busy, staff generally seem accommodating and helpful... ”

Furniture, Bedding & Decor	✗	$$$	Prices
Gear & Equipment	✗	❹	Product availability
Nursing & Feeding	✗	❹	Staff knowledge
Safety & Babycare	✗	❹	Customer service
Clothing, Shoes & Accessories	✓	❹	Decor
Books, Toys & Entertainment	✗		

WWW.GAP.COM

ALPHARETTA—1082 NORTH POINT CIR (AT NORTH POINT MALL); 770.751.9114; M-SA 10-9, SU 12-6; PARKING IN FRONT OF BLDG

Children's Place, The ★★★½☆

“...great bargains on cute clothing... shoes, socks, swimsuits, sunglasses and everything in between... lots of '3 for $20' type deals on sleepers, pants and mix-and-match separates... so much more affordable than the other 'big chains'... don't expect the most unique stuff here, but it wears and washes well... cheap clothing for cheap prices... you can leave the store with bags full of clothes without putting a huge dent in your wallet... ”

Furniture, Bedding & Decor	✗	$$	Prices
Gear & Equipment	✗	❹	Product availability
Nursing & Feeding	✗	❹	Staff knowledge
Safety & Babycare	✗	❹	Customer service
Clothing, Shoes & Accessories	✓	❹	Decor
Books, Toys & Entertainment	✓		

WWW.CHILDRENSPLACE.COM

ALPHARETTA—2034 NORTH POINT CIR (AT NORTH POINT MALL); 770.521.9065; M-SA 10-9, SU 12-6; MALL PARKING

Costco ★★★½☆

“...dependable place for bulk diapers, wipes and formula at discount prices... clothing selection is very hit-or-miss... avoid shopping there during nights and weekends if possible, because parking and checkout lines are brutal... they don't have a huge selection of brands, but the brands they do have are almost always in stock and at a great price... lowest prices around for diapers and formula... kid's clothing tends to be picked through, but it's worth looking for great deals on name-brand items like Carter's... ”

Furniture, Bedding & Decor	✓	$$	Prices
Gear & Equipment	✓	❸	Product availability
Nursing & Feeding	✓	❸	Staff knowledge
Safety & Babycare	✓	❸	Customer service
Clothing, Shoes & Accessories	✓	❷	Decor
Books, Toys & Entertainment	✓		

WWW.COSTCO.COM

ALPHARETTA—2855 JORDAN CT (AT WINDWARD PKWY W); 678.823.4950; M-F 10-8:30, SA 9-7, SU 10-6

Dillard's ★★★★☆

“...this store has beautiful clothes, and if you catch a sale, you can get great quality clothes at super bargain prices... good customer service and helpful staff... a huge selection of merchandise for boys and girls... nice layette department... some furnishings like little tables and chairs... beautiful displays... the best part is that in addition to shopping for your kids, you can also shop for yourself... ”

Furniture, Bedding & Decor .... ✓	$$$ .... Prices
Gear & Equipment .... ×	❹...................... Product availability
Nursing & Feeding .... ×	❸........................... Staff knowledge
Safety & Babycare .... ×	❹......................... Customer service
Clothing, Shoes & Accessories....... ✓	❹... Decor
Books, Toys & Entertainment .... ✓	

WWW.DILLARDS.COM

ALPHARETTA—7000 NORTH POINT CIR (AT NORTH POINT MALL); 770.410.9020; M-SA 10-9, SU 12-6

Gymboree ★★★★☆

"...beautiful clothing and great quality... colorful and stylish baby and kids wear... lots of fun birthday gift ideas... easy exchange and return policy... items usually go on sale pretty quickly... save money with Gymbucks... many stores have a play area which makes shopping with my kids fun (let alone feasible)..."

Furniture, Bedding & Decor .... ×	$$$ .... Prices
Gear & Equipment .... ×	❹...................... Product availability
Nursing & Feeding .... ×	❹........................... Staff knowledge
Safety & Babycare .... ×	❹......................... Customer service
Clothing, Shoes & Accessories....... ✓	❹... Decor
Books, Toys & Entertainment .... ✓	

WWW.GYMBOREE.COM

ALPHARETTA—1148 NORTH POINT CIR (AT NORTH POINT MALL); 770.664.9490; M-SA 10-9, SU 12-6; PARKING LOT

Jack & Jill Children's Boutique ★★★★★

"...great selection of special occasion wear... perfect for flower girl dresses, christening gowns... very fancy... staff is very helpful... you'll spend a bit more here, but you will enjoy the clothes a bit more too..."

Furniture, Bedding & Decor .... ×	$$$$ .... Prices
Gear & Equipment .... ×	❺...................... Product availability
Nursing & Feeding .... ×	❹........................... Staff knowledge
Safety & Babycare .... ×	❹......................... Customer service
Clothing, Shoes & Accessories....... ✓	❸... Decor
Books, Toys & Entertainment .... ×	

WWW.UPTHEHILL.COM

ALPHARETTA—322 N MAIN ST (AT MAYFIELD RDS); 770.475.2288; T-SA 10-5; PARKING LOT

Janie And Jack ★★★★½

"...gorgeous clothing and some accessories (shoes, socks, etc.)... fun to look at, somewhat pricey, but absolutely adorable clothes for little ones... boutique-like clothes at non-boutique prices—especially on sale... high-quality infant and toddler clothes anyone would love—always good for a baby gift... I always check the clearance racks in the back of the store... their decor is darling—a really fun shopping experience..."

Furniture, Bedding & Decor .... ×	$$$$ .... Prices
Gear & Equipment .... ✓	❹...................... Product availability
Nursing & Feeding .... ×	❹........................... Staff knowledge
Safety & Babycare .... ×	❹......................... Customer service
Clothing, Shoes & Accessories....... ✓	❹... Decor
Books, Toys & Entertainment .... ×	

WWW.JANIEANDJACK.COM

ALPHARETTA—1092 NORTH POINT CIR (AT NORTH POINT MALL); 678.867.0242; M-SA 10-9, SU 12-6; MALL PARKING

JCPenney ★★★½☆

"...always a good place to find clothes and other baby basics... the registry process was seamless... staff is generally friendly but the lines always seem long and slow... they don't have the greatest selection of toddler clothes, but their baby section is great... we had some damaged furniture delivered but customer service was easy and accommodating... a pretty limited selection of gear, but what they have is priced right..."

Furniture, Bedding & Decor	✓	$$	Prices
Gear & Equipment	✓	3	Product availability
Nursing & Feeding	✓	3	Staff knowledge
Safety & Babycare	✓	3	Customer service
Clothing, Shoes & Accessories	✓	3	Decor
Books, Toys & Entertainment	✓		

WWW.JCPENNEY.COM

ALPHARETTA—2000 NORTH POINT CIR (AT NORTH POINT MALL); 770.475.9850; M-SA 10-9, SU 12-6; PARKING LOT

Jelly Beans ★★★★☆

"...resale shopping at it's best... bright, spacious and orderly... gently-used clothing... upscale designers such as Baby Lulu, Lily Pulitzer, Catimini and Sophie Dess... new items too... hair bows, jewelry, stuffed animals, leather shoes and gift baskets... fun shop and you do not feel like you're in a used clothing store..."

Furniture, Bedding & Decor	✗	$$$	Prices
Gear & Equipment	✗	3	Product availability
Nursing & Feeding	✗	4	Staff knowledge
Safety & Babycare	✗	4	Customer service
Clothing, Shoes & Accessories	✓	3	Decor
Books, Toys & Entertainment	✗		

WWW.JELLYBEANSSHOP.COM

ALPHARETTA—11130 STATE BRIDGE RD (AT KIMBALL BRIDGE RD); 770.442.2377; M-F 10-5:30, SA 10-5; FREE PARKING

KB Toys ★★★☆☆

"...hectic and always buzzing... wall-to-wall plastic and blinking lights... more Fisher-Price, Elmo and Sponge Bob than the eye can handle... a toy super store with discounted prices... they always have some kind of special sale going on... if you're looking for the latest and greatest popular toy, then look no further—not the place for unique or unusual toys... perfect for bulk toy shopping—especially around the holidays..."

Furniture, Bedding & Decor	✗	$$	Prices
Gear & Equipment	✗	3	Product availability
Nursing & Feeding	✗	3	Staff knowledge
Safety & Babycare	✗	3	Customer service
Clothing, Shoes & Accessories	✗	3	Decor
Books, Toys & Entertainment	✓		

WWW.KBTOYS.COM

ALPHARETTA—1008 NORTH POINT CIR (AT NORTH POINT MALL); 770.667.8723; M-SA 10-9, SU 12-6

Kid's Room Stuff ★★★★★

"...a high-end nursery furniture store with decent prices... our order was delivered and set up very promptly... the staff is knowledgeable and friendly... the selection is good and it makes shopping for a crib pretty easy and painless..."

Furniture, Bedding & Decor	✓	$$$	Prices
Gear & Equipment	✗	4	Product availability
Nursing & Feeding	✗	4	Staff knowledge

Safety & Babycare ✗
Clothing, Shoes & Accessories ✗
Books, Toys & Entertainment ✗

❹ Customer service
❹ Decor

WWW.KIDSROOMSTUFF.COM

ALPHARETTA—10700 STATE BRIDGE RD (AT MORTON RD); 678.240.0918; M-SA 10-7, SU 12-6; PARKING LOT

Kiddie-Go-Round ★★★★☆

"...I've found some real deals on used Baby Gap and Old Navy clothes... the store is cramped and packed to the rafters with used baby and maternity stuff... staff is friendly and willing to take my number if an item came in I was looking for... it's a consignment store so be ready to dig a little... good variety of merchandise..."

Furniture, Bedding & Decor ✗
Gear & Equipment ✗
Nursing & Feeding ✗
Safety & Babycare ✗
Clothing, Shoes & Accessories ✓
Books, Toys & Entertainment ✓

$$ Prices
❸ Product availability
❹ Staff knowledge
❹ Customer service
❸ Decor

ROSWELL—555 S ATLANTA ST (AT MARIETTA HWY); 770.641.9641; M-SA 10-6; PARKING LOT

Kohl's ★★★★☆

"...nice one-stop shopping for the whole family—everything from clothing to baby gear... great sales on clothing and a good selection of higher-end brands... stylish, inexpensive clothes for babies through 24 months... very easy shopping experience... dirt-cheap sales and clearance prices... nothing super fancy, but just right for those everyday romper outfits... Graco, Eddie Bauer and other well-known brands..."

Furniture, Bedding & Decor ✓
Gear & Equipment ✓
Nursing & Feeding ✓
Safety & Babycare ✓
Clothing, Shoes & Accessories ✓
Books, Toys & Entertainment ✓

$$ Prices
❹ Product availability
❸ Staff knowledge
❸ Customer service
❸ Decor

WWW.KOHLS.COM

ROSWELL—2342 HOLCOMB BRIDGE RD (AT FOUTS RD); 678.795.9645; M-SA 8-10, SU 10-8; PARKING LOT

ROSWELL—620 W CROSSVILLE RD (AT CROSSWAY LN); 678.352.9536; M-SA 8-10, SU 10-8; PARKING IN FRONT OF BLDG

Mint Julep ★★★☆☆

"...children's apparel as well as women's clothing... for the tried-and-true preppy... perfect place to shop for matching mom and baby outfits... lots of Lily Pulitzer stuff... high-end... if you've got the cash, go for it... beautiful items... nice bedding, too..."

Furniture, Bedding & Decor ✓
Gear & Equipment ✗
Nursing & Feeding ✗
Safety & Babycare ✗
Clothing, Shoes & Accessories ✓
Books, Toys & Entertainment ✗

$$$ Prices
❸ Product availability
❸ Staff knowledge
❸ Customer service
❸ Decor

WWW.MINTJULEPGA.COM

ALPHARETTA—11550 WEBB BRIDGE WY (AT KIMBALL BRIDGE RD); 678.762.9575; M-W F 10-5, TH 10-6 ; PARKING LOT

Old Navy ★★★★☆

"...hip and 'in' clothes for infants and tots... plenty of steals on clearance items... T-shirts and pants for $10 or less... busy, busy, busy—long lines, especially on weekends... nothing fancy and you

won't mind when your kids get down and dirty in these clothes... easy to wash, decent quality... you can shop for your baby, your toddler, your teen and yourself all at the same time... clothes are especially affordable when you hit their sales (post-holiday sales are amazing!)... ”

Furniture, Bedding & Decor	✗	$$	Prices
Gear & Equipment	✗	❹	Product availability
Nursing & Feeding	✗	❸	Staff knowledge
Safety & Babycare	✗	❸	Customer service
Clothing, Shoes & Accessories	✓	❸	Decor
Books, Toys & Entertainment	✗		

WWW.OLDNAVY.COM

ALPHARETTA—6100 NORTH POINT PKWY (AT NORTH POINT CT); 770.772.6660; M-SA 9-9, SU 11-7; PARKING LOT

Parisian ★★★★☆

“*...a hip department store with a unique selection of infant and kid's clothes... designer lines like Ralph Lauren... watch for the seasonal sales... organized, but packed so it can be hard to maneuver a stroller... huge selection, especially for boys... nice women's restroom with a comfy chair for nursing...* ”

Furniture, Bedding & Decor	✗	$$$	Prices
Gear & Equipment	✓	❹	Product availability
Nursing & Feeding	✗	❹	Staff knowledge
Safety & Babycare	✗	❹	Customer service
Clothing, Shoes & Accessories	✓	❹	Decor
Books, Toys & Entertainment	✗		

WWW.PARISIAN.COM

ALPHARETTA—4500 NORTH POINT CIR (AT NORTH POINT MALL); 770.754.3200; M-SA 10-9, SU 12-6; MALL PARKING

Payless Shoe Source ★★★☆☆

“*...a good place for deals on children's shoes... staff is helpful with sizing... the selection and prices for kids' shoes can't be beat, but the quality isn't always spectacular... good leather shoes for cheap... great variety of all sizes and widths... I get my son's shoes here and don't feel like I'm wasting my money since he'll outgrow them in 3 months anyway...* ”

Furniture, Bedding & Decor	✗	$$	Prices
Gear & Equipment	✗	❸	Product availability
Nursing & Feeding	✗	❸	Staff knowledge
Safety & Babycare	✗	❸	Customer service
Clothing, Shoes & Accessories	✓	❸	Decor
Books, Toys & Entertainment	✗		

WWW.PAYLESS.COM

ALPHARETTA—7500 NORTH POINT PKWY (AT NORTH POINT MALL); 678.566.0099; M-SA 10-9, SU 12:30-5:30

SANDY SPRINGS—6015 ROSWELL RD NE (AT HAMMOND DR NE); 404.843.8580; M-F 10-8, SA 10-7, SU 12-5

Peek-a-Boo Kids ★★★☆☆

“*...great for traditional clothes and special occasionas... the girl's outfits are much cuter than the boy's outfits... high-end selections...* ”

Furniture, Bedding & Decor	✗	$$$$	Prices
Gear & Equipment	✗	❸	Product availability
Nursing & Feeding	✗	❹	Staff knowledge
Safety & Babycare	✗	❹	Customer service
Clothing, Shoes & Accessories	✓	❹	Decor
Books, Toys & Entertainment	✗		

WWW.PEEKABOOKIDS.COM

ALPHARETTA—5075 ABBOTTS BRIDGE RD (AT JONES BRIDGE); 770.777.1777; M-TH 10-6, F-SA 10-5; PARKING LOT

Pottery Barn Kids ★★★★½

"...stylish furniture, rugs, rockers and much more... they've found the right mix between quality and price... finally a company that stands behind what they sell—their customer service is great... gorgeous baby decor and furniture that will make your nursery to-die-for... the play area is so much fun—my daughter never wants to leave... a beautiful store with tons of ideas for setting up your nursery or kid's room... bright colors and cute patterns with basics to mix and match... if you see something in the catalog, but not in the store, just ask because they often have it in the back..."

Furniture, Bedding & Decor	✓	$$$$	Prices
Gear & Equipment	✗	❹	Product availability
Nursing & Feeding	✗	❹	Staff knowledge
Safety & Babycare	✗	❹	Customer service
Clothing, Shoes & Accessories	✗	❺	Decor
Books, Toys & Entertainment	✓		

WWW.POTTERYBARNKIDS.COM

ALPHARETTA—1000 NORTH POINT CIR (AT NORTH POINT MALL); 678.624.0149; M-SA 9-9, SU 12-6; MALL PARKING

Stride Rite Shoes ★★★½☆

"...wonderful selection of baby and toddler shoes... sandals, sneakers, and even special-occasion shoes... decent quality shoes that last... they know a lot about kids' shoes and take the time to get it right—they always measure my son's feet before fittings... store sizes vary, but they always have something in stock that works... they've even special ordered shoes for my daughter... a fun 'first shoe' buying experience..."

Furniture, Bedding & Decor	✗	$$$	Prices
Gear & Equipment	✗	❹	Product availability
Nursing & Feeding	✗	❹	Staff knowledge
Safety & Babycare	✗	❹	Customer service
Clothing, Shoes & Accessories	✓	❹	Decor
Books, Toys & Entertainment	✗		

WWW.STRIDERITE.COM

ALPHARETTA—1096 NORTH POINT CIR (AT NORTH POINT MALL); 770.751.9919; M-SA 10-9, SU 12-6; PARKING LOT

Talbots Kids ★★★½☆

"...a nice alternative to the typical department store experience... expensive, but fantastic quality... great for holiday and special occasion outfits including christening outfits... well-priced, conservative children's clothing... cute selections for infants, toddlers and kids... sales are fantastic—up to half off at least a couple times a year... the best part is, you can also shop for yourself while shopping for baby..."

Furniture, Bedding & Decor	✗	$$$$	Prices
Gear & Equipment	✗	❹	Product availability
Nursing & Feeding	✗	❹	Staff knowledge
Safety & Babycare	✗	❹	Customer service
Clothing, Shoes & Accessories	✓	❹	Decor
Books, Toys & Entertainment	✗		

WWW.TALBOTS.COM

ALPHARETTA—78300 NORTH POINT PKWY (AT NORTH POINT VILLAGE SHOPPING CTR); 770.442.2303; M-F 10-7, SA 10-6, SU 12-5; PARKING LOT

Target ★★★★☆

"...our favorite place to shop for kids' stuff—good selection and very affordable... guilt-free shopping—kids grow so fast so I don't want to

pay high department-store prices... everything from diapers and sippy cups to car seats and strollers... easy return policy... generally helpful staff, but you don't go for the service—you go for the prices... decent registry that won't freak your friends out with outrageous prices... easy, convenient shopping for well-priced items... all the big-box brands available—Graco, Evenflo, Eddie Bauer, etc.... ”

Furniture, Bedding & Decor	✓	$$	Prices
Gear & Equipment	✓	❹	Product availability
Nursing & Feeding	✓	❸	Staff knowledge
Safety & Babycare	✓	❸	Customer service
Clothing, Shoes & Accessories	✓	❸	Decor
Books, Toys & Entertainment	✓		

WWW.TARGET.COM

ROSWELL—1135 WOODSTOCK RD (AT HARDSCRABBLE RD); 770.998.0144; M-SA 8-10, SU 8-9; PARKING IN FRONT OF BLDG

Toys R Us ★★★½☆

“*...not just toys, but also tons of gear and supplies including diapers and formula... a hectic shopping experience but the prices make it all worthwhile... I've experienced good and bad service at the same store on the same day... the stores are huge and can be overwhelming... most big brand-names available... leave the kids at home unless you want to end up with a cart full of toys...* ”

Furniture, Bedding & Decor	✓	$$$	Prices
Gear & Equipment	✓	❹	Product availability
Nursing & Feeding	✓	❸	Staff knowledge
Safety & Babycare	✓	❸	Customer service
Clothing, Shoes & Accessories	✓	❸	Decor
Books, Toys & Entertainment	✓		

WWW.TOYSRUS.COM

ALPHARETTA—7731 NORTH POINT PKWY (AT MANSELL RD); 770.518.9188; M-SA 9:30-9:30, SU 11-7; PARKING LOT

Twin Star Consignment

Furniture, Bedding & Decor	×	×	Gear & Equipment
Nursing & Feeding	×	×	Safety & Babycare
Clothing, Shoes & Accessories	✓	×	Books, Toys & Entertainment

WWW.TWINSTARCONSIGNMENT.COM

ALPHARETTA—214 S MAIN ST (AT OLD MILTON PKWY); 770.772.0957; M-F 10-5:30, SA 10-5; PARKING LOT

Value City ★★★☆☆

“*...if you are looking for bargain merchandise for the whole family, you'll find it here... you can always find something and lots of inexpensive baby and toddler clothes... very low prices with many sizes... chaotic atmosphere and hard to find staff, once you do they are very helpful... lines can be long...* ”

Furniture, Bedding & Decor	✓	$$	Prices
Gear & Equipment	✓	❸	Product availability
Nursing & Feeding	✓	❸	Staff knowledge
Safety & Babycare	✓	❸	Customer service
Clothing, Shoes & Accessories	✓	❸	Decor
Books, Toys & Entertainment	✓		

WWW.VALUECITY.COM

ROSWELL—610 HOLCOMB BRIDGE RD (AT ROSWELL MALL); 770.993.0742; M-SA 9:30-9:30, SU 10-7; MALL PARKING

South Fulton, Fayette & Clayton

★★★★★

"lila picks"

★Serendipity Baby & Co

Babies R Us ★★★★☆

"...everything baby under one roof... they have a wide selection and carry most 'mainstream' items such as Graco, Fisher-Price, Avent and Britax... great customer service—given how big the stores are, I was pleasantly surprised at how attentive the staff was... easy return policy... super busy on weekends so try to visit on a weekday for the best service... keep an eye out for great coupons, deals and frequent sales... easy and comprehensive registry... shopping here is so easy—you've got to check it out..."

Furniture, Bedding & Decor	✓	$$$	Prices
Gear & Equipment	✓	❹	Product availability
Nursing & Feeding	✓	❹	Staff knowledge
Safety & Babycare	✓	❹	Customer service
Clothing, Shoes & Accessories	✓	❹	Decor
Books, Toys & Entertainment	✓		

WWW.BABIESRUS.COM

MORROW—1960 MT ZION RD (AT MT ZION BLVD); 770.477.5111; M-SA 9:30-9:30, SU 11-7; PARKING IN FRONT OF BLDG

Baby Depot At Burlington Coat Factory ★★★½☆

"...a large, 'super store' layout with a ton of baby gear... wide aisles, packed shelves, barely existent customer service and awesome prices... everything from bottles, car seats and strollers to gliders, cribs and clothes... I always find something worth getting... a little disorganized and hard to locate items you're looking for... the staff is not always knowledgeable about their merchandise... return policy is store credit only..."

Furniture, Bedding & Decor	✓	$$	Prices
Gear & Equipment	✓	❸	Product availability
Nursing & Feeding	✓	❸	Staff knowledge
Safety & Babycare	✓	❸	Customer service
Clothing, Shoes & Accessories	✓	❸	Decor
Books, Toys & Entertainment	✓		

WWW.BABYDEPOT.COM

MORROW—1516 SOUTHLAKE PKWY (AT BARTON RD); 770.960.7555; M-SA 10-9:30, SU 11-6

Children's Place, The ★★★½☆

"...great bargains on cute clothing... shoes, socks, swimsuits, sunglasses and everything in between... lots of '3 for $20' type deals on

sleepers, pants and mix-and-match separates... so much more affordable than the other 'big chains'... don't expect the most unique stuff here, but it wears and washes well... cheap clothing for cheap prices... you can leave the store with bags full of clothes without putting a huge dent in your wallet... ”

Furniture, Bedding & Decor .... ✗
Gear & Equipment .... ✗
Nursing & Feeding .... ✗
Safety & Babycare .... ✗
Clothing, Shoes & Accessories ...... ✓
Books, Toys & Entertainment .... ✓

$$ .... Prices
❹ .... Product availability
❹ .... Staff knowledge
❹ ....Customer service
❹ .... Decor

WWW.CHILDRENSPLACE.COM

MORROW—1238 SOUTHLAKE MALL (AT MORROW INDUSTRIAL BLVD); 678.422.0315; M-SA 10-9, SU 11-7; MALL PARKING

PEACHTREE CITY—226 CITY CIR (AT CLOVER RANCH); 678.364.0021; M-SA 10-9, SU 11-7

Costco ★★★½☆

“*...dependable place for bulk diapers, wipes and formula at discount prices... clothing selection is very hit-or-miss... avoid shopping there during nights and weekends if possible, because parking and checkout lines are brutal... they don't have a huge selection of brands, but the brands they do have are almost always in stock and at a great price... lowest prices around for diapers and formula... kid's clothing tends to be picked through, but it's worth looking for great deals on name-brand items like Carter's...* ”

Furniture, Bedding & Decor .... ✓
Gear & Equipment .... ✓
Nursing & Feeding .... ✓
Safety & Babycare .... ✓
Clothing, Shoes & Accessories ...... ✓
Books, Toys & Entertainment .... ✓

$$ .... Prices
❸ .... Product availability
❸ .... Staff knowledge
❸ ....Customer service
❷ .... Decor

WWW.COSTCO.COM

MORROW—1700 MT ZION RD (AT JONESBORO RD); 678.201.0003; M-F 11-8:30, SA 9-7, SU 10-6

JCPenney ★★★½☆

“*...always a good place to find clothes and other baby basics... the registry process was seamless... staff is generally friendly but the lines always seem long and slow... they don't have the greatest selection of toddler clothes, but their baby section is great... we had some damaged furniture delivered but customer service was easy and accommodating... a pretty limited selection of gear, but what they have is priced right...* ”

Furniture, Bedding & Decor .... ✓
Gear & Equipment .... ✓
Nursing & Feeding .... ✓
Safety & Babycare .... ✓
Clothing, Shoes & Accessories ...... ✓
Books, Toys & Entertainment .... ✓

$$ .... Prices
❸ .... Product availability
❸ .... Staff knowledge
❸ ....Customer service
❸ .... Decor

WWW.JCPENNEY.COM

FOREST PARK—5500 FRONTAGE RD (AT OLD DIXIE RD); 404.363.3713; M-F 10-9, SA 9-9, SU 10-6; MALL PARKING

MORROW—1400 SOUTHLAKE CIR (AT SOUTHLAKE MALL); 770.961.6211; M-SA 10-9, SU 12-6; MALL PARKING

Kid's Foot Locker ★★★½☆

“*...Nike, Reebok and Adidas for your little ones... hip, trendy and quite pricey... perfect for the sports addict dad who wants his kid* *sporting the latest NFL duds... shoes cost close to what the adult variety costs... generally good quality... they carry infant and toddler sizes...* ”

Furniture, Bedding & Decor	✗	$$$	Prices
Gear & Equipment	✗	❸	Product availability
Nursing & Feeding	✗	❸	Staff knowledge
Safety & Babycare	✗	❸	Customer service
Clothing, Shoes & Accessories	✓	❸	Decor
Books, Toys & Entertainment	✗		

WWW.KIDSFOOTLOCKER.COM

MORROW—2407 SOUTHLAKE CIR (AT SOUTHLAKE MALL); 770.968.3741; M-SA 10-9, SU 12-6

Macy's ★★★½☆

“*...Macy's has it all and I never leave empty-handed... if you time your visit right you can find some great deals... go during the week so you don't get overwhelmed with the weekend crowd... good for staples as well as beautiful party dresses for girls... lots of brand-names like Carter's, Guess, and Ralph Lauren... not much in terms of assistance... newspaper coupons and sales help keep the cost down... some stores are better organized and maintained than others... if you're going to shop at a department store for your baby, then Macy's is a safe bet...* ”

Furniture, Bedding & Decor	✓	$$$	Prices
Gear & Equipment	✗	❸	Product availability
Nursing & Feeding	✗	❸	Staff knowledge
Safety & Babycare	✗	❸	Customer service
Clothing, Shoes & Accessories	✓	❸	Decor
Books, Toys & Entertainment	✓		

WWW.MACYS.COM

MORROW—1500 SOUTHLAKE CIR (AT SOUTHLAKE MALL); 770.961.3111; M-SA 10-9, SU 12-7; MALL PARKING

Marshalls ★★½☆☆

“*...the ultimate hit or miss... you can generally find all the basics—pajamas, onesies, and booties for a fraction of the regular price... I love to browse the toy aisle for inexpensive shower and birthday gifts... I only go when I am feeling patient and persistent... the aisles are crammed with goods...* ”

Furniture, Bedding & Decor	✗	$$	Prices
Gear & Equipment	✗	❸	Product availability
Nursing & Feeding	✗	❷	Staff knowledge
Safety & Babycare	✗	❷	Customer service
Clothing, Shoes & Accessories	✓	❸	Decor
Books, Toys & Entertainment	✓		

WWW.MARSHALLSONLINE.COM

FAYETTEVILLE—109 PAVILLION PKWY (AT HWY 85); 770.719.4699; M-SA 9:30-9:30, SU 11-7

Mud Pies Baby & Kids ★★★★☆

“*...unique items for babies and children... gorgeous dresses and nursery furnishings... out-of-this-world customer service... a dream store to fill your nursery... worth every penny... a great place to go with your friends, but it's best to leave your kids at home... friendly staff will go out of their way to find what you need... I love dressing my girls in adorable outfits that can't be found on every other child in town... high-end items and a pricetag to go along with it...* ”

Furniture, Bedding & Decor	✓	$$$$	Prices
Gear & Equipment	✗	❹	Product availability
Nursing & Feeding	✗	❹	Staff knowledge
Safety & Babycare	✗	❹	Customer service
Clothing, Shoes & Accessories	✓	❺	Decor
Books, Toys & Entertainment	✓		

WWW.MUDPIESBABYANDKIDS.COM

PEACHTREE CITY—250 CITY CIR (AT CIRCLE GATE); 770.631.4453; M-TH 10-8, F-SA 10-9, SU 12-6; PARKING LOT

Old Navy ★★★★☆

"...hip and 'in' clothes for infants and tots... plenty of steals on clearance items... T-shirts and pants for $10 or less... busy, busy, busy—long lines, especially on weekends... nothing fancy and you won't mind when your kids get down and dirty in these clothes... easy to wash, decent quality... you can shop for your baby, your toddler, your teen and yourself all at the same time... clothes are especially affordable when you hit their sales (post-holiday sales are amazing!)..."

Furniture, Bedding & Decor	✗	$$	Prices
Gear & Equipment	✗	❹	Product availability
Nursing & Feeding	✗	❸	Staff knowledge
Safety & Babycare	✗	❸	Customer service
Clothing, Shoes & Accessories	✓	❸	Decor
Books, Toys & Entertainment	✗		

WWW.OLDNAVY.COM

FAYETTEVILLE—116 PAVILLION PKWY (AT HWY 85); 678.817.7266; M-SA 9-9, SU 11-7; PARKING LOT

MORROW—1865 MT ZION RD (AT MEADOWBROOK LN); 678.422.0687; M-SA 9-9, SU 11-7

Rainbow Kids ★★½☆☆

"...fun clothing styles for infants and tots at low prices... the quality isn't the same as the more expensive brands, but the sleepers and play outfits always hold up well... great place for basics... cute trendy shoe selection for your little walker... we love the prices... up-to-date selection..."

Furniture, Bedding & Decor	✗	$$	Prices
Gear & Equipment	✓	❸	Product availability
Nursing & Feeding	✗	❸	Staff knowledge
Safety & Babycare	✗	❸	Customer service
Clothing, Shoes & Accessories	✓	❸	Decor
Books, Toys & Entertainment	✓		

WWW.RAINBOWSHOPS.COM

COLLEGE PARK—6055B OLD NATIONAL HWY (AT FLAT SHOALS RD); 770.997.7805; M-SA 10-8, SU 12-6

FOREST PARK—4849 JONESBORO RD (AT FOREST PKWY); 404.361.4060; M-SA 10-8, SU 11-6

MORROW—1532 SOUTHLAKE PKWY (AT MT ZION RD); 770.968.8778; M-SA 10-9, SU 1-6

Sears ★★★☆☆

"...a decent selection of clothes and basic baby equipment... check out the Kids Club program—it's a great way to save money... you go to Sears to save money, not to be pampered... the quality of their merchandise is better than Wal-Mart, but don't expect anything too special or different... not much in terms of gear, but tons of well-priced baby and toddler clothing..."

Furniture, Bedding & Decor	✓	$$	Prices
Gear & Equipment	✓	❸	Product availability
Nursing & Feeding	✓	❸	Staff knowledge
Safety & Babycare	✓	❸	Customer service
Clothing, Shoes & Accessories	✓	❸	Decor
Books, Toys & Entertainment	✓		

WWW.SEARS.COM

MORROW—1300 SOUTHLAKE CIR (AT SOUTHLAKE MALL); 770.961.7110; M-SA 10-9, SU 11-6; MALL PARKING

UNION CITY—600 SHANNON SOUTHPARK (AT SHANNON MALL); 770.969.3200; M-F 10-9, SA 8-9, SU 11-5

Serendipity Baby & Co ★★★★★

"...a beautiful selection of hand-painted items... incredible selection and sales support... beautiful bedding, furniture and gift items... everyone here is extremely helpful and willing to go the extra mile... specialty items at reasonable prices... join their e-mail list and you'll get notified about monthly 'e-mail-only' specials... new products arrive frequently... my questions are always answered quickly—the owner is either working in the store, or is available to her staff by telephone..."

Furniture, Bedding & Decor	✓	$$$$	Prices
Gear & Equipment	✗	4	Product availability
Nursing & Feeding	✓	4	Staff knowledge
Safety & Babycare	✗	5	Customer service
Clothing, Shoes & Accessories	✓	5	Decor
Books, Toys & Entertainment	✓		

WWW.SERENDIPITYBABY.COM

FAYETTEVILLE—286 HWY 314 (AT BANKS RD); 770.460.5410; T-F 11-6, SA 10-6; PARKING IN FRONT OF BLDG

Stride Rite Shoes ★★★½☆

"...wonderful selection of baby and toddler shoes... sandals, sneakers, and even special-occasion shoes... decent quality shoes that last... they know a lot about kids' shoes and take the time to get it right—they always measure my son's feet before fittings... store sizes vary, but they always have something in stock that works... they've even special ordered shoes for my daughter... a fun 'first shoe' buying experience..."

Furniture, Bedding & Decor	✗	$$$	Prices
Gear & Equipment	✗	4	Product availability
Nursing & Feeding	✗	4	Staff knowledge
Safety & Babycare	✗	4	Customer service
Clothing, Shoes & Accessories	✓	4	Decor
Books, Toys & Entertainment	✗		

WWW.STRIDERITE.COM

PEACHTREE CITY—232 PEACHTREE CIR; 770.632.2787; M-F 10-9, SA 10-9, SU 12-6

Target ★★★★☆

"...our favorite place to shop for kids' stuff—good selection and very affordable... guilt-free shopping—kids grow so fast so I don't want to pay high department-store prices... everything from diapers and sippy cups to car seats and strollers... easy return policy... generally helpful staff, but you don't go for the service—you go for the prices... decent registry that won't freak your friends out with outrageous prices... easy, convenient shopping for well-priced items... all the big-box brands available—Graco, Evenflo, Eddie Bauer, etc...."

Furniture, Bedding & Decor	✓	$$	Prices
Gear & Equipment	✓	4	Product availability
Nursing & Feeding	✓	3	Staff knowledge
Safety & Babycare	✓	3	Customer service
Clothing, Shoes & Accessories	✓	3	Decor
Books, Toys & Entertainment	✓		

WWW.TARGET.COM

EAST POINT—3660 MARKETPLACE BLVD (AT WELCOME ALL RD SW); 404.267.0063; M-SA 8-10, SU 8-9; PARKING IN FRONT OF BLDG

FAYETTEVILLE—107 PAVILION PKWY (AT HWY 85); 770.719.9766; M-SA 8-10, SU 8-9; PARKING IN FRONT OF BLDG

MORROW—1940 MT ZION RD (AT MT ZION CIR); 770.472.3355; M-SA 8-10, SU 8-9; PARKING IN FRONT OF BLDG

Toys R Us ★★★½☆

"...not just toys, but also tons of gear and supplies including diapers and formula... a hectic shopping experience but the prices make it all worthwhile... I've experienced good and bad service at the same store on the same day... the stores are huge and can be overwhelming... most big brand-names available... leave the kids at home unless you want to end up with a cart full of toys..."

Furniture, Bedding & Decor	✓	$$$	Prices
Gear & Equipment	✓	❹	Product availability
Nursing & Feeding	✓	❸	Staff knowledge
Safety & Babycare	✓	❸	Customer service
Clothing, Shoes & Accessories	✓	❸	Decor
Books, Toys & Entertainment	✓		

WWW.TOYSRUS.COM

FAYETTEVILLE—132 PAVILLION PKWY (AT HWY 85); 678.817.0359; M-SA 10-9, SU 11-6

MORROW—1496 MT ZION RD (AT HWY 54); 770.961.1331; M-SA 9:30-9:30, SU 10-7

Dekalb

★★★★★

"lila picks"

★Babies R Us

Babies R Us ★★★★★

"...everything baby under one roof... they have a wide selection and carry most 'mainstream' items such as Graco, Fisher-Price, Avent and Britax... great customer service—given how big the stores are, I was pleasantly surprised at how attentive the staff was... easy return policy... super busy on weekends so try to visit on a weekday for the best service... keep an eye out for great coupons, deals and frequent sales... easy and comprehensive registry... shopping here is so easy—you've got to check it out..."

Furniture, Bedding & Decor ✓	$$$ Prices
Gear & Equipment ✓	❹ Product availability
Nursing & Feeding ✓	❹ Staff knowledge
Safety & Babycare ✓	❹ Customer service
Clothing, Shoes & Accessories ✓	❹ Decor
Books, Toys & Entertainment ✓	

WWW.BABIESRUS.COM

LITHONIA—8160 MALL PKWY (AT THE MALL AT STONECREST); 770.484.9697; M-SA 9:30-9:30, SU 11-7; PARKING IN FRONT OF BLDG

Baby Depot At Burlington Coat Factory ★★★½☆

"...a large, 'super store' layout with a ton of baby gear... wide aisles, packed shelves, barely existent customer service and awesome prices... everything from bottles, car seats and strollers to gliders, cribs and clothes... I always find something worth getting... a little disorganized and hard to locate items you're looking for... the staff is not always knowledgeable about their merchandise... return policy is store credit only..."

Furniture, Bedding & Decor ✓	$$ Prices
Gear & Equipment ✓	❸ Product availability
Nursing & Feeding ✓	❸ Staff knowledge
Safety & Babycare ✓	❸ Customer service
Clothing, Shoes & Accessories ✓	❸ Decor
Books, Toys & Entertainment ✓	

WWW.BABYDEPOT.COM

DECATUR—2032 LAWRENCEVILLE HWY (AT N DECALB MALL); 480.248.1182; M-SA 10-9, SU 11-7; PARKING LOT

Children's Place, The ★★★½☆

"...great bargains on cute clothing... shoes, socks, swimsuits, sunglasses and everything in between... lots of '3 for $20' type deals on sleepers, pants and mix-and-match separates... so much more affordable than the other 'big chains'... don't expect the most unique

stuff here, but it wears and washes well... cheap clothing for cheap prices... you can leave the store with bags full of clothes without putting a huge dent in your wallet... ❞

Furniture, Bedding & Decor	✗	$$	Prices
Gear & Equipment	✗	❹	Product availability
Nursing & Feeding	✗	❹	Staff knowledge
Safety & Babycare	✗	❹	Customer service
Clothing, Shoes & Accessories	✓	❹	Decor
Books, Toys & Entertainment	✓		

WWW.CHILDRENSPLACE.COM

DECATUR—2050 LAWRENCEVILLE HWY (AT NORTH DEKALB MALL); 404.248.9750; M-SA 10-9, SU 11-7; MALL PARKING

LITHONIA—2929 TURNER HILL RD (AT THE MALL AT STONECREST); 770.484.4498; M-SA 10-9, SU 11-7; MALL PARKING

Dillard's ★★★★☆

❝*...this store has beautiful clothes, and if you catch a sale, you can get great quality clothes at super bargain prices... good customer service and helpful staff... a huge selection of merchandise for boys and girls... nice layette department... some furnishings like little tables and chairs... beautiful displays... the best part is that in addition to shopping for your kids, you can also shop for yourself...* ❞

Furniture, Bedding & Decor	✓	$$$	Prices
Gear & Equipment	✗	❹	Product availability
Nursing & Feeding	✗	❸	Staff knowledge
Safety & Babycare	✗	❹	Customer service
Clothing, Shoes & Accessories	✓	❹	Decor
Books, Toys & Entertainment	✓		

WWW.DILLARDS.COM

LITHONIA—8000 MALL PKWY (AT TURNER HILL RD); 770.666.0000; M-SA 10-9, SU 12-6

JCPenney ★★★½☆

❝*...always a good place to find clothes and other baby basics... the registry process was seamless... staff is generally friendly but the lines always seem long and slow... they don't have the greatest selection of toddler clothes, but their baby section is great... we had some damaged furniture delivered but customer service was easy and accommodating... a pretty limited selection of gear, but what they have is priced right...* ❞

Furniture, Bedding & Decor	✓	$$	Prices
Gear & Equipment	✓	❸	Product availability
Nursing & Feeding	✓	❸	Staff knowledge
Safety & Babycare	✓	❸	Customer service
Clothing, Shoes & Accessories	✓	❸	Decor
Books, Toys & Entertainment	✓		

WWW.JCPENNEY.COM

LITHONIA—8040 MALL PKWY (AT TURNER HILL RD); 770.484.5604; M-SA 10-9, SU 12-6; MALL PARKING

Kid To Kid ★★★½☆

❝*...best selection and best finds of all the secondhand children's stores that I have been to... wonderful resale outlet for high-end children's clothing, furniture, and toys... I make out really well there with books... beautifully arranged, the stock and the prices are great... the place to go for used equipment... they only accept items in excellent condition, many of them look brand new... finally I can actually fit my double stroller in the aisle of a children's clothing store...* ❞

Furniture, Bedding & Decor	✗	$$	Prices
Gear & Equipment	✗	❹	Product availability

Nursing & Feeding	✗	❹	Staff knowledge
Safety & Babycare	✗	❹	Customer service
Clothing, Shoes & Accessories	✓	❸	Decor
Books, Toys & Entertainment	✓		

WWW.KIDTOKID.COM

STONE MOUNTAIN—5370 HYW 78 (AT W PARK PLACE BLVD); 770.879.1170; M-SA 10-7, SU 1-5; PARKING LOT

Kid's Foot Locker ★★★½☆

"...Nike, Reebok and Adidas for your little ones... hip, trendy and quite pricey... perfect for the sports addict dad who wants his kid sporting the latest NFL duds... shoes cost close to what the adult variety costs... generally good quality... they carry infant and toddler sizes..."

Furniture, Bedding & Decor	✗	$$$	Prices
Gear & Equipment	✗	❸	Product availability
Nursing & Feeding	✗	❸	Staff knowledge
Safety & Babycare	✗	❸	Customer service
Clothing, Shoes & Accessories	✓	❸	Decor
Books, Toys & Entertainment	✗		

WWW.KIDSFOOTLOCKER.COM

DECATUR—2050 LAWRENCEVILLE HWY (AT N DEKALB MALL); 404.982.9130; M-SA 10-9, SU 12-6

DECATUR—2801 CANDLER RD (AT S RAINBOW DR); 404.212.0610

Macy's ★★★½☆

"...Macy's has it all and I never leave empty-handed... if you time your visit right you can find some great deals... go during the week so you don't get overwhelmed with the weekend crowd... good for staples as well as beautiful party dresses for girls... lots of brand-names like Carter's, Guess, and Ralph Lauren... not much in terms of assistance... newspaper coupons and sales help keep the cost down... some stores are better organized and maintained than others... if you're going to shop at a department store for your baby, then Macy's is a safe bet..."

Furniture, Bedding & Decor	✓	$$$	Prices
Gear & Equipment	✗	❸	Product availability
Nursing & Feeding	✗	❸	Staff knowledge
Safety & Babycare	✗	❸	Customer service
Clothing, Shoes & Accessories	✓	❸	Decor
Books, Toys & Entertainment	✓		

WWW.MACYS.COM

DECATUR—2144 LAWRENCEVILLE HWY (AT N DEKALB SQ SHOPPPING CTR); 404.329.2600; M-SA 10-9, SU 12-7

DECATUR—2731 CANDLER RD (AT THE GALLERY AT S DE KALB); 404.243.2600; M-SA 10-9, SU 12-7

Old Navy ★★★★☆

"...hip and 'in' clothes for infants and tots... plenty of steals on clearance items... T-shirts and pants for $10 or less... busy, busy, busy—long lines, especially on weekends... nothing fancy and you won't mind when your kids get down and dirty in these clothes... easy to wash, decent quality... you can shop for your baby, your toddler, your teen and yourself all at the same time... clothes are especially affordable when you hit their sales (post-holiday sales are amazing!)..."

Furniture, Bedding & Decor	✗	$$	Prices
Gear & Equipment	✗	❹	Product availability
Nursing & Feeding	✗	❸	Staff knowledge
Safety & Babycare	✗	❸	Customer service
Clothing, Shoes & Accessories	✓	❸	Decor
Books, Toys & Entertainment	✗		

WWW.OLDNAVY.COM

STONE MOUNTAIN—5370 US HWY 78 (AT ROCKRIDGE RD SW); 770.413.9911; M-SA 9-9, SU 11-7

Payless Shoe Source ★★★☆☆

"...a good place for deals on children's shoes... staff is helpful with sizing... the selection and prices for kids' shoes can't be beat, but the quality isn't always spectacular... good leather shoes for cheap... great variety of all sizes and widths... I get my son's shoes here and don't feel like I'm wasting my money since he'll outgrow them in 3 months anyway..."

Furniture, Bedding & Decor	✗	$$	Prices
Gear & Equipment	✗	❸	Product availability
Nursing & Feeding	✗	❸	Staff knowledge
Safety & Babycare	✗	❸	Customer service
Clothing, Shoes & Accessories	✓	❸	Decor
Books, Toys & Entertainment	✗		

WWW.PAYLESS.COM

DORAVILLE—5707 BUFORD HWY NE (AT LONGMIRE EXT); 770.451.3883; M-SA 10-9, SU 12-6

Rainbow Kids ★★½☆☆

"...fun clothing styles for infants and tots at low prices... the quality isn't the same as the more expensive brands, but the sleepers and play outfits always hold up well... great place for basics... cute trendy shoe selection for your little walker... we love the prices... up-to-date selection..."

Furniture, Bedding & Decor	✗	$$	Prices
Gear & Equipment	✓	❸	Product availability
Nursing & Feeding	✗	❸	Staff knowledge
Safety & Babycare	✗	❸	Customer service
Clothing, Shoes & Accessories	✓	❸	Decor
Books, Toys & Entertainment	✓		

WWW.RAINBOWSHOPS.COM

DECATUR—2801 CANDLER RD (AT RAINBOW DR); 404.381.5177; M-SA 10-9, SU 12-6:30

LITHONIA—8130 MALL PKWY (AT IRIS DR SW); 770.484.6128; M-SA 10-9, SU 12-6

STONE MOUNTAIN—5160 MEMORIAL DR (AT RAYS RD); 404.292.8990; M-SA 10-9, SU 11-6

Ross Dress For Less ★★★☆☆

"...if you're in the mood for bargain hunting and are okay with potentially coming up empty-handed, then Ross is for you... don't expect to get educated about baby products here... go early on a week day and you'll find an organized store and staff that is helpful and available—forget weekends... their selection is pretty inconsistent, but I have found some incredible bargains... a great place to stock up on birthday presents or stocking stuffers..."

Furniture, Bedding & Decor	✗	$$	Prices
Gear & Equipment	✗	❸	Product availability
Nursing & Feeding	✗	❸	Staff knowledge
Safety & Babycare	✗	❸	Customer service
Clothing, Shoes & Accessories	✓	❸	Decor
Books, Toys & Entertainment	✓		

WWW.ROSSSTORES.COM

LITHONIA—8090 MALL PKWY (AT HONEYCREEK CT); 770.482.0139; M-SA 9:30-9:30, SU 11-7; MALL PARKING

Sears ★★★☆☆

"...a decent selection of clothes and basic baby equipment... check out the Kids Club program—it's a great way to save money... you go to Sears to save money, not to be pampered... the quality of their merchandise is better than Wal-Mart, but don't expect anything too special or different... not much in terms of gear, but tons of well-priced baby and toddler clothing..."

Furniture, Bedding & Decor .... ✓
Gear & Equipment .... ✓
Nursing & Feeding .... ✓
Safety & Babycare .... ✓
Clothing, Shoes & Accessories .... ✓
Books, Toys & Entertainment .... ✓

$$ .... Prices
❸ .... Product availability
❸ .... Staff knowledge
❸ .... Customer service
❸ .... Decor

WWW.SEARS.COM

LITHONIA—8020 MALL PKWY (AT TURNER HILL RD); 678.629.5000; M-F 10-9, SA 8-9, SU 11-7

Stride Rite Shoes ★★★½☆

"...wonderful selection of baby and toddler shoes... sandals, sneakers, and even special-occasion shoes... decent quality shoes that last... they know a lot about kids' shoes and take the time to get it right—they always measure my son's feet before fittings... store sizes vary, but they always have something in stock that works... they've even special ordered shoes for my daughter... a fun 'first shoe' buying experience..."

Furniture, Bedding & Decor .... ✗
Gear & Equipment .... ✗
Nursing & Feeding .... ✗
Safety & Babycare .... ✗
Clothing, Shoes & Accessories .... ✓
Books, Toys & Entertainment .... ✗

$$$ .... Prices
❹ .... Product availability
❹ .... Staff knowledge
❹ .... Customer service
❹ .... Decor

WWW.STRIDERITE.COM

LITHONIA—1270-2929 TURNER HILL RD (MALL AT STONECREST); 678.526.0676; M-SA 10-9, SU 12-6

Target ★★★★☆

"...our favorite place to shop for kids' stuff—good selection and very affordable... guilt-free shopping—kids grow so fast so I don't want to pay high department-store prices... everything from diapers and sippy cups to car seats and strollers... easy return policy... generally helpful staff, but you don't go for the service—you go for the prices... decent registry that won't freak your friends out with outrageous prices... easy, convenient shopping for well-priced items... all the big-box brands available—Graco, Evenflo, Eddie Bauer, etc...."

Furniture, Bedding & Decor .... ✓
Gear & Equipment .... ✓
Nursing & Feeding .... ✓
Safety & Babycare .... ✓
Clothing, Shoes & Accessories .... ✓
Books, Toys & Entertainment .... ✓

$$ .... Prices
❹ .... Product availability
❸ .... Staff knowledge
❸ .... Customer service
❸ .... Decor

WWW.TARGET.COM

STONE MOUNTAIN—2055 W PARK PL BLVD (AT BERMUDA RD); 770.879.5898; M-SA 8-10, SU 8-9; PARKING IN FRONT OF BLDG

TUCKER—4241 LAVISTA RD (AT NORTHLAKE PKWY); 770.270.5375; M-SA 8-10, SU 8-9; PARKING IN FRONT OF BLDG

Toys R Us ★★★½☆

"...not just toys, but also tons of gear and supplies including diapers and formula... a hectic shopping experience but the prices make it all worthwhile... I've experienced good and bad service at the same store

on the same day... the stores are huge and can be overwhelming... most big brand-names available... leave the kids at home unless you want to end up with a cart full of toys... **”**

Furniture, Bedding & Decor	✓	$$$	Prices
Gear & Equipment	✓	❹	Product availability
Nursing & Feeding	✓	❸	Staff knowledge
Safety & Babycare	✓	❸	Customer service
Clothing, Shoes & Accessories	✓	❸	Decor
Books, Toys & Entertainment	✓		

WWW.TOYSRUS.COM

LITHONIA—2918 TURNER HILL RD (AT MALL AT STONECREST); 770.484.6757; M-SA 10-9, SU 11-6; MALL PARKING

TUCKER—4033 LA VISTA RD (AT BRIARCLIFF RD NE); 770.938.4321; M-SA 10-9, SU 11-6; PARKING LOT

Gwinnett

★★★★★

"lila picks"

- ★Baby Cakes Children's Decor 'n More
- ★Baby's Room & Child Space
- ★Georgia Baby & Kids
- ★New Baby Products

April Cornell ★★★½☆

"...beautiful, classic dresses and accessories for special occasions... I love the matching 'mommy and me' outfits... lots of fun knickknacks for sale... great selection of baby wear on their web site... rest assured your baby won't look like every other child in these adorable outfits... very frilly and girlie—beautiful..."

Furniture, Bedding & Decor	✗	$$$	Prices
Gear & Equipment	✗	❸	Product availability
Nursing & Feeding	✗	❹	Staff knowledge
Safety & Babycare	✗	❹	Customer service
Clothing, Shoes & Accessories	✓	❹	Decor
Books, Toys & Entertainment	✗		

WWW.APRILCORNELL.COM

NORCROSS—5155 PEACHTREE PKY (AT THE FORUM SHOPPING CENTER); 770.447.8021; M-SA 10-9, SU 11-7

Babies R Us ★★★★☆

"...everything baby under one roof... they have a wide selection and carry most 'mainstream' items such as Graco, Fisher-Price, Avent and Britax... great customer service—given how big the stores are, I was pleasantly surprised at how attentive the staff was... easy return policy... super busy on weekends so try to visit on a weekday for the best service... keep an eye out for great coupons, deals and frequent sales... easy and comprehensive registry... shopping here is so easy—you've got to check it out..."

Furniture, Bedding & Decor	✓	$$$	Prices
Gear & Equipment	✓	❹	Product availability
Nursing & Feeding	✓	❹	Staff knowledge
Safety & Babycare	✓	❹	Customer service
Clothing, Shoes & Accessories	✓	❹	Decor
Books, Toys & Entertainment	✓		

WWW.BABIESRUS.COM

DULUTH—3925 VENTURA DR (AT STEVE REYNOLDS BLVD NW); 770.622.8888; M-SA 9:30-9:30, SU 11-7; PARKING IN FRONT OF BLDG

Baby Cakes Children's Decor 'n More ★★★★★

"...the perfect store for finding a nice baby gift... cute clothes, bedding and accessories—perfect for finding a special shower gift... very nice customer service... always offering to help before you have to ask!.. easy delivery... a comprehensive line of baby gear and accessories... a beautiful store with lots of wonderful furniture and custom bedding... you're going to want to buy something here, so plan on spending some money..."

Furniture, Bedding & Decor	✓	$$$$	Prices
Gear & Equipment	✓	4	Product availability
Nursing & Feeding	×	4	Staff knowledge
Safety & Babycare	×	4	Customer service
Clothing, Shoes & Accessories	×	4	Decor
Books, Toys & Entertainment	✓		

WWW.EBABYCAKES.COM

DULUTH—10305 MEDLOCK BRIDGE RD (AT WILSON RD); 678.584.5995; M-SA 10-6, SU 1-5; PARKING LOT

Baby Depot At Burlington Coat Factory ★★★½☆

"...a large, 'super store' layout with a ton of baby gear... wide aisles, packed shelves, barely existent customer service and awesome prices... everything from bottles, car seats and strollers to gliders, cribs and clothes... I always find something worth getting... a little disorganized and hard to locate items you're looking for... the staff is not always knowledgeable about their merchandise... return policy is store credit only..."

Furniture, Bedding & Decor	✓	$$	Prices
Gear & Equipment	✓	3	Product availability
Nursing & Feeding	✓	3	Staff knowledge
Safety & Babycare	✓	3	Customer service
Clothing, Shoes & Accessories	✓	3	Decor
Books, Toys & Entertainment	✓		

WWW.BABYDEPOT.COM

LAWRENCEVILLE—5900 SUGARLOAF PKWY NW (AT BROWN RD NW); 678.847.5101; M-SA 10-9, SU 12-6; PARKING LOT

Baby's Room & Child Space ★★★★★

"...lovely upscale baby gear store... quality name brands for all the basics—cribs, strollers, highchairs... lots of cute items you can't find anywhere else... we ordered our crib here and it was a very smooth process... great selection of toys and furniture with a range of prices... customer service is relaxed and never pushy..."

Furniture, Bedding & Decor	✓	$$$$	Prices
Gear & Equipment	✓	4	Product availability
Nursing & Feeding	✓	4	Staff knowledge
Safety & Babycare	✓	4	Customer service
Clothing, Shoes & Accessories	×	4	Decor
Books, Toys & Entertainment	✓		

WWW.TBRGA.COM

NORCROSS—5270 PEACHTREE PKWY (AT DAVIN CT NW); 678.646.0640; M-SA 10-6; PARKING LOT

BabyGap/GapKids ★★★★☆

"...colorful baby and toddler clothing in clean, well-lit stores... great return policy... it's the Gap, so you know what you're getting—colorful, cute and well-made clothing... best place for baby hats... prices are reasonable especially since there's always a sale of some sort going *on... sales, sales, sales—frequent and fantastic... everything I'm looking for in infant clothing—snap crotches, snaps up the front, all natural fabrics and great styling... fun seasonal selections—a great place to shop for gifts as well as for your own kids... although it can get busy, staff generally seem accommodating and helpful...* ”

Furniture, Bedding & Decor .... ✗
Gear & Equipment .... ✗
Nursing & Feeding .... ✗
Safety & Babycare .... ✗
Clothing, Shoes & Accessories....... ✓
Books, Toys & Entertainment .... ✗

$$$ .... Prices
❹ .... Product availability
❹ .... Staff knowledge
❹ .... Customer service
❹ .... Decor

WWW.GAP.COM

BUFORD—3333 BUFORD DR (AT MALL OF GEORGIA); 678.482.7144; M-SA 10-9, SU 12-6; PARKING IN FRONT OF BLDG

DULUTH—2100 PLEASANT HILL RD NW (AT GWINNETT PL MALL); 770.476.0117; M-SA 10-9; FREE PARKING

Back By Popular Demand

Furniture, Bedding & Decor .... ✗
Nursing & Feeding .... ✗
Clothing, Shoes & Accessories....... ✓

✗ .... Gear & Equipment
✗ .... Safety & Babycare
✗ .... Books, Toys & Entertainment

WWW.GWINNETTWEBPAGES.COM/BACKBYPOPULARDEMAND.HTM

LILBURN—97 MAIN ST (OFF HWY 29); 770.923.2968; M W F-SA 10-6, T TH 10-8; PARKING LOT

Carter's ★★★★☆

“*...always a great selection of inexpensive baby basics—everything from clothing to linens... I always find something at 'giveaway prices' during one of their frequent sales... busy and crowded—it can be a chaotic shopping experience... 30 to 50 percent less than what you would pay at other boutiques... I bought five pieces of baby clothing for less than $40... durable, adorable and affordable... most stores have a small play area for kids in center of store so you can get your shopping done...* ”

Furniture, Bedding & Decor .... ✓
Gear & Equipment .... ✗
Nursing & Feeding .... ✗
Safety & Babycare .... ✗
Clothing, Shoes & Accessories....... ✓
Books, Toys & Entertainment .... ✓

$$ .... Prices
❹ .... Product availability
❹ .... Staff knowledge
❹ .... Customer service
❹ .... Decor

WWW.CARTERS.COM

LAWRENCEVILLE—5900 SUGARLOAF PKWY (AT DISCOVER MILLS MALL); 678.847.5323; M-SA 10-9, SU 12-6; MALL PARKING

Children's Place, The ★★★½☆

“*...great bargains on cute clothing... shoes, socks, swimsuits, sunglasses and everything in between... lots of '3 for $20' type deals on sleepers, pants and mix-and-match separates... so much more affordable than the other 'big chains'... don't expect the most unique stuff here, but it wears and washes well... cheap clothing for cheap prices... you can leave the store with bags full of clothes without putting a huge dent in your wallet...* ”

Furniture, Bedding & Decor .... ✗
Gear & Equipment .... ✗
Nursing & Feeding .... ✗
Safety & Babycare .... ✗
Clothing, Shoes & Accessories....... ✓
Books, Toys & Entertainment .... ✓

$$ .... Prices
❹ .... Product availability
❹ .... Staff knowledge
❹ .... Customer service
❹ .... Decor

WWW.CHILDRENSPLACE.COM

BUFORD—3333 BUFORD DR NE (AT WOODWARD CROSSING RD); 678.482.6240; M-SA 10-9, SU 12-6; PARKING LOT

DULUTH—2100 PLEASANT HILL RD (AT GWINNETT PLACE MALL); 678.584.0030; M-SA 10-6; FREE PARKING

LAWRENCEVILLE—5900 SUGARLOAF PKWY (AT DISCOVER MILLS MALL); 678.847.5020; M-SA 10-9, SU 12-6; PARKING LOT

Dillard's ★★★★☆

"...this store has beautiful clothes, and if you catch a sale, you can get great quality clothes at super bargain prices... good customer service and helpful staff... a huge selection of merchandise for boys and girls... nice layette department... some furnishings like little tables and chairs... beautiful displays... the best part is that in addition to shopping for your kids, you can also shop for yourself..."

Furniture, Bedding & Decor	✓	$$$	Prices
Gear & Equipment	✗	❹	Product availability
Nursing & Feeding	✗	❸	Staff knowledge
Safety & Babycare	✗	❹	Customer service
Clothing, Shoes & Accessories	✓	❹	Decor
Books, Toys & Entertainment	✓		

WWW.DILLARDS.COM

BUFORD—3333 BUFORD DR NE (AT MALL OF GEORGIA); 678.482.5241; M-SA 10-9, SU 12-6

Encore Consignment Boutique

Furniture, Bedding & Decor	✗	✗	Gear & Equipment
Nursing & Feeding	✗	✗	Safety & Babycare
Clothing, Shoes & Accessories	✓	✗	Books, Toys & Entertainment

WWW.ENCOREBOUTIQUE.NET

NORCROSS—7732 SPALDING DR (AT HOLCOMB BRIDGE RD); 770.446.5040; M-SA 10-6:30, SU 12:30-5; PARKING LOT

Georgia Baby & Kids ★★★★★

"...a store for parents or grandparents who want to go all out for their baby's nursery... a fabulous showroom and the place to go if you want a nice looking nursery... wonderful selection of furniture, toys and books... geared toward the high price-point kid and baby items... can be difficult to get help while shopping... beautiful decor, cribs, etc... for infants and older children..."

Furniture, Bedding & Decor	✓	$$$$	Prices
Gear & Equipment	✗	❹	Product availability
Nursing & Feeding	✗	❹	Staff knowledge
Safety & Babycare	✗	❹	Customer service
Clothing, Shoes & Accessories	✗	❹	Decor
Books, Toys & Entertainment	✓		

WWW.GEORGIABABYANDKIDS.COM

NORCROSS—6410 DAWSON BLVD (AT ENTERPRISE DR NW); 770.448.2455; M-SA 10-7, SU 12-6; PARKING LOT

Gymboree ★★★★☆

"...beautiful clothing and great quality... colorful and stylish baby and kids wear... lots of fun birthday gift ideas... easy exchange and return policy... items usually go on sale pretty quickly... save money with Gymbucks... many stores have a play area which makes shopping with my kids fun (let alone feasible)..."

Furniture, Bedding & Decor	✗	$$$	Prices
Gear & Equipment	✗	❹	Product availability
Nursing & Feeding	✗	❹	Staff knowledge
Safety & Babycare	✗	❹	Customer service
Clothing, Shoes & Accessories	✓	❹	Decor

Books, Toys & Entertainment ....✓

WWW.GYMBOREE.COM

DULUTH—2100 PLEASANT HILL RD (AT GWINNETT PLACE MALL); 770.623.0838; M-SA 10-9, SU 12-6; MALL PARKING

Hansel & Gretel ★★★★☆

"...a wonderful little baby boutique with a great play area to entertain children while you shop... tons of cute outfits for babies and children and great decorations for your baby's room... be prepared to spend some money... not cheap, but the quality is fabulous... the staff is so nice and helpful..."

Furniture, Bedding & Decor	✓	$$$$	Prices
Gear & Equipment	✓	❹	Product availability
Nursing & Feeding	✗	❹	Staff knowledge
Safety & Babycare	✗	❹	Customer service
Clothing, Shoes & Accessories	✓	❺	Decor
Books, Toys & Entertainment	✓		

WWW.HANSELNGRETEL.COM

BUFORD—3205 WOODWARD CROSSING BLVD (AT MALL OF GEORGIA); 770.614.6860; M-SA 10-7, SU 1-6; MALL PARKING

JCPenney ★★★½☆

"...always a good place to find clothes and other baby basics... the registry process was seamless... staff is generally friendly but the lines always seem long and slow... they don't have the greatest selection of toddler clothes, but their baby section is great... we had some damaged furniture delivered but customer service was easy and accommodating... a pretty limited selection of gear, but what they have is priced right..."

Furniture, Bedding & Decor	✓	$$	Prices
Gear & Equipment	✓	❸	Product availability
Nursing & Feeding	✓	❸	Staff knowledge
Safety & Babycare	✓	❸	Customer service
Clothing, Shoes & Accessories	✓	❸	Decor
Books, Toys & Entertainment	✓		

WWW.JCPENNEY.COM

BUFORD—3333 BUFORD DR (AT MALL OF GEORGIA); 770.831.0252; M-SA 10-9, SU 12-6; MALL PARKING

KB Toys ★★★☆☆

"...hectic and always buzzing... wall-to-wall plastic and blinking lights... more Fisher-Price, Elmo and Sponge Bob than the eye can handle... a toy super store with discounted prices... they always have some kind of special sale going on... if you're looking for the latest and greatest popular toy, then look no further—not the place for unique or unusual toys... perfect for bulk toy shopping—especially around the holidays..."

Furniture, Bedding & Decor	✗	$$	Prices
Gear & Equipment	✗	❸	Product availability
Nursing & Feeding	✗	❸	Staff knowledge
Safety & Babycare	✗	❸	Customer service
Clothing, Shoes & Accessories	✗	❸	Decor
Books, Toys & Entertainment	✓		

WWW.KBTOYS.COM

BUFORD—3379 BUFORD DR (AT MALL OF GEORGIA); 678.482.7377; M-SA 10-9, SU 12-6; MALL PARKING

LAWRENCEVILLE—5900 SUGARLOAF PKY (AT DISCOVER MILLS); 678.847.5079; M-F 11-9, SA 12-9, SU 12-6; PARKING LOT

Kid's Room Stuff ★★★★☆

"...a high-end nursery furniture store with decent prices... our order was delivered and set up very promptly... the staff is knowledgeable and friendly... the selection is good and it makes shopping for a crib pretty easy and painless..."

Furniture, Bedding & Decor	✓	$$$	Prices
Gear & Equipment	✗	❹	Product availability
Nursing & Feeding	✗	❹	Staff knowledge
Safety & Babycare	✗	❹	Customer service
Clothing, Shoes & Accessories	✗	❹	Decor
Books, Toys & Entertainment	✗		

WWW.KIDSROOMSTUFF.COM

NORCROSS—10700 STATE BRIDGE RD (AT BEST FRIEND DR NW); 770.416.6003; M-TU 10-5, TH-F 10-5, SA 10-6, SU 12-6; PARKING LOT

Kids Formal Wear ★★★☆☆

"...easy shopping for the perfect special occasion outfit... baptismal gowns, flowergirl dresses, tuxedos and suits... precious... a variety of price ranges... all sales are final so make sure you like what you buy..."

Furniture, Bedding & Decor	✗	$$$	Prices
Gear & Equipment	✓	❸	Product availability
Nursing & Feeding	✗	❸	Staff knowledge
Safety & Babycare	✗	❸	Customer service
Clothing, Shoes & Accessories	✓	❸	Decor
Books, Toys & Entertainment	✗		

WWW.KFWEAR.COM

DULUTH—2100 PLEASANT HILL RD NW (AT GWINNETT PLACE MALL); 770.495.0064; M-SA 10-9, SU 12-6; FREE PARKING

Kohl's ★★★★☆

"...nice one-stop shopping for the whole family—everything from clothing to baby gear... great sales on clothing and a good selection of higher-end brands... stylish, inexpensive clothes for babies through 24 months... very easy shopping experience... dirt-cheap sales and clearance prices... nothing super fancy, but just right for those everyday romper outfits... Graco, Eddie Bauer and other well-known brands..."

Furniture, Bedding & Decor	✓	$$	Prices
Gear & Equipment	✓	❹	Product availability
Nursing & Feeding	✓	❸	Staff knowledge
Safety & Babycare	✓	❸	Customer service
Clothing, Shoes & Accessories	✓	❸	Decor
Books, Toys & Entertainment	✓		

WWW.KOHLS.COM

DULUTH—2050 W LIDDELL RD (AT DULUTH HWY NW); 678.417.1818; M-SA 8-10, SU 10-8

LAWRENCEVILLE—630 COLLINS HILL RD NW (AT HURRICANE SHOALS RD NE); 678.442.6646; M-SA 8-10, SU 10-8; PARKING IN FRONT OF BLDG

SNELLVILLE—2059 SCENIC HWY SW (AT HILLCREST DR SW); 678.344.2126; M-SA 8-10, SU 10-8; PARKING IN FRONT OF BLDG

SUWANEE—3620 PEACHTREE PKWY (AT JOHNS CREEK PKWY); 678.474.4993; M-SA 8-10, SU 10-8; PARKING LOT

New Baby Products ★★★★★

"...great to have an in-town specialty store that offers everything your baby needs... best for looking at gear and nursery bedding... I shop here regularly because they pretty much have it all... they have been around for years and are a staple for new parents... a big selection of nursery furnishings packed into a pretty tight space... the service is

friendly and fast... it's tough to navigate their aisles so leave your stroller in the car... they carry many popular brands and products at much more reasonable prices than other stores... ”

Furniture, Bedding & Decor ✓	$$$ Prices
Gear & Equipment ✓	❹ Product availability
Nursing & Feeding ✓	❹ Staff knowledge
Safety & Babycare ✓	❹ Customer service
Clothing, Shoes & Accessories ✓	❸ Decor
Books, Toys & Entertainment ✓	

WWW.NEWBABYPRODUCTS.COM

SNELLVILLE—2334 HENRY CLOWER BLVD (AT KNOLLWOOD DR SW); 770.978.9810; M F 10-8, T-TH SA 10-6; PARKING LOT

Nordstrom ★★★★☆

“*...quality service and quality clothes... awesome kids shoe department—almost as good as the one for adults... free balloons in the children's shoe area as well as drawing tables... in addition to their own brand, they carry a very nice selection of other high-end baby clothing including Ralph Lauren, Robeez, etc... adorable baby clothes—they make great shower gifts... such a wonderful shopping experience—their lounge is perfect for breastfeeding and for changing diapers... well-rounded selection of baby basics as well as fancy clothes for special events...* ”

Furniture, Bedding & Decor ✓	$$$$ Prices
Gear & Equipment ✓	❹ Product availability
Nursing & Feeding ✗	❹ Staff knowledge
Safety & Babycare ✗	❹ Customer service
Clothing, Shoes & Accessories ✓	❹ Decor
Books, Toys & Entertainment ✓	

WWW.NORDSTROM.COM

BUFORD—3333 BUFORD DR (AT MALL OF GEORGIA); 678.546.1122; M-SA 10-9, SU12-6; PARKING LOT

Old Navy ★★★★☆

“*...hip and 'in' clothes for infants and tots... plenty of steals on clearance items... T-shirts and pants for $10 or less... busy, busy, busy—long lines, especially on weekends... nothing fancy and you won't mind when your kids get down and dirty in these clothes... easy to wash, decent quality... you can shop for your baby, your toddler, your teen and yourself all at the same time... clothes are especially affordable when you hit their sales (post-holiday sales are amazing!)...* ”

Furniture, Bedding & Decor ✗	$$ Prices
Gear & Equipment ✗	❹ Product availability
Nursing & Feeding ✗	❸ Staff knowledge
Safety & Babycare ✗	❸ Customer service
Clothing, Shoes & Accessories ✓	❸ Decor
Books, Toys & Entertainment ✗	

WWW.OLDNAVY.COM

BUFORD—3333 BUFORD DR NE (AT MALL OF GEORGIA); 678.482.4343; M-SA 10-9, SU 12-6; PARKING LOT

DULUTH—2255 PLEASANT HILL RD NW (AT SATELLITE BLVD NW); 770.623.4797; M-SA 9-9, SU 11-7; PARKING LOT

NORCROSS—5135 PEACHTREE PKWY (AT E JONES BRIDGE NW); 770.246.0666; M-SA 9-9, SU 11-7; PARKING LOT

SNELLVILLE—2059 SCENIC HWY N (AT DOGWOD RD SW); 770.972.0291; M-SA 9-9, SU 11-7; PARKING LOT

Once Again Kids Inc ★★★☆☆

“...upscale new and used clothes as well as gear and accessories... the secondhand clothes are in terrific shape... make sure you go when you have time to really dig around... friendly, helpful staff... you generally walk out with something even if it's not what you went looking for...”

Furniture, Bedding & Decor	✓	$$$	Prices
Gear & Equipment	✓	❸	Product availability
Nursing & Feeding	✓	❸	Staff knowledge
Safety & Babycare	✓	❹	Customer service
Clothing, Shoes & Accessories	✓	❸	Decor
Books, Toys & Entertainment	✓		

WWW.ONCEAGAINKIDS.COM

SUWANEE—1000 PEACHTREE INDUSTRIAL BLVD (AT MCGINNIS FERRY RD NW); 770.831.2300; M-SA 10-6 ; PARKING LOT

OshKosh B'Gosh ★★★★☆

“...cute, sturdy clothes for infants and toddlers... frequent sales make their high-quality merchandise a lot more affordable... doesn't every American kid have to get a pair of their overalls?.. great selection of cute clothes for boys... you can't go wrong here—their clothing is fun and worth the price... customer service is pretty hit-or-miss from store to store... we always walk out of here with something fun and colorful...”

Furniture, Bedding & Decor	✗	$$$	Prices
Gear & Equipment	✗	❹	Product availability
Nursing & Feeding	✗	❹	Staff knowledge
Safety & Babycare	✗	❹	Customer service
Clothing, Shoes & Accessories	✓	❹	Decor
Books, Toys & Entertainment	✗		

WWW.OSHKOSHBGOSH.COM

LAWRENCEVILLE—5900 SUGARLOAF PKWY (AT SUGAR VALLEY DR NW); 678.847.5450; M-SA 10-9, SU 12-6; PARKING LOT

Payless Shoe Source ★★★☆☆

“...a good place for deals on children's shoes... staff is helpful with sizing... the selection and prices for kids' shoes can't be beat, but the quality isn't always spectacular... good leather shoes for cheap... great variety of all sizes and widths... I get my son's shoes here and don't feel like I'm wasting my money since he'll outgrow them in 3 months anyway...”

Furniture, Bedding & Decor	✗	$$	Prices
Gear & Equipment	✗	❸	Product availability
Nursing & Feeding	✗	❸	Staff knowledge
Safety & Babycare	✗	❸	Customer service
Clothing, Shoes & Accessories	✓	❸	Decor
Books, Toys & Entertainment	✗		

WWW.PAYLESS.COM

DULUTH—2100 PLEASANT HILL RD (AT GWINNETT PL MALL); 678.957.1199; M-SA 10-9, SU 12-6

Pier 1 Kids ★★★★☆

“...everything from curtains and dressers to teddy bears and piggy banks... attractive furniture and prices are moderate to expensive... staff provided lots of help assembling a 'look' for my child's room... we had an excellent shopping experience here... the salesperson told my kids it was okay to touch everything because it's all kid friendly... takes you out of the crib stage and into the next step...”

Furniture, Bedding & Decor	✓	$$$	Prices
Gear & Equipment	✗	❸	Product availability
Nursing & Feeding	✗	❹	Staff knowledge

Safety & Babycare	×	❹	Customer service
Clothing, Shoes & Accessories	×	❹	Decor
Books, Toys & Entertainment	×		

WWW.PIER1KIDS.COM

NORCROSS—5145 PEACHTREE PKWY (AT PEACHTREE CORNERS CIR); 770.242.6085; M 10-9

Pottery Barn Kids ★★★★½

"...stylish furniture, rugs, rockers and much more... they've found the right mix between quality and price... finally a company that stands behind what they sell—their customer service is great... gorgeous baby decor and furniture that will make your nursery to-die-for... the play area is so much fun—my daughter never wants to leave... a beautiful store with tons of ideas for setting up your nursery or kid's room... bright colors and cute patterns with basics to mix and match... if you see something in the catalog, but not in the store, just ask because they often have it in the back..."

Furniture, Bedding & Decor	✓	$$$$	Prices
Gear & Equipment	×	❹	Product availability
Nursing & Feeding	×	❹	Staff knowledge
Safety & Babycare	×	❹	Customer service
Clothing, Shoes & Accessories	×	❺	Decor
Books, Toys & Entertainment	✓		

WWW.POTTERYBARNKIDS.COM

NORCROSS—5155 PEACHTREE PKWY (AT MEDLOCK BRIDGE RD NW); 770.409.8580; M-SA 10-9, SU 12-6; PARKING LOT

Rooms To Go Kids ★★★½☆

"...solid furniture and nursery decor... helpful, but somewhat aggressive sales staff... I've always been pleased with my purchases... you can get the whole room taken care of in just one-stop... easy shopping and reasonable prices..."

Furniture, Bedding & Decor	✓	$$$	Prices
Gear & Equipment	×	❹	Product availability
Nursing & Feeding	×	❹	Staff knowledge
Safety & Babycare	×	❹	Customer service
Clothing, Shoes & Accessories	×	❹	Decor
Books, Toys & Entertainment	×		

WWW.ROOMSTOGOKIDS.COM

DULUTH—2330 PLEASANT HILL RD (AT SATELLITE BLVD NW); 770.622.6844; M-SA 10-9, SU 11-6; PARKING LOT

Ross Dress For Less ★★★☆☆

"...if you're in the mood for bargain hunting and are okay with potentially coming up empty-handed, then Ross is for you... don't expect to get educated about baby products here... go early on a week day and you'll find an organized store and staff that is helpful and available—forget weekends... their selection is pretty inconsistent, but I have found some incredible bargains... a great place to stock up on birthday presents or stocking stuffers..."

Furniture, Bedding & Decor	×	$$	Prices
Gear & Equipment	×	❸	Product availability
Nursing & Feeding	×	❸	Staff knowledge
Safety & Babycare	×	❸	Customer service
Clothing, Shoes & Accessories	✓	❸	Decor
Books, Toys & Entertainment	✓		

WWW.ROSSSTORES.COM

BUFORD—1600 MALL OF GEORGIA BLVD NE (AT MALL OF GEORGIA); 678.546.2871; M-SA 9:30-9:30, SU 11-7; MALL PARKING

Sears ★★★☆☆

"...a decent selection of clothes and basic baby equipment... check out the Kids Club program—it's a great way to save money... you go to Sears to save money, not to be pampered... the quality of their merchandise is better than Wal-Mart, but don't expect anything too special or different... not much in terms of gear, but tons of well-priced baby and toddler clothing..."

Furniture, Bedding & Decor .... ✓ | $$ .... Prices
Gear & Equipment .... ✓ | ❸ .... Product availability
Nursing & Feeding .... ✓ | ❸ .... Staff knowledge
Safety & Babycare .... ✓ | ❸ .... Customer service
Clothing, Shoes & Accessories .... ✓ | ❸ .... Decor
Books, Toys & Entertainment .... ✓

WWW.SEARS.COM

DULUTH—2100 PLEASANT HILL RD (AT GWINNETT PL MALL); 770.476.6691; M-SA 7:30-9, SU 10-7; MALL PARKING

Strasburg Children ★★★★☆

"...totally adorable special occasion outfits for babies and kids... classic baby, toddler, and kids clothes... dress-up clothes for kids... if you are looking for a flower girl or ring bearer outfit, look no further... handmade clothes that will last through multiple kids or generations... it's not cheap, but you can find great sales if you are patient..."

Furniture, Bedding & Decor .... ✗ | $$$$ .... Prices
Gear & Equipment .... ✗ | ❹ .... Product availability
Nursing & Feeding .... ✗ | ❹ .... Staff knowledge
Safety & Babycare .... ✗ | ❹ .... Customer service
Clothing, Shoes & Accessories .... ✓ | ❹ .... Decor
Books, Toys & Entertainment .... ✗

WWW.STRASBURGCHILDREN.COM

LAWRENCEVILLE—5900 SUGARLOAF PKWY (OFF RT 120); 678.847.5442; M-SA 10-9 SU 12-6

Stride Rite Shoes ★★★½☆

"...wonderful selection of baby and toddler shoes... sandals, sneakers, and even special-occasion shoes... decent quality shoes that last... they know a lot about kids' shoes and take the time to get it right—they always measure my son's feet before fittings... store sizes vary, but they always have something in stock that works... they've even special ordered shoes for my daughter... a fun 'first shoe' buying experience..."

Furniture, Bedding & Decor .... ✗ | $$$ .... Prices
Gear & Equipment .... ✗ | ❹ .... Product availability
Nursing & Feeding .... ✗ | ❹ .... Staff knowledge
Safety & Babycare .... ✗ | ❹ .... Customer service
Clothing, Shoes & Accessories .... ✓ | ❹ .... Decor
Books, Toys & Entertainment .... ✗

WWW.STRIDERITE.COM

BUFORD—1081-3333 BUFORD DR (AT MALL OF GEORGIA); 678.482.4244; M-SA 10-10, SU 11-6

SNELLVILLE—1905 SCENIC HWY (AT RONALD REAGAN); 770.978.9008; M-SA 10-6, SU 1-5; PARKING LOT

Target ★★★★☆

"...our favorite place to shop for kids' stuff—good selection and very affordable... guilt-free shopping—kids grow so fast so I don't want to pay high department-store prices... everything from diapers and sippy cups to car seats and strollers... easy return policy... generally helpful staff, but you don't go for the service—you go for the prices... decent registry that won't freak your friends out with outrageous prices... easy,

convenient shopping for well-priced items... all the big-box brands available—Graco, Evenflo, Eddie Bauer, etc.... ”

Furniture, Bedding & Decor ✓	$$ Prices
Gear & Equipment ✓	❹ Product availability
Nursing & Feeding ✓	❸ Staff knowledge
Safety & Babycare ✓	❸ Customer service
Clothing, Shoes & Accessories ✓	❸ Decor
Books, Toys & Entertainment ✓	

WWW.TARGET.COM

BUFORD—3205 WOODWARD CROSSING BLVD (AT MALL OF GEORGIA); 678.482.2367; M-SA 8-10, SU 8-9; PARKING IN FRONT OF BLDG

DULUTH—3935 VENTURE DR (AT STEVE REYNOLDS BLVD NW); 770.232.1929; M-SA 8-10, SU 8-9; PARKING IN FRONT OF BLDG

NORCROSS—3200 HOLCOMB BRIDGE RD (AT PEACHTREE INDUSTRIAL BLVD NW); 770.849.0885; M-SA 8-10, SU 8-9; PARKING IN FRONT OF BLDG

Toys R Us ★★★½☆

“*...not just toys, but also tons of gear and supplies including diapers and formula... a hectic shopping experience but the prices make it all worthwhile... I've experienced good and bad service at the same store on the same day... the stores are huge and can be overwhelming... most big brand-names available... leave the kids at home unless you want to end up with a cart full of toys...*”

Furniture, Bedding & Decor ✓	$$$ Prices
Gear & Equipment ✓	❹ Product availability
Nursing & Feeding ✓	❸ Staff knowledge
Safety & Babycare ✓	❸ Customer service
Clothing, Shoes & Accessories ✓	❸ Decor
Books, Toys & Entertainment ✓	

WWW.TOYSRUS.COM

BUFORD—1705 MALL OF GEORGIA BLVD (AT MALL OF GEORGIA); 770.932.6100; M-SA 9:30-9:30, SU 11-7; MALL PARKING

DULUTH—2205 PLEASANT HILL RD (AT GWINNETT PLACE MALL); 770.476.4646; M-SA 10-9, SU 11-6; MALL PARKING

Cobb & Douglas

★★★★★

"lila picks"

- ★Babes & Kids Furniture
- ★Baby's Room & Child Space
- ★Coggins Shoes For Kids

Babes & Kids Furniture ★★★★★

"...several nursery displays throughout the store so you definitely get a sense of what your baby's room will look like... so many accessories for all ages... beautiful products... everything you could ever need or want... pricey, but you definitely get your money's worth..."

Furniture, Bedding & Decor	✓	$$$	Prices
Gear & Equipment	✗	4	Product availability
Nursing & Feeding	✗	4	Staff knowledge
Safety & Babycare	✗	3	Customer service
Clothing, Shoes & Accessories	✗	4	Decor
Books, Toys & Entertainment	✗		

WWW.BABESANDKIDS.COM

MARIETTA—4880 LOWER ROSWELL RD (AT JOHNSON FERRY RD); 770.565.1420; M-SA 10-6, SU 1-5; PARKING LOT

Babies R Us ★★★★☆

"...everything baby under one roof... they have a wide selection and carry most 'mainstream' items such as Graco, Fisher-Price, Avent and Britax... great customer service—given how big the stores are, I was pleasantly surprised at how attentive the staff was... easy return policy... super busy on weekends so try to visit on a weekday for the best service... keep an eye out for great coupons, deals and frequent sales... easy and comprehensive registry... shopping here is so easy—you've got to check it out..."

Furniture, Bedding & Decor	✓	$$$	Prices
Gear & Equipment	✓	4	Product availability
Nursing & Feeding	✓	4	Staff knowledge
Safety & Babycare	✓	4	Customer service
Clothing, Shoes & Accessories	✓	4	Decor
Books, Toys & Entertainment	✓		

WWW.BABIESRUS.COM

DOUGLASVILLE—6875 DOUGLAS BLVD (AT ARBOR PL); 770.949.2209; M-SA 9:30-9:30, SU 11-7; PARKING IN FRONT OF BLDG

KENNESAW—1875 GREERS CHAPEL RD (AT BARRETT PKWY); 770.919.2229; M-SA 9:30-9:30, SU 11-7; PARKING IN FRONT OF BLDG

Baby Depot At Burlington Coat Factory ★★★½☆

"...a large, 'super store' layout with a ton of baby gear... wide aisles, packed shelves, barely existent customer service and awesome prices... everything from bottles, car seats and strollers to gliders, cribs and clothes... I always find something worth getting... a little disorganized and hard to locate items you're looking for... the staff is not always knowledgeable about their merchandise... return policy is store credit only..."

Furniture, Bedding & Decor ✓
Gear & Equipment ✓
Nursing & Feeding ✓
Safety & Babycare ✓
Clothing, Shoes & Accessories ✓
Books, Toys & Entertainment ✓

$$ Prices
❸ Product availability
❸ Staff knowledge
❸ Customer service
❸ Decor

WWW.BABYDEPOT.COM

MARIETTA—1255 ROSWELL RD (AT I-75); 770.971.6540; M-SA 10-9, SU 11-6; PARKING LOT

Baby's Room & Child Space ★★★★★

"...lovely upscale baby gear store... quality name brands for all the basics—cribs, strollers, highchairs... lots of cute items you can't find anywhere else... we ordered our crib here and it was a very smooth process... great selection of toys and furniture with a range of prices... customer service is relaxed and never pushy..."

Furniture, Bedding & Decor ✓
Gear & Equipment ✓
Nursing & Feeding ✓
Safety & Babycare ✓
Clothing, Shoes & Accessories ✗
Books, Toys & Entertainment ✓

$$$$ Prices
❹ Product availability
❹ Staff knowledge
❹ Customer service
❹ Decor

WWW.TBRGA.COM

MARIETTA—4400 ROSWELL RD NE (AT JOHNSON FERRY RD NE); 770.565.0892; M-SA 10-6; PARKING LOT

BabyGap/GapKids ★★★★☆

"...colorful baby and toddler clothing in clean, well-lit stores... great return policy... it's the Gap, so you know what you're getting—colorful, cute and well-made clothing... best place for baby hats... prices are reasonable especially since there's always a sale of some sort going on... sales, sales, sales—frequent and fantastic... everything I'm looking for in infant clothing—snap crotches, snaps up the front, all natural fabrics and great styling... fun seasonal selections—a great place to shop for gifts as well as for your own kids... although it can get busy, staff generally seem accommodating and helpful..."

Furniture, Bedding & Decor ✗
Gear & Equipment ✗
Nursing & Feeding ✗
Safety & Babycare ✗
Clothing, Shoes & Accessories ✓
Books, Toys & Entertainment ✗

$$$ Prices
❹ Product availability
❹ Staff knowledge
❹ Customer service
❹ Decor

WWW.GAP.COM

KENNESAW—400 ERNEST W BARRETT PKWY NW (AT MALL BLVD NW); 770.425.6003; M-SA 10-9, SU 12:30-6; PARKING IN FRONT OF BLDG

MARIETTA—4475 ROSWELL RD (AT HERITAGE GLEN DR NE); 770.579.5678; M-SA 10-9, SU 12-6; PARKING LOT

Bombay Kids ★★★★☆

"...the kids section of this furniture store carries out-of-the-ordinary items... whimsical, pastel grandfather clocks... zebra bean bags... perfect for my eclectic taste... I now prefer my daughter's room to my own... clean bathroom with changing area and wipes... they have a little table with crayons and coloring books for the kids... easy and relaxed shopping destination..."

Furniture, Bedding & Decor	✓	$$$	Prices
Gear & Equipment	×	❹	Product availability
Nursing & Feeding	×	❹	Staff knowledge
Safety & Babycare	×	❹	Customer service
Clothing, Shoes & Accessories	×	❹	Decor
Books, Toys & Entertainment	×		

WWW.BOMBAYKIDS.COM

MARIETTA—3625 DALLAS HWY SW (OFF DUE W RD); 678.594.6559; M-SA 10-9, SU 12-6

Children's Place, The ★★★½☆

"...great bargains on cute clothing... shoes, socks, swimsuits, sunglasses and everything in between... lots of '3 for $20' type deals on sleepers, pants and mix-and-match separates... so much more affordable than the other 'big chains'... don't expect the most unique stuff here, but it wears and washes well... cheap clothing for cheap prices... you can leave the store with bags full of clothes without putting a huge dent in your wallet..."

Furniture, Bedding & Decor	×	$$	Prices
Gear & Equipment	×	❹	Product availability
Nursing & Feeding	×	❹	Staff knowledge
Safety & Babycare	×	❹	Customer service
Clothing, Shoes & Accessories	✓	❹	Decor
Books, Toys & Entertainment	✓		

WWW.CHILDRENSPLACE.COM

DOUGLASVILLE—6700 DOUGLAS BLVD (AT ARBOR PLACE MALL); 678.838.9443; M-SA 10-9, SU 12-6; MALL PARKING

KENNESAW—400 ERNEST W BARRETT PKWY NW (TOWN CTR AT COBB); 770.792.1996; M-SA 10-9, SU 12:30-6; PARKING LOT

Coggins Shoes For Kids ★★★★★

"...the best place to buy your baby's first shoes... the staff is so helpful and friendly and the selection is outstanding... lots of hair accessories for girls... socks and tights to match the perfect outfit... there is even a fort for kids to play in while you browse... shoe shopping for my children is always a pleasant experience here... they even give your child a balloon when you're all done..."

Furniture, Bedding & Decor	×	$$$	Prices
Gear & Equipment	×	❺	Product availability
Nursing & Feeding	×	❺	Staff knowledge
Safety & Babycare	×	❺	Customer service
Clothing, Shoes & Accessories	✓	❺	Decor
Books, Toys & Entertainment	×		

WWW.SHOESFORKIDS.COM

MARIETTA—2207 ROSWELL RD NE (AT ROBINSON RD NE); 770.973.5335; M-W 10-7, TH-SA 10-6; PARKING LOT

Comfortable Chair Store, The ★★★½☆

"...they have every kind of rocking chair with many styles of fabric to choose from... we bought our glider here and couldn't be happier... the decor has much to be desired... warehouse feel... awesome store with wonderful sales staff... they will beat other stores prices so it pays to do your research..."

Furniture, Bedding & Decor .... ✓	$$$ .... Prices
Gear & Equipment .... ✗	❹ .... Product availability
Nursing & Feeding .... ✗	❹ .... Staff knowledge
Safety & Babycare .... ✗	❹ .... Customer service
Clothing, Shoes & Accessories .... ✗	❸ .... Decor
Books, Toys & Entertainment .... ✗	

WWW.THECOMFORTABLECHAIRSTORE.COM

KENNESAW—425 ERNEST W BARRETT PKWY PKY (AT TOWN CENTER PLAZA); 770.419.1992; M-SA 10-6:30, SU 12-6; MALL PARKING

Deja Vous ★★★½☆

“...an excellent consignment shop with an especially good maternity selection... I frequent this store often and never leave empty-handed... they carry new and gently used items for both mom and baby... great little shop with a lot to choose from... I'm so excited they now carry the Robeez shoes, so I don't have to travel far to get a pair... friendly owner who chooses well...”

Furniture, Bedding & Decor .... ✗	$$$ .... Prices
Gear & Equipment .... ✗	❹ .... Product availability
Nursing & Feeding .... ✗	❹ .... Staff knowledge
Safety & Babycare .... ✗	❹ .... Customer service
Clothing, Shoes & Accessories .... ✓	❸ .... Decor
Books, Toys & Entertainment .... ✗	

SMYRNA—W-4480 S COBB DR (AT COBB PKWY); 678.503.0702; T-F 10-6, SA 11-5; PARKING LOT

Dillard's ★★★★☆

“...this store has beautiful clothes, and if you catch a sale, you can get great quality clothes at super bargain prices... good customer service and helpful staff... a huge selection of merchandise for boys and girls... nice layette department... some furnishings like little tables and chairs... beautiful displays... the best part is that in addition to shopping for your kids, you can also shop for yourself...”

Furniture, Bedding & Decor .... ✓	$$$ .... Prices
Gear & Equipment .... ✗	❹ .... Product availability
Nursing & Feeding .... ✗	❸ .... Staff knowledge
Safety & Babycare .... ✗	❹ .... Customer service
Clothing, Shoes & Accessories .... ✓	❹ .... Decor
Books, Toys & Entertainment .... ✓	

WWW.DILLARDS.COM

DOUGLASVILLE—6720 DOUGLAS BLVD (NEXT TO ARBOR PL); 770.577.4271; M-SA 10-9, SU 12-6

Doodlebug Children's Clothing

Furniture, Bedding & Decor .... ✗	✗ .... Gear & Equipment
Nursing & Feeding .... ✗	✗ .... Safety & Babycare
Clothing, Shoes & Accessories .... ✓	✓ .... Books, Toys & Entertainment

WWW.DOODLEBUGSMYRNA.COM

SMYRNA—1290 W SPRING ST SE (AT ATLANTA RD SE); 770.432.2516; M-SA 9:30-5:30

Gymboree ★★★★☆

“...beautiful clothing and great quality... colorful and stylish baby and kids wear... lots of fun birthday gift ideas... easy exchange and return policy... items usually go on sale pretty quickly... save money with Gymbucks... many stores have a play area which makes shopping with my kids fun (let alone feasible)...”

Furniture, Bedding & Decor .... ✗	$$$ .... Prices
Gear & Equipment .... ✗	❹ .... Product availability
Nursing & Feeding .... ✗	❹ .... Staff knowledge
Safety & Babycare .... ✗	❹ .... Customer service

Clothing, Shoes & Accessories ✓	❹ Decor
Books, Toys & Entertainment ✓	

WWW.GYMBOREE.COM

DOUGLASVILLE—6700 DOUGLAS BLVD (AT ARBOR PLACE); 770.920.0947; M-SA 10-9, SU 12-6; PARKING LOT

KENNESAW—400 ERNEST BARRETT PKWY NW (AT TOWN CTR AT COBB); 770.514.9141; M-SA 10-9, SU 12-6; MALL PARKING

MARIETTA—3625 DALLAS HWY SW (AT LARGENT WAY NW); 678.331.8590; M-SA 10-9, SU 12-6; PARKING LOT

MARIETTA—4475 ROSWELL RD (AT HERITAGE GLEN DR); 678.560.0527; M-SA 10-9, SU 12-6; PARKING LOT

JCPenney ★★★½☆

"...always a good place to find clothes and other baby basics... the registry process was seamless... staff is generally friendly but the lines always seem long and slow... they don't have the greatest selection of toddler clothes, but their baby section is great... we had some damaged furniture delivered but customer service was easy and accommodating... a pretty limited selection of gear, but what they have is priced right..."

Furniture, Bedding & Decor ✓	$$ Prices
Gear & Equipment ✓	❸ Product availability
Nursing & Feeding ✓	❸ Staff knowledge
Safety & Babycare ✓	❸ Customer service
Clothing, Shoes & Accessories ✓	❸ Decor
Books, Toys & Entertainment ✓	

WWW.JCPENNEY.COM

DOUGLASVILLE—6650 DOUGLAS BLVD (AT HWY 5); 678.715.5669; M-SA 10-9, SU 12-6; PARKING IN FRONT OF BLDG

KENNESAW—667 ERNEST W BARRETT PKWY (AT COBB PLACE BLVD NW); 770.514.7101; M-SA 10-9, SU 12-6; MALL PARKING

Kiddie City ★★★★☆

"...fantastic consignment store... they only have high-quality wear and gear... staff is very helpful... willing to contact other stores to see if item is available elsewhere... anything from maternity to baby clothing, and furniture, accessories and toys... lots of brand-names..."

Furniture, Bedding & Decor ✓	$ Prices
Gear & Equipment ✓	❹ Product availability
Nursing & Feeding ✓	❺ Staff knowledge
Safety & Babycare ✓	❺ Customer service
Clothing, Shoes & Accessories ✓	❹ Decor
Books, Toys & Entertainment ✓	

WWW.KIDDIECITY.NET

MARIETTA—3430 CANTON RD (AT CHASTAIN); 770.795.9555; M-SA 10-6; PARKING LOT

Kohl's ★★★★☆

"...nice one-stop shopping for the whole family—everything from clothing to baby gear... great sales on clothing and a good selection of higher-end brands... stylish, inexpensive clothes for babies through 24 months... very easy shopping experience... dirt-cheap sales and clearance prices... nothing super fancy, but just right for those everyday romper outfits... Graco, Eddie Bauer and other well-known brands..."

Furniture, Bedding & Decor ✓	$$ Prices
Gear & Equipment ✓	❹ Product availability
Nursing & Feeding ✓	❸ Staff knowledge
Safety & Babycare ✓	❸ Customer service
Clothing, Shoes & Accessories ✓	❸ Decor
Books, Toys & Entertainment ✓	

WWW.KOHLS.COM

ACWORTH—3354 COBB PKWY (AT NANCE RD NW); 678.574.5370; M-SA 8-10, SU 10-8; PARKING LOT

AUSTELL—1825 E-W CONNECTOR SW (AT S HOSPITAL WY SW); 770.941.3032; M-SA 8-10, SU 10-8; PARKING LOT

MARIETTA—1289 JOHNSON FERRY RD NE (AT E COBB DR NE); 678.560.1296; M-SA 8-10, SU 10-8; PARKING LOT

Lullabies 'n Mudpies ★★★★½

"...one-of-a kind gifts and clothing... geared toward little girls (and their mommies)... adorable hats, shoes and rain gear... perfect for a special something... I love most of their clothing lines—high-quality and they wear very well... easy option for gift buying..."

Furniture, Bedding & Decor	✗	$$$	Prices
Gear & Equipment	✗	❹	Product availability
Nursing & Feeding	✗	❹	Staff knowledge
Safety & Babycare	✗	❹	Customer service
Clothing, Shoes & Accessories	✓	❹	Decor
Books, Toys & Entertainment	✓		

WWW.LULLABIESNMUDPIES.COM

MARIETTA—2145 ROSWELL RD (AT EASTLAKE SHOPPING CTR); 770.973.2383; M-SA 10-6, SA 10-5; PARKING LOT

Old Navy ★★★★☆

"...hip and 'in' clothes for infants and tots... plenty of steals on clearance items... T-shirts and pants for $10 or less... busy, busy, busy—long lines, especially on weekends... nothing fancy and you won't mind when your kids get down and dirty in these clothes... easy to wash, decent quality... you can shop for your baby, your toddler, your teen and yourself all at the same time... clothes are especially affordable when you hit their sales (post-holiday sales are amazing!)..."

Furniture, Bedding & Decor	✗	$$	Prices
Gear & Equipment	✗	❹	Product availability
Nursing & Feeding	✗	❸	Staff knowledge
Safety & Babycare	✗	❸	Customer service
Clothing, Shoes & Accessories	✓	❸	Decor
Books, Toys & Entertainment	✗		

WWW.OLDNAVY.COM

AUSTELL—4155 AUSTELL RD (AT E-W CONNECTOR); 770.944.6665; M-SA 9-9, SU 10-7; PARKING LOT

DOUGLASVILLE—6588 DOUGLAS BLVD (AT ARBOR PL); 678.838.0771; M-SA 10-9, SU 12-6; PARKING LOT

KENNESAW—680 ERNEST W BARRETT PKWY NW (AT COBB PLACE BLVD NW); 770.426.5888; M-SA 9-9, SU 11-7; PARKING LOT

MARIETTA—1291 JOHNSON FERRY RD (AT PROVIDENCE CHURCH RD); 770.321.0008; M-SA 9-9, SU 11-7; PARKING LOT

OshKosh B'Gosh ★★★★☆

"...cute, sturdy clothes for infants and toddlers... frequent sales make their high-quality merchandise a lot more affordable... doesn't every American kid have to get a pair of their overalls?.. great selection of cute clothes for boys... you can't go wrong here—their clothing is fun and worth the price... customer service is pretty hit-or-miss from store to store... we always walk out of here with something fun and colorful..."

Furniture, Bedding & Decor	✗	$$$	Prices
Gear & Equipment	✗	❹	Product availability
Nursing & Feeding	✗	❹	Staff knowledge
Safety & Babycare	✗	❹	Customer service

Clothing, Shoes & Accessories	✓	❹	Decor
Books, Toys & Entertainment	✗		

WWW.OSHKOSHBGOSH.COM

MARIETTA—3625 DALLAS HWY (AT LANGENT WAY NW); 678.354.2118; M-SA 10-9, SU 12-6; PARKING LOT

Payless Shoe Source ★★★☆☆

"...a good place for deals on children's shoes... staff is helpful with sizing... the selection and prices for kids' shoes can't be beat, but the quality isn't always spectacular... good leather shoes for cheap... great variety of all sizes and widths... I get my son's shoes here and don't feel like I'm wasting my money since he'll outgrow them in 3 months anyway..."

Furniture, Bedding & Decor	✗	$$	Prices
Gear & Equipment	✗	❸	Product availability
Nursing & Feeding	✗	❸	Staff knowledge
Safety & Babycare	✗	❸	Customer service
Clothing, Shoes & Accessories	✓	❸	Decor
Books, Toys & Entertainment	✗		

WWW.PAYLESS.COM

MARIETTA—1293 JOHNSON FERRY RD (AT PRINCETON WALK NE); 770.579.2443

PB & J Classic For Kids ★★★★☆

"...resale boutique that specializes in high-end clothes and toys... cash or credit for your consignment... make sure to check the clothes carefully before you buy... they offer a lot of maternity items and will contact you if you're looking for something in particular... consignment is great for grandparents who want duplicates at their own home... this store offers many secondhand toys... carries many basic items for babies..."

Furniture, Bedding & Decor	✗	$	Prices
Gear & Equipment	✗	❹	Product availability
Nursing & Feeding	✗	❹	Staff knowledge
Safety & Babycare	✗	❹	Customer service
Clothing, Shoes & Accessories	✓	❸	Decor
Books, Toys & Entertainment	✗		

WWW.PBJKIDS.COM

MARIETTA—2100 ROSWELL RD (AT E PIEDMONT); 770.509.5437; M-SA 10-6; PARKING LOT

Pier 1 Kids ★★★★☆

"...everything from curtains and dressers to teddy bears and piggy banks... attractive furniture and prices are moderate to expensive... staff provided lots of help assembling a 'look' for my child's room... we had an excellent shopping experience here... the salesperson told my kids it was okay to touch everything because it's all kid friendly... takes you out of the crib stage and into the next step..."

Furniture, Bedding & Decor	✓	$$$	Prices
Gear & Equipment	✗	❸	Product availability
Nursing & Feeding	✗	❹	Staff knowledge
Safety & Babycare	✗	❹	Customer service
Clothing, Shoes & Accessories	✗	❹	Decor
Books, Toys & Entertainment	✗		

WWW.PIER1KIDS.COM

MARIETTA—3625 DALLAS HWY SW (AT LARGENT WAY NW); 678.581.2622; M-SA 10-9 SU 11-7

MARIETTA—50 ERNEST W BARRETT PKWY (AT BARRETT PKWY); 770.579.9922; M-SA 10-9, SU 11-7; PARKING LOT

Polka Dot Kids ★★★½☆

"...mainly a consignment store with some new merchandise... I love this store, we frequent it at least once a week... barely used and new designer items in a boutique atmosphere... I always find great maternity clothes and cheap baby clothes... the selection of boys' clothing is small... the new (handmade) clothing is beautiful..."

Furniture, Bedding & Decor	✗	$$	Prices
Gear & Equipment	✓	❸	Product availability
Nursing & Feeding	✗	❹	Staff knowledge
Safety & Babycare	✗	❹	Customer service
Clothing, Shoes & Accessories	✓	❹	Decor
Books, Toys & Entertainment	✓		

WWW.POLKADOTKIDS.COM

MARIETTA—3718 DALLAS HWY (AT CASTEEL RD SW); 770.426.4501; M-W F 10-6, TH SA 10-8, SU 1-6; PARKING LOT

Rainbow Kids ★★½☆☆

"...fun clothing styles for infants and tots at low prices... the quality isn't the same as the more expensive brands, but the sleepers and play outfits always hold up well... great place for basics... cute trendy shoe selection for your little walker... we love the prices... up-to-date selection..."

Furniture, Bedding & Decor	✗	$$	Prices
Gear & Equipment	✓	❸	Product availability
Nursing & Feeding	✗	❸	Staff knowledge
Safety & Babycare	✗	❸	Customer service
Clothing, Shoes & Accessories	✓	❸	Decor
Books, Toys & Entertainment	✓		

WWW.RAINBOWSHOPS.COM

SMYRNA—2464 ATLANTA RD SE (AT WINDY HILL RD SE); 770.803.0356; M-SA 10-7, SU 12-6

Reruns Fashion Boutique

Furniture, Bedding & Decor	✗	✗	Gear & Equipment
Nursing & Feeding	✗	✗	Safety & Babycare
Clothing, Shoes & Accessories	✓	✗	Books, Toys & Entertainment

MARIETTA—2518 E PIEDMONT RD (AT SANDY PLAINS); 770.565.0121; M W F-SA 10-6, T TH 10-8, SU 1-5; PARKING LOT

Rooms To Go Kids ★★★½☆

"...solid furniture and nursery decor... helpful, but somewhat aggressive sales staff... I've always been pleased with my purchases... you can get the whole room taken care of in just one-stop... easy shopping and reasonable prices..."

Furniture, Bedding & Decor	✓	$$$	Prices
Gear & Equipment	✗	❹	Product availability
Nursing & Feeding	✗	❹	Staff knowledge
Safety & Babycare	✗	❹	Customer service
Clothing, Shoes & Accessories	✗	❹	Decor
Books, Toys & Entertainment	✗		

WWW.ROOMSTOGOKIDS.COM

SMYRNA—2190 COBB PKWY SE (AT WINDY HILL RD SE); 770.989.0123; M-SA 10-9, SU 11-6

Ross Dress For Less ★★★☆☆

"...if you're in the mood for bargain hunting and are okay with potentially coming up empty-handed, then Ross is for you... don't expect to get educated about baby products here... go early on a week day and you'll find an organized store and staff that is helpful and available—forget weekends... their selection is pretty inconsistent, but I

have found some incredible bargains... a great place to stock up on birthday presents or stocking stuffers... ”

Furniture, Bedding & Decor	✗	$$	Prices
Gear & Equipment	✗	❸	Product availability
Nursing & Feeding	✗	❸	Staff knowledge
Safety & Babycare	✗	❸	Customer service
Clothing, Shoes & Accessories	✓	❸	Decor
Books, Toys & Entertainment	✓		

WWW.ROSSSTORES.COM

AUSTELL—1825 E-W CONNECTOR SW (AT CHAMPION DR); 678.945.0219; M-SA 9:30-9:30, SU 11-7; PARKING LOT

MARIETTA—50 ERNEST W BARRETT PKWY NW (AT BELLS FERRY RD NE); 770.419.1203; M-SA 9:30-9:30, SU 11-7; PARKING LOT

Sears ★★★☆☆

“...a decent selection of clothes and basic baby equipment... check out the Kids Club program—it's a great way to save money... you go to Sears to save money, not to be pampered... the quality of their merchandise is better than Wal-Mart, but don't expect anything too special or different... not much in terms of gear, but tons of well-priced baby and toddler clothing... ”

Furniture, Bedding & Decor	✓	$$	Prices
Gear & Equipment	✓	❸	Product availability
Nursing & Feeding	✓	❸	Staff knowledge
Safety & Babycare	✓	❸	Customer service
Clothing, Shoes & Accessories	✓	❸	Decor
Books, Toys & Entertainment	✓		

WWW.SEARS.COM

DOUGLASVILLE—6580 DOUGLAS BLVD (AT GA-5); 770.577.5200; M-F 10-9, SA 10-6, SU 11-5; PARKING LOT

KENNESAW—400 ERNEST W BARRETT PKWY (AT TOWN CTR AT COBB); 770.429.4155; M-F 10-9, SA 8-9, SU 11-6; PARKING LOT

Silver Spoon Children's Boutique

Furniture, Bedding & Decor	✗	✗	Gear & Equipment
Nursing & Feeding	✗	✗	Safety & Babycare
Clothing, Shoes & Accessories	✓	✗	Books, Toys & Entertainment

SMYRNA—1675 CUMBERLAND PKWY (AT S ATLANTA RD); 404.216.9885; M-SA 10-7

Strasburg Children ★★★★☆

“...totally adorable special occasion outfits for babies and kids... classic baby, toddler, and kids clothes... dress-up clothes for kids... if you are looking for a flower girl or ring bearer outfit, look no further... handmade clothes that will last through multiple kids or generations... it's not cheap, but you can find great sales if you are patient... ”

Furniture, Bedding & Decor	✗	$$$$	Prices
Gear & Equipment	✗	❹	Product availability
Nursing & Feeding	✗	❹	Staff knowledge
Safety & Babycare	✗	❹	Customer service
Clothing, Shoes & Accessories	✓	❹	Decor
Books, Toys & Entertainment	✗		

WWW.STRASBURGCHILDREN.COM

DOUGLASVILLE—6700 DOUGLAS BLVD (AT ARBOR PL MALL); 770.489.9233; M-SA 10-9 SU 12-6

Stride Rite Shoes ★★★½☆

“...wonderful selection of baby and toddler shoes... sandals, sneakers, and even special-occasion shoes... decent quality shoes that last... they

know a lot about kids' shoes and take the time to get it right—they always measure my son's feet before fittings... store sizes vary, but they always have something in stock that works... they've even special ordered shoes for my daughter... a fun 'first shoe' buying experience... ”

Furniture, Bedding & Decor	✗	$$$	Prices
Gear & Equipment	✗	❹	Product availability
Nursing & Feeding	✗	❹	Staff knowledge
Safety & Babycare	✗	❹	Customer service
Clothing, Shoes & Accessories	✓	❹	Decor
Books, Toys & Entertainment	✗		

WWW.STRIDERITE.COM

DOUGLASVILLE—6700 DOUGLAS BLVD (AT ARBOR PLACE MALL); 678.838.1282; M-SA 10-9, SU 12-6

KENNESAW—Y04-400 ERNEST W BARRETT PKWY (AT TOWN CTR MALL); 770.428.6102; M-SA 10-9, SU 12:30-6; PARKING LOT

MARIETTA—210-4475 ROSWELL RD (AT JOHNSON FERRY RD NE); 770.971.1001; M-SA 10-9, SU 12-6

Tadpoles ★★★★☆

“*...I recommend this store to anyone willing to buy used clothes... the quality and style of the clothing is as good in many retail stores... my daughter gets complimented on outfits I've bought for here for less than $5... great frequent customer program... I felt the staff could have been a little friendlier... maternity to kids' sizes... well laid out and not crowded...* ”

Furniture, Bedding & Decor	✓	$$	Prices
Gear & Equipment	✓	❹	Product availability
Nursing & Feeding	✓	❹	Staff knowledge
Safety & Babycare	✓	❹	Customer service
Clothing, Shoes & Accessories	✓	❹	Decor
Books, Toys & Entertainment	✓		

WWW.TADPOLESINC.COM

KENNESAW—425 ERNEST W BARRETT PKWY NW (AT TOWN CTR AT COBB); 770.499.7010; M-W 9-5, TH-SA 9-7, SU 12-5; PARKING LOT

Talbots Kids ★★★½☆

“*...a nice alternative to the typical department store experience... expensive, but fantastic quality... great for holiday and special occasion outfits including christening outfits... well-priced, conservative children's clothing... cute selections for infants, toddlers and kids... sales are fantastic—up to half off at least a couple times a year... the best part is, you can also shop for yourself while shopping for baby...* ”

Furniture, Bedding & Decor	✗	$$$$	Prices
Gear & Equipment	✗	❹	Product availability
Nursing & Feeding	✗	❹	Staff knowledge
Safety & Babycare	✗	❹	Customer service
Clothing, Shoes & Accessories	✓	❹	Decor
Books, Toys & Entertainment	✗		

WWW.TALBOTS.COM

MARIETTA—4475 ROSWELL RD (AT JOHNSON FERRY RD NE); 770.321.2464; M-SA 10-9, SU 12-6; PARKING LOT

Target ★★★★☆

“*...our favorite place to shop for kids' stuff—good selection and very affordable... guilt-free shopping—kids grow so fast so I don't want to pay high department-store prices... everything from diapers and sippy cups to car seats and strollers... easy return policy... generally helpful staff, but you don't go for the service—you go for the prices... decent registry that won't freak your friends out with outrageous prices... easy,* *convenient shopping for well-priced items... all the big-box brands available—Graco, Evenflo, Eddie Bauer, etc.... ”*

Furniture, Bedding & Decor ✓	$$ Prices
Gear & Equipment ✓	❹ Product availability
Nursing & Feeding ✓	❸ Staff knowledge
Safety & Babycare ✓	❸ Customer service
Clothing, Shoes & Accessories ✓	❸ Decor
Books, Toys & Entertainment ✓	

WWW.TARGET.COM

AUSTELL—4125 AUSTELL RD (AT E-W CONNECTOR); 678.945.4550; M-SA 8-10, SU 8-9; PARKING IN FRONT OF BLDG

DOUGLASVILLE—2950 CHAPEL HILL RD (OFF ARBOR PL BLVD); 770.947.5303; M-SA 8-10, SU 8-9; PARKING IN FRONT OF BLDG

KENNESAW—740 ERNEST W BARRETT PKWY NW (AT COBB PL BLVD NW); 770.425.6895; M-SA 8-10, SU 8-9; PARKING IN FRONT OF BLDG

MARIETTA—2535 DALLAS HWY SW (AT ERNEST W BARRETT PKWY NW); 770.792.7933; M-SA 8-10, SU 8-9; PARKING IN FRONT OF BLDG

MARIETTA—3040 SHALLOWFORD RD (AT SANDY PLAINS RD NE); 770.321.8545; M-SA 8-10, SU 8-9; PARKING IN FRONT OF BLDG

SMYRNA—2201 COBB PKWY SE (AT LAKE PARK DR SE); 770.952.2241; M-F 8-10, SU 8-9; PARKING IN FRONT OF BLDG

Toys R Us ★★★½☆

“...not just toys, but also tons of gear and supplies including diapers and formula... a hectic shopping experience but the prices make it all worthwhile... I've experienced good and bad service at the same store on the same day... the stores are huge and can be overwhelming... most big brand-names available... leave the kids at home unless you want to end up with a cart full of toys... ”

Furniture, Bedding & Decor ✓	$$$ Prices
Gear & Equipment ✓	❹ Product availability
Nursing & Feeding ✓	❸ Staff knowledge
Safety & Babycare ✓	❸ Customer service
Clothing, Shoes & Accessories ✓	❸ Decor
Books, Toys & Entertainment ✓	

WWW.TOYSRUS.COM

DOUGLASVILLE—9365 THE LANDING DR (AT ARBOR PLACE); 770.577.5755; M-SA 10:00-9:00, SU 11-7

KENNESAW—501 ROBERTS CT (AT ERNEST W BARRETT PKY NW); 770.424.9100; M-SA 9:30-9:30, SU 11-7; PARKING LOT

Online

★★★★★

"lila picks"

- ★babycenter.com
- ★babystyle.com
- ★babyuniverse.com
- ★joggingstroller.com

ababy.com

Furniture, Bedding & Decor	✓	✓	Gear & Equipment
Nursing & Feeding	✗	✓	Safety & Babycare
Clothing, Shoes & Accessories	✓	✗	Books, Toys & Entertainment

aikobaby.com ★★★☆☆

"...high end clothes that are so cute... everything from Catamini to Jack and Lily... you can find super expensive infant and baby clothes at discounted prices... amazing selection of diaper bags so you don't have to look like a frumpy mom (or dad)..."

Furniture, Bedding & Decor	✗	✓	Gear & Equipment
Nursing & Feeding	✗	✗	Safety & Babycare
Clothing, Shoes & Accessories	✓	✗	Books, Toys & Entertainment

albeebaby.com ★★★★☆

"...they offer a really comprehensive selection of baby gear... their prices are some of the best online... great discounts on Maclarens before the new models come out... good product availability—fast shipping and easy transactions... the site is pretty easy to use... the prices are surprisingly great..."

Furniture, Bedding & Decor	✓	✓	Gear & Equipment
Nursing & Feeding	✓	✓	Safety & Babycare
Clothing, Shoes & Accessories	✓	✓	Books, Toys & Entertainment

amazon.com ★★★★½

"...unless you've been living under a rock, you know that in addition to books, Amazon carries an amazing amount of baby stuff too... they have the best prices and offer free shipping on bigger purchases... you can even buy used items for dirt cheap... I always read the comments written by others—they're very useful in helping make my decisions... I love Amazon for just about everything, but their baby selection only carries the big box standards..."

Furniture, Bedding & Decor	✗	✓	Gear & Equipment
Nursing & Feeding	✓	✓	Safety & Babycare
Clothing, Shoes & Accessories	✓	✓	Books, Toys & Entertainment

arunningstroller.com ★★★★½

"...the prices are very competitive and the customer service is great... I talked to them on the phone for a while and they totally hooked me up with the right model... if you're looking for a new stroller, look no further... talk to Marilyn—she's the best... shipping costs are reasonable and their prices overall are good..."

Furniture, Bedding & Decor	✓	✓	Gear & Equipment
Nursing & Feeding	✗	✗	Safety & Babycare
Clothing, Shoes & Accessories	✗	✗	Books, Toys & Entertainment

babiesinthesun.com ★★★★☆

"...one-stop shopping for cloth diapers... run by a fantastic woman who had 3 cloth diapered babies herself and is a wealth of knowledge... if you live in South Florida, the owner will let you into her home to see the merchandise and ask questions... great selection and the customer service is the best..."

Furniture, Bedding & Decor	✗	✓	Gear & Equipment
Nursing & Feeding	✗	✓	Safety & Babycare
Clothing, Shoes & Accessories	✗	✗	Books, Toys & Entertainment

babiesrus.com ★★★★☆

"...terrific web site with all the baby gear you'll need... registering online made it easy for my family and friends... getting the registry activated was a bit tricky... super convenient and ideal for the moms-to-be who are on bedrest... web site prices are comparable to in-store prices... shipping is usually free... a very efficient way to buy and send baby gifts... our local Babies R Us said they will accept returns if they carry the same item... not all online items are available in your local store..."

Furniture, Bedding & Decor	✓	✓	Gear & Equipment
Nursing & Feeding	✓	✓	Safety & Babycare
Clothing, Shoes & Accessories	✓	✓	Books, Toys & Entertainment

babiestravellite.com ★★★★½

"...caters to traveling families... they deliver baby items to your hotel room anywhere in the country... all of the different baby supplies you will need when you travel with a baby or a toddler... they sell almost every major brand for each product and their prices are sometimes cheaper than you would find at your local store..."

Furniture, Bedding & Decor	✗	✗	Gear & Equipment
Nursing & Feeding	✓	✓	Safety & Babycare
Clothing, Shoes & Accessories	✗	✓	Books, Toys & Entertainment

babyage.com ★★★★☆

"...fast shipping and the best prices around... flat rate shipping is great after the baby has arrived and you don't have time to go to the store... very attentive customer service... clearance items are a great deal (regular items are very competitive too)... ordering and delivery were super smooth... I usually check this web site before I purchase any baby gear... sign up for their newsletter and they'll notify you when they are having a sale..."

Furniture, Bedding & Decor	✓	✓	Gear & Equipment
Nursing & Feeding	✓	✓	Safety & Babycare
Clothing, Shoes & Accessories	✓	✓	Books, Toys & Entertainment

babyant.com ★★★★☆

"...wide variety of brands and products available through their site... super easy to navigate... fun, whimsical ideas... nice people and helpful... easy to return items and you can call them with questions... often has the best prices and low shipping costs..."

Furniture, Bedding & Decor	✓	✓	Gear & Equipment
Nursing & Feeding	✓	✓	Safety & Babycare
Clothing, Shoes & Accessories	✓	✓	Books, Toys & Entertainment

babybazaar.com

"...high-end baby stuff available on an easy-to-use web site... lots of European styles... quick processing and shipping... mom's tips, educational toys, exclusive favorites Bugaboo and Stokke..."

Furniture, Bedding & Decor .... ✓ | ✓ .... Gear & Equipment
Nursing & Feeding .... ✓ | ✓ .... Safety & Babycare
Clothing, Shoes & Accessories....... ✓ | ✓ .... Books, Toys & Entertainment

babybestbuy.com

Furniture, Bedding & Decor .... ✓ | ✓ .... Gear & Equipment
Nursing & Feeding .... ✓ | ✓ .... Safety & Babycare
Clothing, Shoes & Accessories....... ✓ | ✓ .... Books, Toys & Entertainment

babycatalog.com ★★★★☆

"...great deals on many essentials... wide selection of rockers but fewer options in other categories... the web site could be more user-friendly... customer service and delivery was fast and efficient... check out their seasonal specials... the baby club is a great way to save additional money... sign up for their wonderful pregnancy/new baby email newsletter... check this web site before you buy anywhere else..."

Furniture, Bedding & Decor .... ✓ | ✓ .... Gear & Equipment
Nursing & Feeding .... ✓ | ✓ .... Safety & Babycare
Clothing, Shoes & Accessories....... ✓ | ✓ .... Books, Toys & Entertainment

babycenter.com ★★★★★

"...a terrific selection of all things baby, plus quick shipping... free shipping on big orders... makes shopping convenient for new parents... web site is very user friendly... they always email you about sale items and special offers... lots of useful information for parents... carries everything you may need... online registry is simple, easy and a great way to get what you need... includes helpful products ratings by parents... they've created a nice online community in addition to their online store..."

Furniture, Bedding & Decor .... ✓ | ✓ .... Gear & Equipment
Nursing & Feeding .... ✓ | ✓ .... Safety & Babycare
Clothing, Shoes & Accessories....... ✓ | ✓ .... Books, Toys & Entertainment

babydepot.com ★★★☆☆

"...carries everything you'll find in a big department store but at cheaper prices and with everything all in one place... be certain you know what you want because returns can be difficult... site could be more user-friendly... online selection can differ from instore selection... love the online registry..."

Furniture, Bedding & Decor .... ✓ | ✓ .... Gear & Equipment
Nursing & Feeding .... ✓ | ✓ .... Safety & Babycare
Clothing, Shoes & Accessories....... ✓ | ✓ .... Books, Toys & Entertainment

babygeared.com

Furniture, Bedding & Decor .... ✓ | ✓ .... Gear & Equipment
Nursing & Feeding .... ✓ | ✓ .... Safety & Babycare
Clothing, Shoes & Accessories....... ✓ | ✓ .... Books, Toys & Entertainment

babyphd.com

Furniture, Bedding & Decor .... ✓ | ✗ .... Gear & Equipment
Nursing & Feeding .... ✗ | ✗ .... Safety & Babycare
Clothing, Shoes & Accessories....... ✓ | ✓ .... Books, Toys & Entertainment

babystyle.com ★★★★★

"...their web site is just like their stores—terrific... an excellent source for everything a parent needs... fantastic maternity and baby clothes...

they always respond quickly by email... their site seems to have even more merchandise than their stores... I started shopping on their site after receiving a gift card—very easy and convenient... wonderful selection... ”

Furniture, Bedding & Decor	✓	✓	Gear & Equipment
Nursing & Feeding	✓	✓	Safety & Babycare
Clothing, Shoes & Accessories	✓	✓	Books, Toys & Entertainment

babysupermall.com

Furniture, Bedding & Decor	✓	✓	Gear & Equipment
Nursing & Feeding	✓	✓	Safety & Babycare
Clothing, Shoes & Accessories	✓	✓	Books, Toys & Entertainment

babyuniverse.com ★★★★★

“...nice large selection of specialty and basic items... easy-to-use web site with decent prices... carries Carter's clothes and many other popular brands... great bedding selection - they're one of the few places with the Kidsline bedding I wanted... adorable backpacks for toddlers and preschoolers... check out the site for strollers and car seats... this was my first online shopping experience and they made it so easy, convenient and fast, I was hooked... fine customer service... flat rate (if not free) shipping takes the 'ouch' factor out of those big ticket purchases... ”

Furniture, Bedding & Decor	✓	✓	Gear & Equipment
Nursing & Feeding	✓	✓	Safety & Babycare
Clothing, Shoes & Accessories	✓	✓	Books, Toys & Entertainment

barebabies.com

Furniture, Bedding & Decor	✓	✓	Gear & Equipment
Nursing & Feeding	✓	✓	Safety & Babycare
Clothing, Shoes & Accessories	✓	✓	Books, Toys & Entertainment

birthandbaby.com ★★★★☆

“...incredible site for buying a nursing bra... there is more information about different manufacturers than you can imagine... I've even received a phone call from the owner after placing an order to clarify something... free shipping, so it's easy to buy multiple sizes and send back the ones that don't fit... their selection of nursing bras is better than any other place I've found... if you are a hard to fit size, this is the place to go... ”

Furniture, Bedding & Decor	×	✓	Gear & Equipment
Nursing & Feeding	✓	✓	Safety & Babycare
Clothing, Shoes & Accessories	×	✓	Books, Toys & Entertainment

blueberrybabies.com

Furniture, Bedding & Decor	✓	✓	Gear & Equipment
Nursing & Feeding	✓	✓	Safety & Babycare
Clothing, Shoes & Accessories	✓	✓	Books, Toys & Entertainment

buybuybaby.com ★★★★½

“...this is the web site for the popular New York-based baby retailer... you name it, they've got it... all the items in their store can also be found on their web site... prices are fair - especially since things get shipped right to your door... we had some items that were damaged and their online customer service took care of it without any problems... ”

Furniture, Bedding & Decor	✓	✓	Gear & Equipment
Nursing & Feeding	✓	✓	Safety & Babycare
Clothing, Shoes & Accessories	✓	✓	Books, Toys & Entertainment

childcarriers.com

Furniture, Bedding & Decor	×	✓	Gear & Equipment

Nursing & Feeding ✗ ✗ Safety & Babycare
Clothing, Shoes & Accessories ✗ ✗ Books, Toys & Entertainment

clothdiaper.com

Furniture, Bedding & Decor ✗ ✓ Gear & Equipment
Nursing & Feeding ✓ ✓ Safety & Babycare
Clothing, Shoes & Accessories ✗ ✗ Books, Toys & Entertainment

cocoacrayon.com

Furniture, Bedding & Decor ✓ ✓ Gear & Equipment
Nursing & Feeding ✓ ✓ Safety & Babycare
Clothing, Shoes & Accessories ✓ ✓ Books, Toys & Entertainment

cvs.com ★★★★☆

"...super convenient web site for any 'drug store' items... items are delivered in a reasonable amount of time... decent selection of baby products... prices are competitive and ordering online definitely beats making the trip out to the drugstore... order a bunch of stuff at a time so shipping is free... I used them for my baby announcements and everyone loved them... super easy to refill prescriptions... it was a real relief to order all my formula, baby wipes and diapers online..."

Furniture, Bedding & Decor ✗ ✗ Gear & Equipment
Nursing & Feeding ✓ ✓ Safety & Babycare
Clothing, Shoes & Accessories ✗ ✗ Books, Toys & Entertainment

dreamtimebaby.com

Furniture, Bedding & Decor ✓ ✓ Gear & Equipment
Nursing & Feeding ✓ ✓ Safety & Babycare
Clothing, Shoes & Accessories ✓ ✓ Books, Toys & Entertainment

drugstore.com ★★★★☆

Furniture, Bedding & Decor ✗ ✗ Gear & Equipment
Nursing & Feeding ✓ ✓ Safety & Babycare
Clothing, Shoes & Accessories ✗ ✗ Books, Toys & Entertainment

ebay.com ★★★★☆

"...great way to save money on everything from maternity clothes to breast pumps... be careful with whom you do business... it's always worth checking out what's available... I picked up a brand new jogger for dirt cheap... great deals to be had if you have patience to browse and be willing to resell or exchange what you don't like... baby stuff is easily found and often reasonably priced... keep an eye on shipping costs when you're bidding..."

Furniture, Bedding & Decor ✓ ✓ Gear & Equipment
Nursing & Feeding ✓ ✓ Safety & Babycare
Clothing, Shoes & Accessories ✓ ✓ Books, Toys & Entertainment

egiggle.com ★★★★☆

"...nice selection—not overwhelming... don't expect the big box store brands here—they carry higher-end, specialty items that you won't find elsewhere... smooth shopping experience... nice site—convenient and easy to use..."

Furniture, Bedding & Decor ✓ ✓ Gear & Equipment
Nursing & Feeding ✓ ✓ Safety & Babycare
Clothing, Shoes & Accessories ✓ ✓ Books, Toys & Entertainment

gagagifts.com ★★★★☆

"...great online store that carries fun clothes and unique gifts and toys for kids and adults... unique and special gifts like designer diaper bags, Whoozit learning toys and handmade quilts... this site makes gift buying incredibly easy—I'm done in less than 5 minutes... prices are high but products are special..."

Furniture, Bedding & Decor	✓	✓	Gear & Equipment
Nursing & Feeding	✓	✓	Safety & Babycare
Clothing, Shoes & Accessories	✓	✓	Books, Toys & Entertainment

gap.com ★★★★☆

"...I love the Gap's online store—all the cool things in their stores available via my computer... terrific selection of boys and girls clothes plus cute shoes... you can find awesome deals and return online purchases to Gap stores... their clothes are very durable... it's easy to purchase items online and delivery is prompt... a very practical and affordable way to shop... site makes it easy to quickly find what you need... sign up for the weekly newsletter and you'll find out about online sales..."

Furniture, Bedding & Decor	✓	✓	Gear & Equipment
Nursing & Feeding	✗	✗	Safety & Babycare
Clothing, Shoes & Accessories	✓	✓	Books, Toys & Entertainment

geniusbabies.com ★★★½☆

"...the best selection available of developmental toys and gifts... the only place to order real puppets from the Baby Einstein video series... cool place for unique baby shower and birthday gifts... their site navigation could use an upgrade..."

Furniture, Bedding & Decor	✗	✗	Gear & Equipment
Nursing & Feeding	✗	✗	Safety & Babycare
Clothing, Shoes & Accessories	✗	✓	Books, Toys & Entertainment

gymboree.com ★★★★☆

"...beautiful clothing and great quality... colorful and stylish baby and kids wear... lots of fun birthday gift ideas... easy exchange and return policy... items usually go on sale pretty quickly... save money with gymbucks... many stores have a play area which makes shopping with my kids fun (let alone feasible)..."

Furniture, Bedding & Decor	✗	✗	Gear & Equipment
Nursing & Feeding	✗	✗	Safety & Babycare
Clothing, Shoes & Accessories	✓	✓	Books, Toys & Entertainment

hannaandersson.com

Furniture, Bedding & Decor	✓	✗	Gear & Equipment
Nursing & Feeding	✓	✗	Safety & Babycare
Clothing, Shoes & Accessories	✓	✓	Books, Toys & Entertainment

jcpenney.com

Furniture, Bedding & Decor	✓	✗	Gear & Equipment
Nursing & Feeding	✗	✓	Safety & Babycare
Clothing, Shoes & Accessories	✓	✗	Books, Toys & Entertainment

joggingstroller.com ★★★★★

"...an excellent resource when you're choosing a jogging stroller... the entire site is devoted to joggers... very helpful information that's worth checking whether you plan to buy from them or not... the best online guide for researching jogging strollers... includes helpful comparisons and parent reviews on the top strollers..."

Furniture, Bedding & Decor	✗	✓	Gear & Equipment
Nursing & Feeding	✗	✗	Safety & Babycare
Clothing, Shoes & Accessories	✗	✗	Books, Toys & Entertainment

kidsurplus.com

Furniture, Bedding & Decor	✓	✗	Gear & Equipment
Nursing & Feeding	✓	✗	Safety & Babycare
Clothing, Shoes & Accessories	✓	✓	Books, Toys & Entertainment

landofnod.com

★★★★☆

"...cool site with adorable and unique furnishings... hip kid style art work... fabulous furniture and bedding... the catalog is amusing and nicely laid out... lots of sweet selections for both boys and girls... good customer service... fun but small selection of music, books, toys and more... a great way to get ideas for putting rooms together..."

Furniture, Bedding & Decor	✓	✗	Gear & Equipment
Nursing & Feeding	✗	✗	Safety & Babycare
Clothing, Shoes & Accessories	✗	✓	Books, Toys & Entertainment

landsend.com

★★★★☆

"...carries the best quality in children's wear—their stuff lasts forever... durable and adorable clothing, shoes and bedding... they offer a huge variety of casual clothing and awesome pajamas... not as inexpensive as other sites, but you can't beat the quality... the very best diaper bags... site is easy to navigate and has great finds for the entire family... love the flannel sheets, maternity clothes and shoes for mom..."

Furniture, Bedding & Decor	✓	✗	Gear & Equipment
Nursing & Feeding	✗	✗	Safety & Babycare
Clothing, Shoes & Accessories	✓	✗	Books, Toys & Entertainment

letsgostrolling.com

Furniture, Bedding & Decor	✓	✓	Gear & Equipment
Nursing & Feeding	✓	✗	Safety & Babycare
Clothing, Shoes & Accessories	✓	✓	Books, Toys & Entertainment

llbean.com

★★★★☆

"...high quality clothing for babies, toddlers and kids at reasonable prices... the clothes are extremely durable and stand up to wear and tear very well... a great site for winter clothing and gear shopping... wonderful selection for older kids, too... fewer options for infants... an awesome way to shop for clothing basics... you can't beat the diaper bags..."

Furniture, Bedding & Decor	✗	✗	Gear & Equipment
Nursing & Feeding	✗	✗	Safety & Babycare
Clothing, Shoes & Accessories	✓	✗	Books, Toys & Entertainment

modernseed.com

★★★★½

"...it was fun finding many unique items for my son's nursery... I wanted a contemporary theme and they had lots of wonderful items including crib linens, wall art and lighting... the place to find super cool baby and kid stuff and the best place for modern nursery decor... they also carry children and adult clothing and furniture and toys... not cheap but one of my favorite places..."

Furniture, Bedding & Decor	✓	✓	Gear & Equipment
Nursing & Feeding	✓	✓	Safety & Babycare
Clothing, Shoes & Accessories	✓	✓	Books, Toys & Entertainment

naturalbaby-catalog.com

★★★½☆

"...all natural products—clothes, toys, herbal medicines, bathing, etc... fine quality and a great alternative to the usual products... site is fairly easy to navigate and has a good selection... dealing with returns is pretty painless... love the catalogue and the products... excellent customer service... lots of organic clothing made with natural materials... high quality shoes in a range of prices..."

Furniture, Bedding & Decor	✓	✓	Gear & Equipment
Nursing & Feeding	✓	✓	Safety & Babycare
Clothing, Shoes & Accessories	✓	✓	Books, Toys & Entertainment

netkidswear.com

Furniture, Bedding & Decor .... ✓ ✓ .... Gear & Equipment
Nursing & Feeding .... ✓ ✓ .... Safety & Babycare
Clothing, Shoes & Accessories ...... ✓ ✓ .... Books, Toys & Entertainment

nordstrom.com ★★★★☆

"...just like their stores, the site carries a great selection of high-quality items... you can't go wrong with Nordstrom—even online... quick shipping and easy site navigation... a little pricey, but great quality items... I've purchased a bunch of baby stuff from their website and have never had a problem... a great shoe selection for all ages..."

Furniture, Bedding & Decor .... ✓ ✓ .... Gear & Equipment
Nursing & Feeding .... ✗ ✓ .... Safety & Babycare
Clothing, Shoes & Accessories ...... ✓ ✓ .... Books, Toys & Entertainment

oldnavy.com ★★★★☆

"...shopping online with Old Navy makes it easy to find incredible bargains... site was easy to use and my products arrived quickly... site carries items that aren't necessarily available in their stores... an inexpensive way to get trendy baby clothes... you can return items directly to any store... check out the sale page of this web site for deep discounts on current season clothing... I signed up for the email savings and get free shipping several times a year..."

Furniture, Bedding & Decor .... ✗ ✗ .... Gear & Equipment
Nursing & Feeding .... ✗ ✗ .... Safety & Babycare
Clothing, Shoes & Accessories ...... ✓ ✗ .... Books, Toys & Entertainment

oliebollen.com ★★★★½

"...perfect for the busy mom looking for a fun baby shower gift... this online-only store has all the best brands—Catamini and Tea Collection to name a couple... great for gifts and home stuff, too... lots of style... very easy to use... 30 days full refund, 60 days store credit..."

Furniture, Bedding & Decor .... ✓ ✗ .... Gear & Equipment
Nursing & Feeding .... ✓ ✗ .... Safety & Babycare
Clothing, Shoes & Accessories ...... ✓ ✓ .... Books, Toys & Entertainment

onestepahead.com ★★★★½

"...one stop shopping site with everything parents are looking for... huge variety of items to choose from... I bought everything from a crib to a nursery bottle... high quality items, many of which are developmental in nature... great line of safety equipment... easy to order and fast delivery but you will pay for shipping... web site has helpful reviews... great site for hard to find items..."

Furniture, Bedding & Decor .... ✓ ✓ .... Gear & Equipment
Nursing & Feeding .... ✓ ✓ .... Safety & Babycare
Clothing, Shoes & Accessories ...... ✓ ✓ .... Books, Toys & Entertainment

peapods.com

Furniture, Bedding & Decor .... ✓ ✓ .... Gear & Equipment
Nursing & Feeding .... ✗ ✓ .... Safety & Babycare
Clothing, Shoes & Accessories ...... ✓ ✓ .... Books, Toys & Entertainment

pokkadots.com

Furniture, Bedding & Decor .... ✓ ✓ .... Gear & Equipment
Nursing & Feeding .... ✓ ✗ .... Safety & Babycare
Clothing, Shoes & Accessories ...... ✓ ✓ .... Books, Toys & Entertainment

poshtots.com ★★★★☆

"...incredible selection of whimsical and out-of-the-ordinary nursery decor... beautiful, unique designer room sets in multiple styles... they do boys and girls bedrooms... great for the baby that has everything—

including parents with an unlimited cash account... you can get great ideas about decor just from browsing the site, even if you don't buy... ”

Furniture, Bedding & Decor ✓ ✓ Gear & Equipment
Nursing & Feeding ✓ ✗ Safety & Babycare
Clothing, Shoes & Accessories ✓ ✓ Books, Toys & Entertainment

potterybarnkids.com ★★★★½

“*...beautiful high end furniture and bedding... they have a way with matching everything perfectly and I am always a sucker for that look... adorable merchandise of great quality... you will get what you pay for: high quality furniture at high prices... web site is easy to navigate... items like hooded towels and plush blankets make this place special... if I could afford it I would buy everything in the store...* ”

Furniture, Bedding & Decor ✓ ✓ Gear & Equipment
Nursing & Feeding ✗ ✗ Safety & Babycare
Clothing, Shoes & Accessories ✗ ✓ Books, Toys & Entertainment

preemie.com

Furniture, Bedding & Decor ✗ ✓ Gear & Equipment
Nursing & Feeding ✓ ✓ Safety & Babycare
Clothing, Shoes & Accessories ✓ ✓ Books, Toys & Entertainment

rei.com

Furniture, Bedding & Decor ✗ ✓ Gear & Equipment
Nursing & Feeding ✗ ✗ Safety & Babycare
Clothing, Shoes & Accessories ✓ ✓ Books, Toys & Entertainment

royalnursery.com ★★★½☆

“*...this used to be a store in San Diego and now it is only online... if you need a silver rattle, luxury baby blanket or shower gift—this is the place... a beautiful site with elegant baby clothes, jewelry, and gifts... love the hand print kits—they are my current favorite gift... high end baby wear and gear... be sure to check out the sale items...* ”

Furniture, Bedding & Decor ✓ ✗ Gear & Equipment
Nursing & Feeding ✗ ✓ Safety & Babycare
Clothing, Shoes & Accessories ✓ ✓ Books, Toys & Entertainment

showeryourbaby.com

Furniture, Bedding & Decor ✓ ✓ Gear & Equipment
Nursing & Feeding ✓ ✓ Safety & Babycare
Clothing, Shoes & Accessories ✓ ✓ Books, Toys & Entertainment

snipsnsnails.com ★★★★½

“*...a great boys clothing store for infants to 14 years old... clothes for every occasion, from casual to special occasion... pajamas and swimsuits, too... pricey, but upscale and fun... items on the web site are not always in stock ...* ”

Furniture, Bedding & Decor ✓ ✗ Gear & Equipment
Nursing & Feeding ✗ ✗ Safety & Babycare
Clothing, Shoes & Accessories ✓ ✗ Books, Toys & Entertainment

strollerdepot.com

Furniture, Bedding & Decor ✗ ✓ Gear & Equipment
Nursing & Feeding ✗ ✗ Safety & Babycare
Clothing, Shoes & Accessories ✗ ✓ Books, Toys & Entertainment

strollers4less.com ★★★½☆

“*...some of the best prices on strollers... I love this site... we purchased our stroller online for a lot less than it costs locally... online ordering went smoothly—from ordering through receiving... wide* selection and some incredible deals... shipping is relatively fast... free shipping if you spend $100, which isn't hard to do... ”

Furniture, Bedding & Decor	✗	✓	Gear & Equipment
Nursing & Feeding	✗	✗	Safety & Babycare
Clothing, Shoes & Accessories	✗	✓	Books, Toys & Entertainment

target.com ★★★★☆

“...our favorite place to shop for kids stuff—good selection and very affordable... guilt free shopping—kids grow so fast so I don't want to pay high department store prices... everything from diapers and sippy cups to car seats and strollers... easy return policy... decent registry that won't freak your friends out with outrageous prices... easy, convenient shopping for well-priced items... all the big box brands available—Graco, Evenflo, Eddie Bauer, etc.... ”

Furniture, Bedding & Decor	✓	✓	Gear & Equipment
Nursing & Feeding	✓	✓	Safety & Babycare
Clothing, Shoes & Accessories	✓	✓	Books, Toys & Entertainment

teddylux.com

Furniture, Bedding & Decor	✗	✗	Gear & Equipment
Nursing & Feeding	✗	✗	Safety & Babycare
Clothing, Shoes & Accessories	✗	✓	Books, Toys & Entertainment

thebabyhammock.com ★★★★☆

“...a family owned business selling parent-tested products from morning sickness relief products to baby carriers, natural skincare, gift sets and more... fast friendly service... natural products and waldorf influenced toys... ”

Furniture, Bedding & Decor	✓	✓	Gear & Equipment
Nursing & Feeding	✓	✓	Safety & Babycare
Clothing, Shoes & Accessories	✓	✗	Books, Toys & Entertainment

thebabyoutlet.com

Furniture, Bedding & Decor	✗	✓	Gear & Equipment
Nursing & Feeding	✓	✓	Safety & Babycare
Clothing, Shoes & Accessories	✗	✓	Books, Toys & Entertainment

tinyride.com

Furniture, Bedding & Decor	✗	✓	Gear & Equipment
Nursing & Feeding	✓	✗	Safety & Babycare
Clothing, Shoes & Accessories	✗	✗	Books, Toys & Entertainment

toadsandtulips.com

Furniture, Bedding & Decor	✗	✗	Gear & Equipment
Nursing & Feeding	✗	✗	Safety & Babycare
Clothing, Shoes & Accessories	✗	✗	Books, Toys & Entertainment

toysrus.com ★★★★☆

“...makes shopping incredibly easy... well organized site with discount prices... makes registering for gifts super simple... even more products are online than in the actual stores... check out the outlet section and coupon codes for even more discounts... I did most of my Christmas shopping here, paid no shipping and had my gifts delivered in 3 days... web site includes helpful toy reviews... use this to send your wish lists to relatives... ”

Furniture, Bedding & Decor	✓	✓	Gear & Equipment
Nursing & Feeding	✓	✓	Safety & Babycare
Clothing, Shoes & Accessories	✓	✓	Books, Toys & Entertainment

tuttibella.com ★★★★☆

“...well designed web site with beautiful, original clothing, toys, bedding and accessories... cute vintage stuff for babies and kids...

stylish designer goods from here and abroad... your child will stand out among the Baby Gap-clothed masses... gorgeous fabrics... a great place to find that perfect gift for someone special and stylish... **”**

Furniture, Bedding & Decor .... ✓ ✓ .... Gear & Equipment
Nursing & Feeding .... ✗ ✗ .... Safety & Babycare
Clothing, Shoes & Accessories....... ✓ ✗ .... Books, Toys & Entertainment

usillygoose.com

Furniture, Bedding & Decor .... ✓ ✗ .... Gear & Equipment
Nursing & Feeding .... ✗ ✗ .... Safety & Babycare
Clothing, Shoes & Accessories....... ✗ ✓ .... Books, Toys & Entertainment

walmart.com ★★★⯪☆

“*...the site is packed with information, which can be a little difficult to navigate... anything and everything you need at a huge discount... good idea to browse the site and research prices before you visit a store... my order was delivered well before the estimated delivery date... I've found cheaper deals online than in the store...* **”**

Furniture, Bedding & Decor .... ✓ ✓ .... Gear & Equipment
Nursing & Feeding .... ✓ ✓ .... Safety & Babycare
Clothing, Shoes & Accessories....... ✓ ✓ .... Books, Toys & Entertainment

maternity clothing

City of Atlanta

★★★★★

"lila picks"

★Bloom Maternity

★Due Maternity

★Northside Hospital (Women's Place)

Alexis Maternity ★★★★☆

"...some of the cutest maternity clothes I have seen... helpful staff that know what will look good... a nice combination of trendy and conservative clothes... high-quality clothes that have lasted through multiple pregnancies... a good selection of hard-to-find fashionable and comfortable plus-sized clothes... pricey, but good to get something for a special occasion... good sales..."

Casual wear	✓	$$$$	Prices
Business wear	✓	❹	Product availability
Intimate apparel	✓	❹	Customer service
Nursing wear	×	❸	Decor

WWW.ALEXISMATERNITYCOLLECTIONS.COM

ATLANTA—6631 ROSWELL RD NE (AT ABERNATHY RD NW); 404.236.0105; M-W F-SA 10-6, TH 10-7, SU 12-4

Baby Depot At Burlington Coat Factory ★★★☆☆

"...a surprisingly good selection of maternity clothes at great prices... staff can be hard to find so be prepared to dig... cute pants, skirts and sets... I wouldn't have thought that their selection would be as good as it is... not much other than casual items, but what they have is pretty good..."

Casual wear	✓	$$	Prices
Business wear	×	❸	Product availability
Intimate apparel	×	❸	Customer service
Nursing wear	×	❸	Decor

WWW.BABYDEPOT.COM

ATLANTA—2841 GREENBRIAR PKWY SW (AT HEADLAND DR SW); 404.349.6300; M-SA 10-9, SU 11-6; PARKING LOT

ATLANTA—4166 BUFORD HWY NE (AT OAK SHADOW DR NE); 404.634.5566; M-SA 10-9, SU 10-6 ; PARKING LOT

Bloom Maternity ★★★★★

"...a great selection of hip and fashionable maternity wear... this is where I go for a little pick-me-up—I always leave with something fun... a nice variety of clothing from casual to dressy... they also have bras, diaper bags and other adorable accessories... the staff is attentive, but not pushy... nice designer apparel to make you look and feel great..."

Casual wear	✓	$$$$	Prices

Business wear	✓	❹	Product availability
Intimate apparel	✓	❹	Customer service
Nursing wear	✓	❹	Decor

ATLANTA—2140 PEACHTREE RD (AT PEACHTREE PARK DR NE); 404.351.6262; M-F 10-6, SA 10-5

Consignkidz

Casual wear	✓	×	Nursing wear
Business wear	✓	✓	Intimate apparel

ATLANTA—2205 LAVISTA RD NE (AT N DRUID HILLS); 404.929.0222; M-SA 10-5:45; PARKING LOT

Due Maternity ★★★★★

"...a lovely boutique that will help you find something pretty to cover that growing belly... the hippest, specialty maternity boutique in town... cute things that are a little pricier than the average maternity fare, but you can't beat their selection and service... plenty of choices for a variety of looks... a fun shopping experience—they make you feel like you're celebrating you pregnancy..."

Casual wear	✓	$$$$	Prices
Business wear	✓	❹	Product availability
Intimate apparel	✓	❺	Customer service
Nursing wear	✓	❺	Decor

WWW.DUEMATERNITY.COM

ATLANTA—4300 PACES FERRY RD SE (AT COCHISE DR SE); 770.384.0009; M-SA 10-6, SU 11-5; FREE PARKING

Great Beginnings ★★★★★

"...a smallish boutique with a limited stock of fun, hip maternity clothes... they have their own label which they actually design and make... they do carry other brands too, but mostly their own... prices are reasonable compared to other maternity shops... the owner is fun and helpful... great place for business casual clothes..."

Casual wear	✓	$$$	Prices
Business wear	×	❸	Product availability
Intimate apparel	×	❹	Customer service
Nursing wear	×	❸	Decor

WWW.GBMATERNITY.COM

ATLANTA—1945 CLIFF VALLEY WY (AT LAVISTA RD NE); 404.633.1711; CALL FOR APPT

Hanger-roo For Moms And Tots

Casual wear	✓	×	Nursing wear
Business wear	×	×	Intimate apparel

WWW.HANGER-ROO.COM

ATLANTA—5352 PEACHTREE RD (AT PIERCE DR NE); 770.451.8911; T-SA 10-4

JCPenney ★★★☆☆

"...competitive prices and a surprisingly cute selection... they carry bigger sizes that are very hard to find at other stores... much cheaper than most maternity boutiques and they always seem to have some sort of sale going on... an especially large selection of maternity jeans for plus sizes... a more conservative collection than the smaller, hipper boutiques... good for casual basics, but not much for special occasions..."

Casual wear	✓	$$	Prices
Business wear	✓	❸	Product availability
Intimate apparel	✓	❸	Customer service

Nursing wear .... ✗ ❸ .... Decor

WWW.JCPENNEY.COM

ATLANTA—2100 PLEASANT HILL RD NW (AT N CASTLEGATE DR); 770.476.3220; M-SA 10-9, SU 12-6; MALL PARKING

Macy's ★★★½☆

"...if your local Macy's has a maternity section, you're in luck... I bought my entire pregnancy work wardrobe at Macy's... the styles are all relatively recent and the brands are well known... you can generally find some attractive dresses at very reasonable prices on their sales rack... like other large department stores, you're bound to find something that works if you dig enough... very convenient because you can get your other shopping done at the same time... the selection isn't huge, but what they have is nice..."

Casual wear .... ✓ $$$ .... Prices
Business wear .... ✓ ❸ .... Product availability
Intimate apparel .... ✓ ❸ .... Customer service
Nursing wear .... ✗ ❸ .... Decor

WWW.MACYS.COM

ATLANTA—1300 CUMBERLAND MALL (AT RT 407); 770.434.2611; M-SA 10-9, SU 12-7; MALL PARKING

ATLANTA—2841 GREENBRIAR PKWY (AT GREENBRIAR MALL); 404.346.2690; M-SA 10-9, SU 12-7; MALL PARKING

ATLANTA—3393 PEACHTREE RD NE (AT LENOX SQ MALL); 404.231.2800; M-SA 10-9, SU 12-7; MALL PARKING

ATLANTA—4300 ASHFORD DUNWOODY RD (AT PERIMETER MALL); 770.396.2800; M-SA 10-9, SU 12-7; MALL PARKING

ATLANTA—4800 BRIARCLIFF RD (AT NORTHLAKE SHOPPING MALL); 770.491.2800; M-SA 10-9, SU 12-7; MALL PARKING

Mimi Maternity ★★★★☆

"...it's definitely worth stopping here if you're still working and need some good-looking outfits... not cheap, but the quality is fantastic... not as expensive as A Pea In The Pod, but better quality than Motherhood Maternity... nice for basics that will last you through multiple pregnancies... perfect for work clothes, but pricey for the everyday stuff... good deals to be found on their sales racks... a good mix of high-end fancy clothes and items you can wear every day..."

Casual wear .... ✓ $$$$ .... Prices
Business wear .... ✓ ❹ .... Product availability
Intimate apparel .... ✓ ❹ .... Customer service
Nursing wear .... ✓ ❹ .... Decor

WWW.MIMIMATERNITY.COM

ATLANTA—3393 PEACHTREE RD NE (AT LENOX SQUARE MALL); 404.365.0426; M-SA 10-9, SU 12-6; MALL PARKING

Motherhood Maternity ★★★★☆

"...a wide variety of styles, from business to weekend wear, all at a good price... affordable and cute... everything from bras and swimsuits to work outfits... highly recommended for those who don't want to spend a fortune on maternity clothes... less fancy and pricey than their sister stores—A Pea in the Pod and Mimi Maternity... they have frequent sales, so you just need to keep dropping in—you're bound to find something good..."

Casual wear .... ✓ $$$ .... Prices
Business wear .... ✓ ❹ .... Product availability
Intimate apparel .... ✓ ❹ .... Customer service
Nursing wear .... ✓ ❸ .... Decor

WWW.MOTHERHOOD.COM

ATLANTA—1312 NORTHLAKE MALL (AT NORTHLAKE SHOPPING MALL); 770.939.2626; M-SA 10-9, SU 12-6; MALL PARKING

ATLANTA—1405 CUMBERLAND MALL (AT COBB PKY); 770.432.4184; M-SA 10-9, SU 12-6 ; MALL PARKING

ATLANTA—4800 BRIARCLIFF RD NE (AT NORTHLAKE SHOPPING MALL); 770.939.2626; M-SA 10-9, SU 12-6; MALL PARKING

Northside Hospital (Women's Place) ★★★★★

“...perfect for nursing bras and prenatal support... very wide range of sizes... they take your measurements in order to get the perfect size... they carry hard-to-find sizes... good selection of the most beautiful pajamas... staff is extremely knowledgeable about breastfeeding troubles and products... ”

Casual wear	✗	$$$	Prices
Business wear	✗	❹	Product availability
Intimate apparel	✗	❺	Customer service
Nursing wear	✓	❹	Decor

WWW.NORTHSIDE.COM/AWOMANSPLACE/MAIN.HTM

ATLANTA—1000 JOHNSON FERRY RD NE (AT MERIDIAN MARK RD NE); 404.845.5555; M-F 9-5; PARKING LOT AT HOSPITAL

Old Navy ★★★½☆

“...the best for casual maternity clothing like stretchy T-shirts with Lycra and comfy jeans... prices are so reasonable it's ridiculous... not much for the workplace, but you can't beat the prices on casual clothes... not all Old Navy locations carry their maternity line... don't expect a huge or diverse selection... the staff is not always knowledgeable about maternity clothing and can't really help with questions about sizing... they have the best return policy—order online and return to the nearest store location... perfect for inexpensive maternity duds... ”

Casual wear	✓	$$	Prices
Business wear	✗	❹	Product availability
Intimate apparel	✗	❸	Customer service
Nursing wear	✗	❸	Decor

WWW.OLDNAVY.COM

ATLANTA—1 BUCKHEAD LOOP NE (AT TURNER MCDONALD PKWY); 404.467.0670; M-SA 9-9, SU 11-7; PARKING LOT

ATLANTA—4800 BRIARCLIFF RD NE (AT NORTHLAKE SHOPPING MALL); 770.270.0131; M-SA 10-9, SU 12-6; MALL PARKING

Ross Dress For Less ★★½☆☆

“...if you don't mind looking through a lot of clothes you can find some good pieces at great prices... they sometimes have larger sizes too... totally hit or miss depending on their most recent shipment... not the most fashionable clothing, but great for that everyday, casual T-shirt or stretchy pair of pants... ”

Casual wear	✓	$$$	Prices
Business wear	✓	❸	Product availability
Intimate apparel	✗	❷	Customer service
Nursing wear	✗	❷	Decor

WWW.ROSSSTORES.COM

ATLANTA—5932 ROSWELL RD NE (AT CLIFTWOOD DR NE); 404.843.1474; M-SA 9:30-9:30, SU 11-7; PARKING LOT

Sears ★★★☆☆

“...good place to get maternity clothes for a low price... the clearance rack always has good deals and their sales are quite frequent... not necessarily super high-quality, but if you just need them for nine

months, who cares... good selection of nursing bras... I love the fact that they carry maternity wear in larger sizes—I got so tired of looking in those cutesy boutiques and then being disappointed because they didn't have my size... the only place I found maternity for plus-sized women... ❞

Casual wear	✓	$$	Prices
Business wear	✗	❸	Product availability
Intimate apparel	✓	❸	Customer service
Nursing wear	✓	❸	Decor

WWW.SEARS.COM

ATLANTA—1500 CUMBERLAND MALL (AT RT 407); 770.433.7400; M-F 10-9, SA 10-6, SU 11-5; MALL PARKING

ATLANTA—2201 HENDERSON MILL RD NE (AT NORTHLAKE SHOPPING MALL); 770.493.3210; M-SA 10-9, SU 11-7

Sweet Repeats

Casual wear	✓	✓	Nursing wear
Business wear	✓	✗	Intimate apparel

ATLANTA—321 PHARR RD (AT FULTON DR); 404.261.7519; M-SA 10-5 ; PARKING LOT

Target ★★★★☆

❝*...I was surprised at how fashionable their selection is—they carry Liz Lange and other really cute selections... the price is right—especially since you'll only be wearing these clothes for a few months... great for maternity basics—T-shirts, skirts, sweaters, even maternity bras... best of all, you can do some maternity shopping while you're shopping for other household basics... shirts for $10—you can't beat that... not the most exciting or romantic maternity shopping, but once you see the prices you'll get over it... as always, Target provides the perfectly priced solution...* ❞

Casual wear	✓	$$	Prices
Business wear	✓	❸	Product availability
Intimate apparel	✓	❸	Customer service
Nursing wear	✓	❸	Decor

WWW.TARGET.COM

ATLANTA—235 JOHNSON FERRY RD NW (AT ABERNATHY RD NW); 404.256.4600; M-SA 8-10, SU 8-9; PARKING IN FRONT OF BLDG

ATLANTA—2400 N DRUID HILLS RD NE (AT WOODCLIFF DR NE); 404.267.0060; M-SA 8-10, SU 8-9; PARKING IN FRONT OF BLDG

ATLANTA—3535 PEACHTREE RD NE (AT PHIPPS PLAZA); 404.237.9494; M-SA 8-10, SU 8-9; PARKING IN FRONT OF BLDG

Warm Front, The ★★★☆☆

❝*...a good source for business wear and outfits... I found some suits here that worked very well for work and still were reasonably comfortable... some of the outfits just weren't my style, but it is a good source for maternity business clothes...* ❞

Casual wear	✓	$$$$$	Prices
Business wear	✓	❹	Product availability
Intimate apparel	✗	❹	Customer service
Nursing wear	✗	❹	Decor

WWW.THE-WARM-FRONT.COM

ATLANTA—1 GALLERIA PKWY SE (AT AKERS MILL RD SE); 770.859.9122; TH-SU 12-5

North Fulton

★★★★★

"lila picks"

★Izzy Maternity

★Motherhood Maternity

Baby Depot At Burlington Coat Factory ★★★☆☆

"...a surprisingly good selection of maternity clothes at great prices... staff can be hard to find so be prepared to dig... cute pants, skirts and sets... I wouldn't have thought that their selection would be as good as it is... not much other than casual items, but what they have is pretty good..."

Casual wear	✓	$$	Prices
Business wear	×	❸	Product availability
Intimate apparel	×	❸	Customer service
Nursing wear	×	❸	Decor

WWW.BABYDEPOT.COM

ROSWELL—608 HOLCOMB BRIDGE RD (AT ROSWELL MALL), 770.510.0000, M-SA 10-9, SU 11-6; MALL PARKING

Izzy Maternity ★★★★★

"...not your typical maternity store—they have beautiful items and very personalized service... the owner is the consummate salesman and will help you put together a maternity wardrobe that flatters your body's shape and coloring... good store with a convenient mall location... pricey, but you'll always find something different... go here if you need to be gorgeous for a special event... exchanges only..."

Casual wear	✓	$$$$	Prices
Business wear	✓	❹	Product availability
Intimate apparel	✓	❹	Customer service
Nursing wear	✓	❹	Decor

ALPHARETTA—2110 NORTH POINT CIR (AT NORTH POINT MALL); 770.753.0204; M-SA 10-9, SU 12-6; MALL PARKING

JCPenney ★★★☆☆

"...competitive prices and a surprisingly cute selection... they carry bigger sizes that are very hard to find at other stores... much cheaper than most maternity boutiques and they always seem to have some sort of sale going on... an especially large selection of maternity jeans for plus sizes... a more conservative collection than the smaller, hipper boutiques... good for casual basics, but not much for special occasions..."

Casual wear	✓	$$	Prices
Business wear	✓	❸	Product availability
Intimate apparel	✓	❸	Customer service
Nursing wear	×	❸	Decor

WWW.JCPENNEY.COM

ALPHARETTA—2000 NORTH POINT CIR (AT NORTH POINT MALL); 770.475.9850; M-SA 10-9, SU 12-6; PARKING LOT

Kiddie-Go-Round

Casual wear	✗	✗	Nursing wear
Business wear	✗	✗	Intimate apparel

ROSWELL—555 S ATLANTA ST (AT MARIETTA HWY); 770.641.9641; M-SA 10-6; PARKING LOT

Kohl's ★★★☆☆

"...a small maternity selection but I always manage to find several items I like... our favorite shopping destination—clean, wide open aisles... not a huge amount of maternity, but if you find something the price is always right... the selection is very inconsistent but sometimes you can find nice casuals... best for the bare-bone basics like T-shirts, shorts or casual pants..."

Casual wear	✓	$$	Prices
Business wear	✗	❸	Product availability
Intimate apparel	✗	❸	Customer service
Nursing wear	✗	❸	Decor

WWW.KOHLS.COM

ROSWELL—2342 HOLCOMB BRIDGE RD (AT FOUTS RD); 678.795.9645; M-SA 8-10, SU 10-8; PARKING LOT

ROSWELL—620 W CROSSVILLE RD (AT CROSSWAY LN); 678.352.9536; M-SA 8-10, SU 10-8; PARKING IN FRONT OF BLDG

Motherhood Maternity ★★★★★

"...a wide variety of styles, from business to weekend wear, all at a good price... affordable and cute... everything from bras and swimsuits to work outfits... highly recommended for those who don't want to spend a fortune on maternity clothes... less fancy and pricey than their sister stores—A Pea in the Pod and Mimi Maternity... they have frequent sales, so you just need to keep dropping in—you're bound to find something good..."

Casual wear	✓	$$$	Prices
Business wear	✓	❹	Product availability
Intimate apparel	✓	❹	Customer service
Nursing wear	✓	❸	Decor

WWW.MOTHERHOOD.COM

ALPHARETTA—6270 NORTH POINT PKWY (AT NORTH POINT CT); 770.521.0929; M-SA 10-9, SU 12-6

Old Navy ★★★½☆

"...the best for casual maternity clothing like stretchy T-shirts with Lycra and comfy jeans... prices are so reasonable it's ridiculous... not much for the workplace, but you can't beat the prices on casual clothes... not all Old Navy locations carry their maternity line... don't expect a huge or diverse selection... the staff is not always knowledgeable about maternity clothing and can't really help with questions about sizing... they have the best return policy—order online and return to the nearest store location... perfect for inexpensive maternity duds..."

Casual wear	✓	$$	Prices
Business wear	✗	❹	Product availability
Intimate apparel	✗	❸	Customer service
Nursing wear	✗	❸	Decor

WWW.OLDNAVY.COM

ALPHARETTA—6100 NORTH POINT PKWY (AT NORTH POINT CT); 770.772.6660; M-SA 9-9, SU 11-7; PARKING LOT

Target ★★★★☆

"...I was surprised at how fashionable their selection is—they carry Liz Lange and other really cute selections... the price is right—especially since you'll only be wearing these clothes for a few months... great for maternity basics—T-shirts, skirts, sweaters, even maternity bras... best of all, you can do some maternity shopping while you're shopping for other household basics... shirts for $10—you can't beat that... not the most exciting or romantic maternity shopping, but once you see the prices you'll get over it... as always, Target provides the perfectly priced solution..."

Casual wear ✓	$$ Prices
Business wear ✓	❸ Product availability
Intimate apparel ✓	❸ Customer service
Nursing wear ✓	❸ Decor

WWW.TARGET.COM

ROSWELL—1135 WOODSTOCK RD (AT HARDSCRABBLE RD); 770.998.0144; M-SA 8-10, SU 8-9; PARKING IN FRONT OF BLDG

South Fulton, Fayette & Clayton

Baby Depot At Burlington Coat Factory ★★★☆☆

"...a surprisingly good selection of maternity clothes at great prices... staff can be hard to find so be prepared to dig... cute pants, skirts and sets... I wouldn't have thought that their selection would be as good as it is... not much other than casual items, but what they have is pretty good..."

Casual wear ✓ | $$ Prices
Business wear ✗ | ❸ Product availability
Intimate apparel ✗ | ❸ Customer service
Nursing wear ✗ | ❸ Decor

WWW.BABYDEPOT.COM

MORROW—1516 SOUTHLAKE PKWY (AT BARTON RD); 770.960.7555; M-SA 10-9:30, SU 11-6

JCPenney ★★★☆☆

"...competitive prices and a surprisingly cute selection... they carry bigger sizes that are very hard to find at other stores... much cheaper than most maternity boutiques and they always seem to have some sort of sale going on... an especially large selection of maternity jeans for plus sizes... a more conservative collection than the smaller, hipper boutiques... good for casual basics, but not much for special occasions..."

Casual wear ✓ | $$ Prices
Business wear ✓ | ❸ Product availability
Intimate apparel ✓ | ❸ Customer service
Nursing wear ✗ | ❸ Decor

WWW.JCPENNEY.COM

FOREST PARK—5500 FRONTAGE RD (AT OLD DIXIE RD); 404.363.3713; M-F 10-9, SA 9-9, SU 10-6; MALL PARKING

MORROW—1400 SOUTHLAKE CIR (AT SOUTHLAKE MALL); 770.961.6211; M-SA 10-9, SU 12-6; MALL PARKING

Kohl's ★★★☆☆

"...a small maternity selection but I always manage to find several items I like... our favorite shopping destination—clean, wide open aisles... not a huge amount of maternity, but if you find something the price is always right... the selection is very inconsistent but sometimes you can find nice casuals... best for the bare-bone basics like T-shirts, shorts or casual pants..."

Casual wear ✓ | $$ Prices
Business wear ✗ | ❸ Product availability
Intimate apparel ✗ | ❸ Customer service
Nursing wear ✗ | ❸ Decor

WWW.KOHLS.COM

FAYETTEVILLE—300 PAVILLION PKWY (AT HWY 314); 678.817.1450; M-SA 8-10, SU 10-8; PARKING IN FRONT OF BLDG

Macy's ★★★½☆

"...if your local Macy's has a maternity section, you're in luck... I bought my entire pregnancy work wardrobe at Macy's... the styles are all relatively recent and the brands are well known... you can generally find some attractive dresses at very reasonable prices on their sales

rack... like other large department stores, you're bound to find something that works if you dig enough... very convenient because you can get your other shopping done at the same time... the selection isn't huge, but what they have is nice... ”

Casual wear	✓	$$$	Prices
Business wear	✓	❸	Product availability
Intimate apparel	✓	❸	Customer service
Nursing wear	✗	❸	Decor

WWW.MACYS.COM

MORROW—1500 SOUTHLAKE CIR (AT SOUTHLAKE MALL); 770.961.3111; M-SA 10-9, SU 12-7; MALL PARKING

Motherhood Maternity ★★★★☆

“...a wide variety of styles, from business to weekend wear, all at a good price... affordable and cute... everything from bras and swimsuits to work outfits... highly recommended for those who don't want to spend a fortune on maternity clothes... less fancy and pricey than their sister stores—A Pea in the Pod and Mimi Maternity... they have frequent sales, so you just need to keep dropping in—you're bound to find something good... ”

Casual wear	✓	$$$	Prices
Business wear	✓	❹	Product availability
Intimate apparel	✓	❹	Customer service
Nursing wear	✓	❸	Decor

WWW.MOTHERHOOD.COM

EAST POINT—3610 MARKETPLACE BLVD (AT WELCOME ALL RD SW); 404.349.7940; M-SA 10-9, SU 12-6

Ross Dress For Less ★★½☆☆

“...if you don't mind looking through a lot of clothes you can find some good pieces at great prices... they sometimes have larger sizes too... totally hit or miss depending on their most recent shipment... not the most fashionable clothing, but great for that everyday, casual T-shirt or stretchy pair of pants... ”

Casual wear	✓	$$$	Prices
Business wear	✓	❸	Product availability
Intimate apparel	✗	❷	Customer service
Nursing wear	✗	❷	Decor

WWW.ROSSSTORES.COM

FAYETTEVILLE—118 PAVILLION PKWY (AT HWY 85); 770.460.8733; M-SA 9:30-9:30, SU 11-7

Sears ★★★☆☆

“...good place to get maternity clothes for a low price... the clearance rack always has good deals and their sales are quite frequent... not necessarily super high-quality, but if you just need them for nine months, who cares... good selection of nursing bras... I love the fact that they carry maternity wear in larger sizes—I got so tired of looking in those cutesy boutiques and then being disappointed because they didn't have my size... the only place I found maternity for plus-sized women... ”

Casual wear	✓	$$	Prices
Business wear	✗	❸	Product availability
Intimate apparel	✓	❸	Customer service
Nursing wear	✓	❸	Decor

WWW.SEARS.COM

MORROW—1300 SOUTHLAKE CIR (AT SOUTHLAKE MALL); 770.961.7110; M-SA 10-9, SU 11-6; MALL PARKING

UNION CITY—600 SHANNON SOUTHPARK (AT SHANNON MALL); 770.969.3200; M-F 10-9, SA 8-9, SU 11-5

Target ★★★★☆

"...I was surprised at how fashionable their selection is—they carry Liz Lange and other really cute selections... the price is right—especially since you'll only be wearing these clothes for a few months... great for maternity basics—T-shirts, skirts, sweaters, even maternity bras... best of all, you can do some maternity shopping while you're shopping for other household basics... shirts for $10—you can't beat that... not the most exciting or romantic maternity shopping, but once you see the prices you'll get over it... as always, Target provides the perfectly priced solution..."

Casual wear	✓	$$	Prices
Business wear	✓	❸	Product availability
Intimate apparel	✓	❸	Customer service
Nursing wear	✓	❸	Decor

WWW.TARGET.COM

EAST POINT—3660 MARKETPLACE BLVD (AT WELCOME ALL RD SW); 404.267.0063; M-SA 8-10, SU 8-9; PARKING IN FRONT OF BLDG

FAYETTEVILLE—107 PAVILION PKWY (AT HWY 85); 770.719.9766; M-SA 8-10, SU 8-9; PARKING IN FRONT OF BLDG

MORROW—1940 MT ZION RD (AT MT ZION CIR); 770.472.3355; M-SA 8-10, SU 8-9; PARKING IN FRONT OF BLDG

Dekalb

Baby Depot At Burlington Coat Factory

★★★☆☆

"...a surprisingly good selection of maternity clothes at great prices... staff can be hard to find so be prepared to dig... cute pants, skirts and sets... I wouldn't have thought that their selection would be as good as it is... not much other than casual items, but what they have is pretty good..."

Casual wear	✓	$$	Prices
Business wear	✗	❸	Product availability
Intimate apparel	✗	❸	Customer service
Nursing wear	✗	❸	Decor

WWW.BABYDEPOT.COM

DECATUR—2032 LAWRENCEVILLE HWY (AT N DECALB MALL); 480.248.1182; M-SA 10-9, SU 11-7; PARKING LOT

Jack & Jill Consignment

★★★½☆

"...a small consignment store... they have tons of maternity and baby gear... they are bound to have something that will work for you... prices are reasonable and the quality is generally quite good—they do a good job of checking their merchandise..."

Casual wear	✓	$$$	Prices
Business wear	✓	❹	Product availability
Intimate apparel	✗	❺	Customer service
Nursing wear	✗	❹	Decor

WWW.JACKANDJILLCONSIGNMENT.COM

AVONDALE ESTATES—31 N AVONDALE RD (AT COVINGTON RD); 404.508.0611; T-W 10:30-5:30, TH 10:30-7, F-SA 10:30-5:30

JCPenney

★★★☆☆

"...competitive prices and a surprisingly cute selection... they carry bigger sizes that are very hard to find at other stores... much cheaper than most maternity boutiques and they always seem to have some sort of sale going on... an especially large selection of maternity jeans for plus sizes... a more conservative collection than the smaller, hipper boutiques... good for casual basics, but not much for special occasions..."

Casual wear	✓	$$	Prices
Business wear	✓	❸	Product availability
Intimate apparel	✓	❸	Customer service
Nursing wear	✗	❸	Decor

WWW.JCPENNEY.COM

LITHONIA—8040 MALL PKWY (AT TURNER HILL RD); 770.484.5604; M-SA 10-9, SU 12-6; MALL PARKING

Macy's

★★★½☆

"...if your local Macy's has a maternity section, you're in luck... I bought my entire pregnancy work wardrobe at Macy's... the styles are all relatively recent and the brands are well known... you can generally find some attractive dresses at very reasonable prices on their sales rack... like other large department stores, you're bound to find something that works if you dig enough... very convenient because you can get your other shopping done at the same time... the selection isn't huge, but what they have is nice..."

Casual wear	✓	$$$	Prices
Business wear	✓	❸	Product availability

Intimate apparel	✓	❸	Customer service
Nursing wear	✗	❸	Decor

WWW.MACYS.COM

DECATUR—2144 LAWRENCEVILLE HWY (AT N DEKALB SQ SHOPPPING CTR); 404.329.2600; M-SA 10-9, SU 12-7

DECATUR—2731 CANDLER RD (AT THE GALLERY AT S DEKALB); 404.243.2600; M-SA 10-9, SU 12-7

Ross Dress For Less ★★½☆☆

"...if you don't mind looking through a lot of clothes you can find some good pieces at great prices... they sometimes have larger sizes too... totally hit or miss depending on their most recent shipment... not the most fashionable clothing, but great for that everyday, casual T-shirt or stretchy pair of pants..."

Casual wear	✓	$$$	Prices
Business wear	✓	❸	Product availability
Intimate apparel	✗	❷	Customer service
Nursing wear	✗	❷	Decor

WWW.ROSSSTORES.COM

LITHONIA—8090 MALL PKWY (AT HONEYCREEK CT); 770.482.0139; M-SA 9:30-9:30, SU 11-7; MALL PARKING

Sears ★★★☆☆

"...good place to get maternity clothes for a low price... the clearance rack always has good deals and their sales are quite frequent... not necessarily super high-quality, but if you just need them for nine months, who cares... good selection of nursing bras... I love the fact that they carry maternity wear in larger sizes—I got so tired of looking in those cutesy boutiques and then being disappointed because they didn't have my size... the only place I found maternity for plus-sized women..."

Casual wear	✓	$$	Prices
Business wear	✗	❸	Product availability
Intimate apparel	✓	❸	Customer service
Nursing wear	✓	❸	Decor

WWW.SEARS.COM

LITHONIA—8020 MALL PKWY (AT TURNER HILL RD); 678.629.5000; M-F 10-9, SA 8-9, SU 11-7

Target ★★★★☆

"...I was surprised at how fashionable their selection is—they carry Liz Lange and other really cute selections... the price is right—especially since you'll only be wearing these clothes for a few months... great for maternity basics—T-shirts, skirts, sweaters, even maternity bras... best of all, you can do some maternity shopping while you're shopping for other household basics... shirts for $10—you can't beat that... not the most exciting or romantic maternity shopping, but once you see the prices you'll get over it... as always, Target provides the perfectly priced solution..."

Casual wear	✓	$$	Prices
Business wear	✓	❸	Product availability
Intimate apparel	✓	❸	Customer service
Nursing wear	✓	❸	Decor

WWW.TARGET.COM

STONE MOUNTAIN—2055 W PARK PL BLVD (AT BERMUDA RD); 770.879.5898; M-SA 8-10, SU 8-9; PARKING IN FRONT OF BLDG

TUCKER—4241 LAVISTA RD (AT NORTHLAKE PKWY); 770.270.5375; M-SA 8-10, SU 8-9; PARKING IN FRONT OF BLDG

Gwinnett

★★★★★

"lila picks"

★Belly Boutique

Alexis Maternity ★★★★☆

"...some of the cutest maternity clothes I have seen... helpful staff that know what will look good... a nice combination of trendy and conservative clothes... high-quality clothes that have lasted through multiple pregnancies... a good selection of hard-to-find fashionable and comfortable plus-sized clothes... pricey, but good to get something for a special occasion... good sales..."

Casual wear	✓	$$$$	Prices
Business wear	✓	❹	Product availability
Intimate apparel	✓	❹	Customer service
Nursing wear	✗	❸	Decor

WWW.ALEXISMATERNITYCOLLECTIONS.COM

LAWRENCEVILLE—1860 DULUTH HWY (AT SUGARLOAF PKWY); 770.962.3646; M-W F-SA 10-6, TH 10-7, SU 12-4

Baby Depot At Burlington Coat Factory ★★★☆☆

"...a surprisingly good selection of maternity clothes at great prices... staff can be hard to find so be prepared to dig... cute pants, skirts and sets... I wouldn't have thought that their selection would be as good as it is... not much other than casual items, but what they have is pretty good..."

Casual wear	✓	$$	Prices
Business wear	✗	❸	Product availability
Intimate apparel	✗	❸	Customer service
Nursing wear	✗	❸	Decor

WWW.BABYDEPOT.COM

LAWRENCEVILLE—5900 SUGARLOAF PKWY NW (AT BROWN RD NW); 678.847.5101; M-SA 10-9, SU 12-6; PARKING LOT

Back By Popular Demand

Casual wear	✓	✓	Nursing wear
Business wear	✓	✓	Intimate apparel

WWW.GWINNETTWEBPAGES.COM/BACKBYPOPULARDEMAND.HTM

LILBURN—97 MAIN ST (OFF HWY 29); 770.923.2968; M W F-SA 10-6, T TH 10-8; PARKING LOT

Belly Boutique ★★★★★

"...a little boutique that carries styles from all the hip maternity designers... they'll help you find something that looks good on you... super nice shopping experience... fun for the occasional splurge, as they have a good selection... I always thought of shopping here as a mini celebration of having such a big belly—very fun atmosphere..."

Casual wear	✓	$$$	Prices
Business wear	✓	❸	Product availability
Intimate apparel	✓	❸	Customer service
Nursing wear	✓	❸	Decor

WWW.BELLYBOUTIQUEMATERNITY.COM

NORCROSS—5165 PEACHTREE PKWY (AT THE FORUM); 770.840.8710; M-SA 10-6 ; PARKING LOT

JCPenney ★★★☆☆

"...competitive prices and a surprisingly cute selection... they carry bigger sizes that are very hard to find at other stores... much cheaper than most maternity boutiques and they always seem to have some sort of sale going on... an especially large selection of maternity jeans for plus sizes... a more conservative collection than the smaller, hipper boutiques... good for casual basics, but not much for special occasions..."

Casual wear	✓	$$	Prices
Business wear	✓	❸	Product availability
Intimate apparel	✓	❸	Customer service
Nursing wear	✗	❸	Decor

WWW.JCPENNEY.COM

BUFORD—3333 BUFORD DR (AT MALL OF GEORGIA); 770.831.0252; M-SA 10-9, SU 12-6; MALL PARKING

Kohl's ★★★☆☆

"...a small maternity selection but I always manage to find several items I like... our favorite shopping destination—clean, wide open aisles... not a huge amount of maternity, but if you find something the price is always right... the selection is very inconsistent but sometimes you can find nice casuals... best for the bare-bone basics like T-shirts, shorts or casual pants..."

Casual wear	✓	$$	Prices
Business wear	✗	❸	Product availability
Intimate apparel	✗	❸	Customer service
Nursing wear	✗	❸	Decor

WWW.KOHLS.COM

DULUTH—2050 W LIDDELL RD (AT DULUTH HWY NW); 678.417.1818; M-SA 8-10, SU 10-8

LAWRENCEVILLE—630 COLLINS HILL RD NW (AT HURRICANE SHOALS RD NE); 678.442.6646; M-SA 8-10, SU 10-8; PARKING IN FRONT OF BLDG

SNELLVILLE—2059 SCENIC HWY SW (AT HILLCREST DR SW); 678.344.2126; M-SA 8-10, SU 10-8; PARKING IN FRONT OF BLDG

SUWANEE—3620 PEACHTREE PKWY (AT JOHNS CREEK PKWY); 678.474.4993; M-SA 8-10, SU 10-8; PARKING LOT

Mimi Maternity ★★★★☆

"...it's definitely worth stopping here if you're still working and need some good-looking outfits... not cheap, but the quality is fantastic... not as expensive as A Pea In The Pod, but better quality than Motherhood Maternity... nice for basics that will last you through multiple pregnancies... perfect for work clothes, but pricey for the everyday stuff... good deals to be found on their sales racks... a good mix of high-end fancy clothes and items you can wear every day..."

Casual wear	✓	$$$	Prices
Business wear	✓	❹	Product availability
Intimate apparel	✓	❹	Customer service
Nursing wear	✓	❹	Decor

WWW.MIMIMATERNITY.COM

BUFORD—3333 BUFORD DR (AT MALL OF GEORGIA); 678.482.4797; M-SA 10-9, SU 12-6; MALL PARKING

DULUTH—2100 PLEASANT HILL RD (AT GWINNETT PL MALL); 770.497.0405; M-SA 10-9, SU 12-6; MALL PARKING

Motherhood Maternity ★★★★☆

“...a wide variety of styles, from business to weekend wear, all at a good price... affordable and cute... everything from bras and swimsuits to work outfits... highly recommended for those who don't want to spend a fortune on maternity clothes... less fancy and pricey than their sister stores—A Pea in the Pod and Mimi Maternity... they have frequent sales, so you just need to keep dropping in—you're bound to find something good...”

Casual wear	✓	$$$	Prices
Business wear	✓	❹	Product availability
Intimate apparel	✓	❹	Customer service
Nursing wear	✓	❸	Decor

WWW.MOTHERHOOD.COM

BUFORD—3385 WOODWARD CROSSING BLVD (AT MALL OF GEORGIA); 678.482.1848; M-SA 10-9, SU 12-6; MALL PARKING

LAWRENCEVILLE—5900 SUGARLOAF PKWY (AT SUGAR VALLEY DR NW); 678.847.5919; M-SA 10-9, SU 12-6

Old Navy ★★★½☆

“...the best for casual maternity clothing like stretchy T-shirts with Lycra and comfy jeans... prices are so reasonable it's ridiculous... not much for the workplace, but you can't beat the prices on casual clothes... not all Old Navy locations carry their maternity line... don't expect a huge or diverse selection... the staff is not always knowledgeable about maternity clothing and can't really help with questions about sizing... they have the best return policy—order online and return to the nearest store location... perfect for inexpensive maternity duds...”

Casual wear	✓	$$	Prices
Business wear	✗	❹	Product availability
Intimate apparel	✗	❸	Customer service
Nursing wear	✗	❸	Decor

WWW.OLDNAVY.COM

BUFORD—3333 BUFORD DR NE (AT MALL OF GEORGIA); 678.482.4343; M-SA 10-9, SU 12-6; PARKING LOT

NORCROSS—5135 PEACHTREE PKWY (AT E JONES BRIDGE NW); 770.246.0666; M-SA 9-9, SU 11-7; PARKING LOT

SNELLVILLE—2059 SCENIC HWY N (AT DOGWOOD RD SW); 770.972.0291; M-SA 9-9, SU 11-7; PARKING LOT

Ross Dress For Less ★★½☆☆

“...if you don't mind looking through a lot of clothes you can find some good pieces at great prices... they sometimes have larger sizes too... totally hit or miss depending on their most recent shipment... not the most fashionable clothing, but great for that everyday, casual T-shirt or stretchy pair of pants...”

Casual wear	✓	$$$	Prices
Business wear	✓	❸	Product availability
Intimate apparel	✗	❷	Customer service
Nursing wear	✗	❷	Decor

WWW.ROSSSTORES.COM

BUFORD—1600 MALL OF GEORGIA BLVD NE (AT MALL OF GEORGIA); 678.546.2871; M-SA 9:30-9:30, SU 11-7; MALL PARKING

Sears ★★★☆☆

“...good place to get maternity clothes for a low price... the clearance rack always has good deals and their sales are quite frequent... not *necessarily super high-quality, but if you just need them for nine months, who cares... good selection of nursing bras... I love the fact that they carry maternity wear in larger sizes—I got so tired of looking in those cutesy boutiques and then being disappointed because they didn't have my size... the only place I found maternity for plus-sized women...* ❞

Casual wear	✓	$$	Prices
Business wear	✗	❸	Product availability
Intimate apparel	✓	❸	Customer service
Nursing wear	✓	❸	Decor

WWW.SEARS.COM

DULUTH—2100 PLEASANT HILL RD (AT GWINNETT PL MALL); 770.476.6691; M-SA 7:30-9, SU 10-7; MALL PARKING

Target ★★★★☆

❝*...I was surprised at how fashionable their selection is—they carry Liz Lange and other really cute selections... the price is right—especially since you'll only be wearing these clothes for a few months... great for maternity basics—T-shirts, skirts, sweaters, even maternity bras... best of all, you can do some maternity shopping while you're shopping for other household basics... shirts for $10—you can't beat that... not the most exciting or romantic maternity shopping, but once you see the prices you'll get over it... as always, Target provides the perfectly priced solution...* ❞

Casual wear	✓	$$	Prices
Business wear	✓	❸	Product availability
Intimate apparel	✓	❸	Customer service
Nursing wear	✓	❸	Decor

WWW.TARGET.COM

BUFORD—3205 WOODWARD CROSSING BLVD (AT MALL OF GEORGIA); 678.482.2367; M-SA 8-10, SU 8-9; PARKING IN FRONT OF BLDG

DULUTH—3935 VENTURE DR (AT STEVE REYNOLDS BLVD NW); 770.232.1929; M-SA 8-10, SU 8-9; PARKING IN FRONT OF BLDG

NORCROSS—3200 HOLCOMB BRIDGE RD (AT PEACHTREE INDUSTRIAL BLVD NW); 770.849.0885; M-SA 8-10, SU 8-9; PARKING IN FRONT OF BLDG

Cobb & Douglas

★★★★★

"lila picks"

★Motherhood Maternity

Baby Depot At Burlington Coat Factory ★★★☆☆

"...a surprisingly good selection of maternity clothes at great prices... staff can be hard to find so be prepared to dig... cute pants, skirts and sets... I wouldn't have thought that their selection would be as good as it is... not much other than casual items, but what they have is pretty good..."

Casual wear	✓	$$	Prices
Business wear	✗	❸	Product availability
Intimate apparel	✗	❸	Customer service
Nursing wear	✗	❸	Decor

WWW.BABYDEPOT.COM

MARIETTA—1255 ROSWELL RD (AT I-75); 770.971.6540; M-SA 10-9, SU 11-6; PARKING LOT

Deja Vous

Casual wear	✓	✓	Nursing wear
Business wear	✓	✗	Intimate apparel

SMYRNA—W-4480 S COBB DR (AT COBB PKWY); 678.503.0702; T-F 10-6, SA 11-5; PARKING LOT

JCPenney ★★★☆☆

"...competitive prices and a surprisingly cute selection... they carry bigger sizes that are very hard to find at other stores... much cheaper than most maternity boutiques and they always seem to have some sort of sale going on... an especially large selection of maternity jeans for plus sizes... a more conservative collection than the smaller, hipper boutiques... good for casual basics, but not much for special occasions..."

Casual wear	✓	$$	Prices
Business wear	✓	❸	Product availability
Intimate apparel	✓	❸	Customer service
Nursing wear	✗	❸	Decor

WWW.JCPENNEY.COM

DOUGLASVILLE—6650 DOUGLAS BLVD (AT HWY 5); 678.715.5669; M-SA 10-9, SU 12-6; PARKING IN FRONT OF BLDG

KENNESAW—667 ERNEST W BARRETT PKWY (AT COBB PLACE BLVD NW); 770.514.7101; M-SA 10-9, SU 12-6; MALL PARKING

Kohl's ★★★☆☆

"...a small maternity selection but I always manage to find several items I like... our favorite shopping destination—clean, wide open aisles... not a huge amount of maternity, but if you find something the

price is always right... the selection is very inconsistent but sometimes you can find nice casuals... best for the bare-bone basics like T-shirts, shorts or casual pants... ❞

Casual wear ✓	$$ Prices
Business wear ✗	❸ Product availability
Intimate apparel ✗	❸ Customer service
Nursing wear ✗	❸ Decor

WWW.KOHLS.COM

ACWORTH—3354 COBB PKWY (AT NANCE RD NW); 678.574.5370; M-SA 8-10, SU 10-8; PARKING LOT

AUSTELL—1825 E-W CONNECTOR SW (AT S HOSPITAL WY SW); 770.941.3032; M-SA 8-10, SU 10-8; PARKING LOT

MARIETTA—1289 JOHNSON FERRY RD NE (AT E COBB DR NE); 678.560.1296; M-SA 8-10, SU 10-8; PARKING LOT

Mimi Maternity ★★★★☆

❝*...it's definitely worth stopping here if you're still working and need some good-looking outfits... not cheap, but the quality is fantastic... not as expensive as A Pea In The Pod, but better quality than Motherhood Maternity... nice for basics that will last you through multiple pregnancies... perfect for work clothes, but pricey for the everyday stuff... good deals to be found on their sales racks... a good mix of high-end fancy clothes and items you can wear every day...* ❞

Casual wear ✓	$$$ Prices
Business wear ✓	❹ Product availability
Intimate apparel ✓	❹ Customer service
Nursing wear ✓	❹ Decor

WWW.MIMIMATERNITY.COM

MARIETTA—4475 ROSWELL RD (AT E COBB SHOPPING CTR); 770.578.4740; M-SA 10-9, SU 12-6

Motherhood Maternity ★★★★★

❝*...a wide variety of styles, from business to weekend wear, all at a good price... affordable and cute... everything from bras and swimsuits to work outfits... highly recommended for those who don't want to spend a fortune on maternity clothes... less fancy and pricey than their sister stores—A Pea in the Pod and Mimi Maternity... they have frequent sales, so you just need to keep dropping in—you're bound to find something good...* ❞

Casual wear ✓	$$$ Prices
Business wear ✓	❹ Product availability
Intimate apparel ✓	❹ Customer service
Nursing wear ✓	❸ Decor

WWW.MOTHERHOOD.COM

DOUGLASVILLE—1510 DOUGLAS BLVD (AT CHAPEL HILL RD); 770.577.5676; M-SA 10-9, SU 12-6

KENNESAW—3316 BUSBEE DR NW (AT TOWN CTR MALL); 678.797.1995; M-SA 10-9, SU 12-6; PARKING LOT

KENNESAW—400 ERNEST W BARRETT PKWY NW (AT MALL BLVD NW); 678.797.1995; M-SA 10-9, SU 12-6; MALL PARKING

Old Navy ★★★½☆

❝*...the best for casual maternity clothing like stretchy T-shirts with Lycra and comfy jeans... prices are so reasonable it's ridiculous... not much for the workplace, but you can't beat the prices on casual clothes... not all Old Navy locations carry their maternity line... don't expect a huge or diverse selection... the staff is not always knowledgeable about maternity clothing and can't really help with questions about sizing... they have the best return policy—order online* *and return to the nearest store location... perfect for inexpensive maternity duds...* ❞

Casual wear ✓ | $$ Prices
Business wear ✗ | ❹ Product availability
Intimate apparel ✗ | ❸ Customer service
Nursing wear ✗ | ❸ Decor

WWW.OLDNAVY.COM

DOUGLASVILLE—6588 DOUGLAS BLVD (AT ARBOR PL); 678.838.0771; M-SA 10-9, SU 12-6; PARKING LOT

PB & J Classic For Kids

Casual wear ✓ | ✓ Nursing wear
Business wear ✓ | ✗ Intimate apparel

WWW.PBJKIDS.COM

MARIETTA—2100 ROSWELL RD (AT E PIEDMONT); 770.509.5437; M-SA 10-6; PARKING LOT

Ross Dress For Less ★★½☆☆

❝*...if you don't mind looking through a lot of clothes you can find some good pieces at great prices... they sometimes have larger sizes too... totally hit or miss depending on their most recent shipment... not the most fashionable clothing, but great for that everyday, casual T-shirt or stretchy pair of pants...* ❞

Casual wear ✓ | $$$ Prices
Business wear ✓ | ❸ Product availability
Intimate apparel ✗ | ❷ Customer service
Nursing wear ✗ | ❷ Decor

WWW.ROSSSTORES.COM

AUSTELL—1825 E-W CONNECTOR SW (AT CHAMPION DR); 678.945.0219; M-SA 9:30-9:30, SU 11-7; PARKING LOT

MARIETTA—50 ERNEST W BARRETT PKWY NW (AT BELLS FERRY RD NE); 770.419.1203; M-SA 9:30-9:30, SU 11-7; PARKING LOT

Sears ★★★☆☆

❝*...good place to get maternity clothes for a low price... the clearance rack always has good deals and their sales are quite frequent... not necessarily super high-quality, but if you just need them for nine months, who cares... good selection of nursing bras... I love the fact that they carry maternity wear in larger sizes—I got so tired of looking in those cutesy boutiques and then being disappointed because they didn't have my size... the only place I found maternity for plus-sized women...* ❞

Casual wear ✓ | $$ Prices
Business wear ✗ | ❸ Product availability
Intimate apparel ✓ | ❸ Customer service
Nursing wear ✓ | ❸ Decor

WWW.SEARS.COM

DOUGLASVILLE—6580 DOUGLAS BLVD (AT GA-5); 770.577.5200; M-F 10-9, SA 10-6, SU 11-5; PARKING LOT

KENNESAW—400 ERNEST W BARRETT PKWY (AT TOWN CTR AT COBB); 770.429.4155; M-F 10-9, SA 8-9, SU 11-6; PARKING LOT

Tadpoles

Casual wear ✓ | ✗ Nursing wear
Business wear ✓ | ✗ Intimate apparel

WWW.TADPOLESINC.COM

KENNESAW—425 ERNEST W BARRETT PKWY NW (AT TOWN CTR AT COBB); 770.499.7010; M-W 9-5, TH-SA 9-7, SU 12-5; PARKING LOT

Target ★★★★☆

"...I was surprised at how fashionable their selection is—they carry Liz Lange and other really cute selections... the price is right—especially since you'll only be wearing these clothes for a few months... great for maternity basics—T-shirts, skirts, sweaters, even maternity bras... best of all, you can do some maternity shopping while you're shopping for other household basics... shirts for $10—you can't beat that... not the most exciting or romantic maternity shopping, but once you see the prices you'll get over it... as always, Target provides the perfectly priced solution..."

Casual wear	✓	$$	Prices
Business wear	✓	❸	Product availability
Intimate apparel	✓	❸	Customer service
Nursing wear	✓	❸	Decor

WWW.TARGET.COM

AUSTELL—4125 AUSTELL RD (AT E-W CONNECTOR); 678.945.4550; M-SA 8-10, SU 8-9; PARKING IN FRONT OF BLDG

DOUGLASVILLE—2950 CHAPEL HILL RD (OFF ARBOR PL BLVD); 770.947.5303; M-SA 8-10, SU 8-9; PARKING IN FRONT OF BLDG

KENNESAW—740 ERNEST W BARRETT PKWY NW (AT COBB PL BLVD NW); 770.425.6895; M-SA 8-10, SU 8-9; PARKING IN FRONT OF BLDG

MARIETTA—2535 DALLAS HWY SW (AT ERNEST W BARRETT PKWY NW); 770.792.7933; M-SA 8-10, SU 8-9; PARKING IN FRONT OF BLDG

MARIETTA—3040 SHALLOWFORD RD (AT SANDY PLAINS RD NE); 770.321.8545; M-SA 8-10, SU 8-9; PARKING IN FRONT OF BLDG

SMYRNA—2201 COBB PKWY SE (AT LAKE PARK DR SE); 770.952.2241; M-F 8-10, SU 8-9; PARKING IN FRONT OF BLDG

Online

★★★★★

"lila picks"

★breastisbest.com ★gap.com

★maternitymall.com ★naissance maternity.com

babiesrus.com ★★★★☆

"...their online store is surprisingly plentiful for maternity wear in addition to all of the baby stuff... they carry everything from Mimi Maternity to Belly Basics... easy shopping and good return policy... the price is right and the selection is really good..."

Casual wear ✓ ✓ Nursing wear
Business wear ✓ ✓ Intimate apparel

babycenter.com ★★★★☆

"...it's babycenter.com—of course it's good... a small but well selected maternity section... I love being able to read other people's comments before purchasing... prices are reasonable and the convenience is priceless... great customer service and easy returns..."

Casual wear ✓ ✓ Nursing wear
Business wear ✗ ✗ Intimate apparel

babystyle.com ★★★★☆

"...beautiful selection of maternity clothes... very trendy, fashionable styles... take advantage of their free shipping offers to keep the cost down... items generally ship quickly... I found a formal maternity outfit for a benefit dinner, bought it on sale and received it on time... a nice variety of things and they ship in a timely manner..."

Casual wear ✓ ✓ Nursing wear
Business wear ✓ ✓ Intimate apparel

bellablumaternity.com

Casual wear ✓ ✓ Nursing wear
Business wear ✓ ✓ Intimate apparel

breakoutbras.com

Casual wear ✗ ✓ Nursing wear
Business wear ✗ ✓ Intimate apparel

breastisbest.com ★★★★★

"...by far the best resource for purchasing good quality nursing bras online... the site is easy to use and they have an extensive online fitting guide... returns are a breeze... since they are only online you may have to try a few before you get it exactly right..."

Casual wear ✓ ✓ Nursing wear
Business wear ✗ ✓ Intimate apparel

childishclothing.com

Casual wear ✓ · ✗ Nursing wear
Business wear ✗ · ✗ Intimate apparel

duematernity.com ★★★★☆

"...refreshing styles... fun and hip clothing... the site is easy to navigate and use... I've ordered a bunch of clothes from them and never had a problem... everything from casual wear to fun, funky items for special occasions... prices are reasonable..."

Casual wear ✓ · ✓ Nursing wear
Business wear ✓ · ✓ Intimate apparel

evalillian.com

Casual wear ✓ · ✓ Nursing wear
Business wear ✓ · ✓ Intimate apparel

expressiva.com ★★★★½

"...the best site for nursing clothes... prices are good and their selection is terrific... lots of selection on dressy, casual, sleep, workout and even bathing suits... if you're going to shop for maternity online then be sure not to miss this cool site... good customer service—quite prompt in answering questions about my order..."

Casual wear ✓ · ✓ Nursing wear
Business wear ✗ · ✓ Intimate apparel

gap.com ★★★★★

"...stylish maternity clothes delivered right to your doorstep... always something worth buying... the best place for functional, comfortable and affordable maternity clothes... classic styles, not too trendy... more available online than in a store... no fancy dresses but lots of casual outfits that are cheap, look good and I don't mind parting with them after my baby is born... easy to use site and deliveries are generally prompt... you can return them to any Gap store..."

Casual wear ✓ · ✓ Nursing wear
Business wear ✓ · ✓ Intimate apparel

japaneseweekend.com ★★★★☆

"...pregnancy clothes that scream 'I am proud of my pregnant body'... a must for comfy, stylish stuff... they make the best maternity pants which cradle your belly as it grows... a little expensive but I lived in their pants my entire pregnancy—I definitely got my money's worth... really nice clothing that just doesn't look and feel like your traditional pregnancy wear—I still wear a couple of the outfits (my baby is now 6 months old)..."

Casual wear ✓ · ✓ Nursing wear
Business wear ✓ · ✓ Intimate apparel

jcpenney.com ★★★☆☆

"...competitive prices and a surprisingly cute selection... they carry bigger sizes that are very hard to find at other stores... much cheaper than most maternity boutiques and they always seem to have some sort of sale going on... an especially large selection of maternity jeans for plus sizes... a more conservative collection than the smaller, hipper boutiques... good for casual basics, but not much for special occasions..."

Casual wear ✓ · ✓ Nursing wear
Business wear ✓ · ✓ Intimate apparel

lizlange.com ★★★★½

"...well-designed and cute... the real buys on this site are definitely in the sale section... cute, hip selection of jeans, skirts, blouses and

bathing suits... their evening and dressy clothes are the best with wonderful fabrics and designs... easy and convenient online shopping... practical but not frumpy styles—their web site made my maternity shopping so easy... ”

Casual wear ✓ ✗ Nursing wear
Business wear ✓ ✗ Intimate apparel

maternitymall.com ★★★★★

“*...I had great luck with maternitymall.com... a large selection of vendors in all price ranges... quick and easy without having to leave my house... found everything I needed... their merchandise tends to be true to size... site is a bit hard to navigate and cluttered with ads... sale and clearance prices are fantastic...* ”

Casual wear ✓ ✓ Nursing wear
Business wear ✓ ✓ Intimate apparel

mommygear.com

Casual wear ✓ ✓ Nursing wear
Business wear ✗ ✓ Intimate apparel

momsnightout.com

“*...for that fashionable-not-frumpy fancy occasion dress... beautiful store with gorgeous selection of dresses from cocktail to bridal... one on one attention... expensive but worth it...* ”

Casual wear ✗ ✗ Nursing wear
Business wear ✓ ✗ Intimate apparel

motherhood.com ★★★★☆

“*...a wide variety of styles, from business to weekend wear—all at a good price... affordable and cute... everything from bras and swimsuits to work outfits... highly recommended for those who don't want to spend a fortune on maternity clothes... less fancy and pricey than their sister stores—A Pea in the Pod and Mimi Maternity... they have frequent sales, so you just need to keep dropping in—you're bound to find something good...* ”

Casual wear ✓ ✓ Nursing wear
Business wear ✓ ✓ Intimate apparel

motherwear.com ★★★★½

“*...excellent selection of cute and practical nursing clothes at reasonable prices... sign up for their e-mail newsletter for great offers, including free shipping... top quality clothes... decent selection of hard to find plus sizes... golden return policy, you can return any item (even used!) you aren't 100% happy with... they sell the only nursing tops I could actually wear outside the house... cute styles that aren't frumpy... so easy... pricey but worth it for the quality... top notch customer service...* ”

Casual wear ✗ ✓ Nursing wear
Business wear ✗ ✓ Intimate apparel

naissancematernity.com ★★★★★

“*...the cutest maternity clothes around... hip and funky clothes for the artsy, well-dressed mom to be... their site is easy to navigate... if you can't make it down to the actual store in LA, just go online... clothes that make you look and feel sexy... it ain't cheap but you will look marvelous and the clothes will grow with you... web site is great and their phone order service was incredible...* ”

Casual wear ✓ ✗ Nursing wear
Business wear ✓ ✗ Intimate apparel

nordstrom.com ★★★☆☆

"...now that they don't carry maternity in stores anymore, this is the only way to get any maternity from Nordstrom... overpriced but nice... makes returns harder, since you have to ship everything instead of just going back to a store... they carry Cadeau, Liz Lange, Belly Basics, etc... nice stuff, not so nice prices..."

Casual wear ✓ ✓ Nursing wear
Business wear ✓ ✓ Intimate apparel

oldnavy.com ★★★★☆

"...since not all Old Navy stores carry maternity clothes, this is the easiest way to go... just like their regular clothes, the maternity selection is great for casual wear... cheap, cheap, cheap... the quality is good and the price is definitely right... frequent sales make great prices even better..."

Casual wear ✓ ✓ Nursing wear
Business wear ✗ ✗ Intimate apparel

onehotmama.com ★★★½☆

"...you'll find many things you must have... cool and very nice clothing... they carry everything from underwear and tights to formal dresses... you can find some real bargains online... super fast shipping... also, lots of choices for nursing and get-back-in-shape wear..."

Casual wear ✓ ✓ Nursing wear
Business wear ✓ ✓ Intimate apparel

showeryourbaby.com

Casual wear ✓ ✓ Nursing wear
Business wear ✗ ✓ Intimate apparel

target.com ★★★★☆

"...lots of Liz Lange at very fair prices... the selection is great and it's so easy to shop online—we bought most of our baby gear here and I managed to slip in a couple of orders for some maternity wear too... maternity shirts for $10—where else can you find deals like that..."

Casual wear ✓ ✓ Nursing wear
Business wear ✓ ✓ Intimate apparel

activities & outings

City of Atlanta

★★★★★

"lila picks"

- ★Center For Puppetry Arts
- ★Imagine It! The Children's Museum
- ★The Music Class
- ★Zoo Atlanta

Abrakadoodle ★★★★☆

"...a national franchise with programs in major markets throughout the country... a curriculum designed by art teachers... lots of painting, coloring and gluing... wonderful art enrichment classes offered at preschools, daycare centers, home schools, community centers, libraries, etc... programs are run by different instructors in different cities..."

Customer service........................❹ $$..Prices
Age range.............20 mths to 12 yrs
WWW.ABRAKADOODLE.COM

ATLANTA—3212 SAYBROOK DR (AT WINDSOR PKWY); 404.949.9409; CHECK SCHEDULE ONLINE; FREE PARKING

Atlanta History Center ★★★★☆

"...primary source of Atlanta regional and national history... beautiful gardens and neat old houses to explore... enjoy story time at Tullie Smith Farm on Magic Mondays... arts and crafts, literature workshops and summer camps in June and July where kids create Indian-inspired art, play croquet and view the exhibitions... a must for school-age kids, but also fun for the younger crowd..."

Customer service........................❹ $$..Prices
Age range....................3 yrs and up
WWW.ATLANTAHISTORYCENTER.COM

ATLANTA—130 W PACES FERRY RD NW (AT VALLEY RD NW); 404.814.4000; M-SA 10-5:30, SU 12-5:30; FREE PARKING

Atlanta Rocks ★★★★★

"...professionally designed climbing structures... offers classes for kids as young as 6 years and summer camps for 8 years and above... harnesses available for 3 years old and above... both locations are available for birthday parties and rent out a portable wall for a party at home... let your kids climb the walls in this safe, but challenging environment... technically not intended for toddlers, but they can can climb around a little, too..."

Customer service........................❹ $$$......................................Prices
Age range....................6 yrs and up
WWW.ATLANTAROCKS.COM

ATLANTA—1019-A COLLIER RD NW (AT WOODLAND HILLS AVE NW); 404.351.3009; M W F 3-10, T TH 11-10, SA 12-8, SU 12-6; FREE PARKING

Barnes & Noble ★★★★½

"...wonderful weekly story times for all ages and frequent author visits for older kids... lovely selection of books and the story times are fun and very well done... they have evening story times—we put our kids in their pjs and come here as a treat before bedtime... they read a story, and then usually have a little craft or related coloring project... times vary by location so give them a call..."

Customer service .... ❹ $.. Prices
Age range .... 6 mths to 6 yrs

WWW.BARNESANDNOBLE.COM

ATLANTA—120 PERIMETER CENTER W (AT PERIMETER MALL); 770.396.1200; CALL FOR SCHEDULE

ATLANTA—1217 CAROLINE ST (AT DEKALB AVE NE); 404.522.0212; CALL FOR SCHEDULE

ATLANTA—2900 PEACHTREE RD NE (AT PEACHTREE AVE NE); 404.261.7747; CALL FOR SCHEDULE

ATLANTA—2952 COBB PKWY (AT AKERS MILL RD SE); 770.953.0966; CALL FOR SCHEDULE

Borders Books ★★★★☆

"...very popular weekly story time held in most branches (check the web site for locations and times)... call before you go since they are very popular and get extremely crowded... kids love the unique blend of songs, stories and dancing... Mr. Hatbox's appearances are a delight to everyone (unfortunately he doesn't make appearances at all locations)... large children's section is well categorized and well priced... they make it fun for young tots to browse through the board-book section by hanging toys around the shelves... the low-key cafe is a great place to have coffee with your baby and leaf through some magazines..."

Customer service .... ❹ $.. Prices
Age range .... 6 mths to 6 yrs

WWW.BORDERSSTORES.COM

ATLANTA—1745 PEACHTREE RD NE (AT HUNTINGTON RD NE); 404.810.9004; CALL FOR SCHEDULE

ATLANTA—3101 COBB PKWY (AT CUMBERLAND BLVD SE); 770.612.0940; CALL FOR SCHEDULE

ATLANTA—3637 PEACHTREE RD NE (AT PEACHTREE DUNWOODY RD NE); 404.237.0707; CALL FOR SCHEDULE

ATLANTA—650 PONCE DE LEON AVE NE (AT MONROE DR NE); 404.607.7903; CALL FOR SCHEDULE

Buckhead Gymnastics Center ★★★½☆

"...this is a serious gymnastics center that also offers a variety of gymnastics classes ranging from toddler to competitive gymnastics... the Roly Poly program is a wonderful way to spend time with tots and meet other moms... dedicated teachers blend imagination and laughter with stretching, strengthening and skills... my daughter loves the staff and they have a great time..."

Customer service .... ❹ $$.. Prices

WWW.BUCKHEADGYMNASTICS.COM

ATLANTA—2335 ADAMS DR (AT HOLCOMB CTR); 404.367.4414; CALL FOR SCHEDULE; FREE PARKING

Candler Park Pool ★★★★☆

"...fun in the summer... I loved going to this pool while I was pregnant... the shallow part of the pool is very large and they have an

activities & outings

adult swim time for 10 minutes every hour... there's a playground just across from the pool... definitely the best Dekalb County pool for children... it can be crowded on nice days... ”

Customer service........................❸ $ ....Prices

WWW.CANDLERPARKPOOL.COM

ATLANTA—1500 MCLENDON AVE NE (AT CANDLER PARK DR NE); 404.373.4849; CALL FOR HOURS; FREE PARKING

Center For Puppetry Arts ★★★★★

“*...the quality of the performances are amazing and the workshops are lots of fun... shows are the perfect length and kids love to play in the museum... cast members talk about the puppets after the show... plan ahead as tickets go fast... preview shows available at a discount... can be overwhelming for little ones when school groups and daycare centers are in attendance...* ”

Customer service........................❹ $$$......................................Prices

Age range.................6 mths and up

WWW.PUPPET.ORG

ATLANTA—1404 SPRING ST (AT 18TH ST NW); 404.873.3391; T-SA 9-5, SU 11-5; PARKING BEHIND BLDG

Chastain Pool ★★★½☆

“*...located in the largest, most popular park in Atlanta... the swim club's motto is 'convenient, fun, clean and refreshing'... offers group and private swim lessons... operated by the North Atlanta Swim Association... subscribers receive unlimited use of pool at no additional charge... they did a great job on the renovation...* ”

Customer service........................❹ $$...Prices

Age range.................6 mths and up

WWW.NORTHATLANTASWIM.ORG

ATLANTA—135 W WIEUCA RD NW (AT POOL RD); 404.255.0863; DAILY 10-8; PARKING LOT

Chuck E Cheese's ★★★☆☆

“*...lots of games, rides, playrooms and very greasy food... the kids can play and eat and parents can unwind a little... a good rainy day activity... the kids love the food, but it's a bit greasy for adults... always crowded and crazy—but that's half the fun... can you ever go wrong with pizza, games and singing?.. although they do have a salad bar for adults, remember, you're not going for the food—you're going because your kids will love it... just about the easiest birthday party around—just pay money and show up...* ”

Customer service........................❸ $$...Prices

Age range...............12 mths to 7 yrs

WWW.CHUCKECHEESE.COM

ATLANTA—2990 CUMBERLAND BLVD SE (AT SPRING HILL PKWY SE); 770.435.9036; SU-TH 9-10, F-SA 9-11; FREE PARKING

Fernbank Museum of Natural History ★★★★☆

“*...one of the best places to take kids where they can see and talk about such a variety of things... drop-in activities and storytelling on the weekend... offers family walks and summer camps... the IMAX theater is wonderful... my daughter loves the dinosaurs... plenty to do and see for all ages... children love the small discovery room...* ”

Customer service........................❹ $$$......................................Prices

Age range.....................3 yrs and up

WWW.FERNBANK.EDU/MUSEUM

ATLANTA—767 CLIFTON RD NE (AT PONCE DE LEON AVE NE); 404.929.6300; M-SA 10-5, SU 12-5; FREE PARKING

Fernbank Science Center ★★★★☆

"...a science, engineering, math & aerospace academy... much more suited to school-aged children, but tots will have fun seeing the dinosaurs and walking through the forest, greenhouses and the rose garden... planetarium offers programs for schools and the public... $4 for adults; under 5 free..."

Customer service .... ❹ $$ .... Prices

WWW.FERNBANKSCIENCECENTER.ORG

ATLANTA—156 HEATON PARK DR NE (AT DYSON DR); 678.874.7102; M-F 8-4; FREE PARKING

Garden Hills Park ★★★½☆

"...a gathering place for Buckhead residents who leased the facility from the city... children can enjoy the main pool and the wading pool... available for birthday parties... reasonably priced memberships, which includes access for nannies and babysitters..."

Customer service .... ❸ $$ .... Prices

Age range ....6 mths and up

WWW.GARDENHILLSPOOL.COM

ATLANTA—E WESLEY RD NE (AT RUMSON RD NE); 404.848.7220; CALL FOR HOURS; FREE PARKING

Georgia Aquarium ★★★★½

"...the newly opened aquarium is gorgeous... an amazing, state-of-the-art aquarium that is guaranteed to fascinate your whole family... located in downtown Atlanta... one of the biggest attractions to hit the city... the biggest and nicest aquarium I've ever been to..."

Customer service .... ❹ $$$ .... Prices

Age range ....6 mths and up

WWW.GEORGIAAQUARIUM.ORG

ATLANTA—CENTENNIAL OLYMPIC PARK DR NW (AT ALEXANDER ST NW); 877.434.7442; FREE PARKING

Grant Park Pool ★★½☆☆

"...no-charge swimming weekday afternoons, and paid swimming on evenings and on weekends... swim lessons and summer camps available... lessons for all ages... $2 adults; under 5 free..."

Customer service .... ❶ $$ .... Prices

WWW.GRANTPARKPOOL.ORG

ATLANTA—840 CHEROKEE AVE SE (AT ORMOND ST SE); 404.622.3041; CHECK SCHEDULE ONLINE; FREE PARKING

Gymboree Play & Music ★★★★½

"...we've done several rounds of classes with our kids and they absolutely love it... colorful, padded environment with tons of things to climb and play on... a good indoor place to meet other families and for kids to learn how to play with each other... the equipment and play areas are generally neat and clean... an easy birthday party spot... a guaranteed nap after class... costs vary, so call before showing up..."

Customer service .... ❹ $$$ .... Prices

Age range .... birth to 5 yrs

WWW.GYMBOREE.COM

ATLANTA—2205 LAVISTA RD NE (AT TOCO HILLS SHOPPING CTR); 404.320.0060; CHECK SCHEDULE ONLINE; PARKING LOT

ATLANTA—4920 ROSWELL RD NE (AT FRANKLIN RD); 404.256.2223; CHECK SCHEDULE ONLINE

Imagine It! The Children's Museum Of Atlanta ★★★★★

"...an awesome place for kids to play, learn and explore... a fun-filled day of creative play... fabulous indoor activities such as sandboxes, a painted wall and a water area where kids can 'fish' for rubber ducks... phenomenal setup... my son lives for places like these where he can touch everything... a membership will pay for itself in a few visits... indoor picnic area and a reasonably-priced deli... nursing room has activities for siblings... can be crazy on a busy day... annual memberships start at $90..."

Customer service........................❹ $$$......................................Prices

Age range.................... 2 yrs to 8 yrs

WWW.IMAGINEIT-CMA.ORG

ATLANTA—275 CENTENNIAL OLYMPIC PARK DR NW (AT BAKER ST NW); 404.659.5437; CALL FOR SCHEDULE

Little Gym, The ★★★★☆

"...a well thought-out program of gym and tumbling geared toward different age groups... a clean facility, excellent and knowledgeable staff... we love the small-sized gym equipment and their willingness to work with kids with special needs... activities are fun and personalized to match the kids' age... great place for birthday parties with a nice party room—they'll organize and do everything for you..."

Customer service........................❹ $$$......................................Prices

Age range...............4 mths to 12 yrs

WWW.THELITTLEGYM.COM

ATLANTA—360 PHARR RD (AT GRANDVIEW AVE NE); 404.848.0420; CALL FOR SCHEDULE

Monkey Joe's Parties & Play ★★★½☆

"...a party and play center... indoor party areas have slides, jumps and obstacle courses... also rents out jumps and slides for parties at home... many parents say their kids are still talking about this place after attending my son's party... kids have lots of fun and are completely worn out at the end of the day... $8 per child..."

Customer service........................❹ $$..Prices

Age range................. 2 yrs to 12 yrs

WWW.MONKEYJOES.COM

ATLANTA—1019 COLLIER RD NW (AT HWY 75); 404.351.1818; M-SA 10-6, SU 11-6; FREE PARKING

Music Class, The ★★★★★

"...an excellent introduction to music for your children... you will sing the songs for years to come... we love the music pups program... classes help children develop an ear for music... friendly and enthusiastic teachers... songs are great, easy to remember, and enjoyed by kids and parents alike... you get more out of the class if you listen to the CD/tape at home or in the car... the 45-minute class is the perfect length for kids to stay interested..."

Customer service........................❺ $$$......................................Prices

Age range................ 3 mths to 4 yrs

WWW.THEMUSICCLASS.COM

ATLANTA—1580 SPALDING DR (AT TEMPLE EMANU-EL); 770.645.5578; CHECK SCHEDULE ONLINE; FREE PARKING

ATLANTA—257 BUCKHEAD AVE (AT BOILING WY NE); 770.645.5578; CHECK SCHEDULE ONLINE; FREE PARKING

ATLANTA—2991-B N DRUID HILLS RD (AT CAPITAL AVE SE); 770.645.5578; CHECK SCHEDULE ONLINE

ATLANTA—301 JOHNSON FERRY RD NW (AT ABERNATHY PARK); 770.645.5578; CHECK SCHEDULE ONLINE; FREE PARKING

Music Together ★★★★½

"...the best mom and baby classes out there... music, singing, dancing—even instruments for tots to play with... liberal make-up policy, great venues, take home books, CDs and tapes which are different each semester... it's a national franchise so instructors vary and have their own style... different age groups get mixed up which makes it a good learning experience for all involved... the highlight of our week—grandma always comes along... be prepared to have your tot sing the songs at home, in the car—everywhere..."

Customer service .... ❹ $$$ .... Prices
Age range .... 2 mths to 5 yrs

WWW.MUSICTOGETHER.COM

ATLANTA—800.728.2692; CALL FOR SCHEDULE AND LOCATION

ATLANTA—404.875.4377; CALL FOR SCHEDULE AND LOCATION

ATLANTA—404.288.5424; CALL FOR SCHEDULE AND LOCATION

ATLANTA—404.287.0087; CALL FOR SCHEDULE AND LOCATION

My Gym Children's Fitness Center ★★★★☆

"...a wonderful gym environment for parents with babies and older tots... classes range from tiny tots to school-aged children and the staff is great about making it fun for all ages... equipment and facilities are really neat—ropes, pulleys, swings, you name it... the kind of place your kids hate to leave... the staff's enthusiasm is contagious... great for memorable birthday parties... although it's a franchise, each gym seems to have its own individual feeling... awesome for meeting playmates and other parents..."

Customer service .... ❹ $$$ .... Prices
Age range .... 3 mths to 9 yrs

WWW.MY-GYM.COM

ATLANTA—267 W WIEUCA RD NE (AT ROSWELL RD NE); 404.252.1201; CHECK SCHEDULE ONLINE; FREE PARKING

Reel Moms (Loews Theatres) ★★★★☆

"...not really an activity for kids, but rather something you can easily do with your baby... first-run movies for people with babies... the sound is low, the lights turned up and no one cares if your baby cries... packed with moms changing diapers all over the place... so nice to be able to go see current movies... don't have to worry about baby noise... relaxed environment with moms, dads and babies wandering all over... the staff is very friendly and there is a real community feel... a great idea and very well done..."

Customer service .... ❹ $$ .... Prices
Age range .... 3 mths to 2 yrs

WWW.ENJOYTHESHOW.COM/REELMOMS

ATLANTA—2841 GREENBRIER PKWY SW (AT HEADLAND DR); 404.629.2377; CHECK SCHEDULE ONLINE

YMCA ★★★★☆

"...most of the Ys in the area have classes and activities for kids... swimming, gym classes, dance—even play groups for the really little ones... ... some facilities are nicer than others, but in general their programs are worth checking out... prices are more than reasonable for what is offered... the best bang for your buck... they have it all—great programs that meet the needs of a diverse range of families... check out their camps during the summer and school breaks..."

Customer service........................❹ $$..Prices
Age range.................3 mths and up

WWW.YMCAATLANTA.ORG

ATLANTA—1160 MOORES MILL RD NW (AT MILMAR DR NW); 404.350.9292; CHECK SCHEDULE ONLINE

ATLANTA—2220 CAMPBELLTON RD SW (AT DELOWE DR SW); 404.753.4169; M-F 5-9:45, SA 8-6, SU 12-6; PARKING LOT

ATLANTA—275 E LAKE BLVD (AT MEMORIAL AVE); 404.373.6561; CHECK SCHEDULE ONLINE; FREE PARKING

ATLANTA—3692 ASHFORD-DUNWOODY RD NE (AT JOHNSON FERRY RD NE); 770.451.9622; M-F 5:30-10, SA 8-6, SU 1-8; PARKING LOT

ATLANTA—555 LUCKIE ST NW (AT COCA-COLA PLZ NW); 404.724.9622; M-F 6-9, SA 9-12, SU 12-5; PARKING LOT

Zoo Atlanta ★★★★★

"...a great place to take the stroller and walk the baby around... always a great outing... can be pricey, but the membership is totally worthwhile if you plan to go often... the new panda exhibit is extra-special... a wonderful African Safari area and reptile house... the children's section has a carousel, train and petting zoo... very shaded, which is great in the summer... bring your own food as there aren't a lot of choices at the snack bar... watch out for field trips in the spring..."

Customer service........................❹ $$$......................................Prices
Age range.................6 mths and up

WWW.ZOOATLANTA.ORG

ATLANTA—800 CHEROKEE AVE SE (AT GRANT PARK PL SE); 404.624.5600; DAILY 9:30-4:30

North Fulton

★★★★★

"lila picks"

★Chattahoochee Nature Center

★The Music Class

Alpharetta City Pool ★★★½☆

"...offers swim lessons for various ages and skill levels... the baby pool is covered all day and is colder than the main pool... main pool is shared with Sharks swim team... 50-meter pool, showers, lockers and concession stand available... open only in the summer (Memorial Day through early September)..."

Customer service .... ❹ $.. Prices

WWW.ALPHARETTA.GA.US

ALPHARETTA—1825 OLD MILTON PKWY (AT WILLS DR); 678.297.6107; CHECK SCHEDULE ONLINE; FREE PARKING

Barnes & Noble ★★★★½

"...wonderful weekly story times for all ages and frequent author visits for older kids... lovely selection of books and the story times are fun and very well done... they have evening story times—we put our kids in their pjs and come here as a treat before bedtime... they read a story, and then usually have a little craft or related coloring project... times vary by location so give them a call..."

Customer service .... ❹ $.. Prices

Age range .... 6 mths to 6 yrs

WWW.BARNESANDNOBLE.COM

ALPHARETTA—7660 NORTH POINT PKWY (AT MANSELL RD); 770.993.8340; CALL FOR SCHEDULE

Borders Books ★★★★☆

"...very popular weekly story time held in most branches (check the web site for locations and times)... call before you go since they are very popular and get extremely crowded... kids love the unique blend of songs, stories and dancing... Mr. Hatbox's appearances are a delight to everyone (unfortunately he doesn't make appearances at all locations)... large children's section is well categorized and well priced... they make it fun for young tots to browse through the board-book section by hanging toys around the shelves... the low-key cafe is a great place to have coffee with your baby and leaf through some magazines..."

Customer service .... ❹ $.. Prices

Age range .... 6 mths to 6 yrs

WWW.BORDERSSTORES.COM

DUNWOODY—4745 ASHFORD-DUNWOODY RD (AT VALLEY VIEW RD); 770.396.0004; CALL FOR SCHEDULE

Build-A-Bear Workshop ★★★½☆

"...design and make your own bear—it's a dream come true... the most cherished toy my daughter owns... they even come with birth certificates... the staff is fun and knows how to play along with the kids' excitement... the basic stuffed animal is only about $15, but the extras add up quickly... great for field trips, birthdays and special occasions... how darling—my nephew is 8 years old now, and still sleeps with his favorite bear..."

Customer service........................❹ $$$......................................Prices
Age range....................3 yrs and up

WWW.BUILDABEAR.COM

ALPHARETTA—1092 NORTH POINT CIR (AT NORTH POINT MALL); 770.442.0900; M-SA 10-9, SU 11-6; MALL PARKING

Chattahoochee Nature Center ★★★★★

"...children love getting close to the birds and snakes... great place for picnics... annual butterfly festival is a favorite... guided canoe trips, story time by the river and animal encounters in the summer... a wonderful place for the entire family... minutes away from downtown Atlanta..."

Customer service........................❹ $ ....Prices
Age range.................6 mths and up

WWW.CHATTNATURECENTER.COM

ROSWELL—9135 WILLEO RD (AT RIVER PARK); 770.992.2055; M-SA 9-5, SU 12-5; PARKING LOT

Chuck E Cheese's ★★★☆☆

"...lots of games, rides, playrooms and very greasy food... the kids can play and eat and parents can unwind a little... a good rainy day activity... the kids love the food, but it's a bit greasy for adults... always crowded and crazy—but that's half the fun... can you ever go wrong with pizza, games and singing?.. although they do have a salad bar for adults, remember, you're not going for the food—you're going because your kids will love it... just about the easiest birthday party around—just pay money and show up..."

Customer service........................❸ $$...Prices
Age range...............12 mths to 7 yrs

WWW.CHUCKECHEESE.COM

ALPHARETTA—925 NORTH POINT DR (AT MILL CREEK AVE); 678.893.0171; SU-TH 9-10, F-SA 9-11

Dancer's Studio Backstage ★★★★☆

"...outstanding dance classes ranging from preschool through advanced professional levels... tot intro classes for 3 year olds... summer camps starting at 5 years old... professional performances of fairytales such as 'Babes in Toyland,' 'Hansel and Gretel' and 'Cinderella'... special emphasis is placed on correct technique and student progress... great teachers..."

Customer service........................❹ $$...Prices
Age range....................3 yrs and up

WWW.DANCERS-BACKSTAGE.COM

ALPHARETTA—8560 HOLCOMB BRIDGE RD (AT NESBITT FERRY RD); 770.993.2623; CALL FOR SCHEDULE; FREE PARKING

Dunwoody Nature Center ★★★★☆

"...hands-on environmental education... located in a public park, it features wetland, woodland and streamside trails, display gardens, a picnic meadow and a shaded playground... fun to explore with kids... beautiful trails... butterfly festival and animal encounters... a precious oasis..."

Customer service .... ❹ $ .... Prices
Age range .... 2 yrs and up
WWW.DUNWOODYNATURE.ORG
DUNWOODY—5343 ROBERTS DR (AT HOLLY BANK CIR); 770.394.3322; M-F 9-5; FREE PARKING

Gymboree Play & Music ★★★★☆

"...we've done several rounds of classes with our kids and they absolutely love it... colorful, padded environment with tons of things to climb and play on... a good indoor place to meet other families and for kids to learn how to play with each other... the equipment and play areas are generally neat and clean... an easy birthday party spot... a guaranteed nap after class... costs vary, so call before showing up..."

Customer service .... ❹ $$$ .... Prices
Age range .... birth to 5 yrs
WWW.GYMBOREE.COM
ALPHARETTA—11005 JONES BRIDGE RD (AT STATE BRIDGE RD); 770.772.4000; CHECK SCHEDULE ONLINE
SANDY SPRINGS—4920 ROSWELL RD (AT FRANKLIN RD NE); 404.256.2223; CHECK SCHEDULE ONLINE; FREE PARKING

Gymnastics World Of Georgia ★★★★★

"...wide variety of classes for all ages in gymnastics, tumbling and 'wee-nastics' for babies and toddlers... parent workout room and sibling waiting area available... good place to take your children... hosts birthday parties on Saturday afternoons... drop off the kids for a monthly parents' night out... helped boost my son's confidence..."

Customer service .... ❺ $$ .... Prices
Age range .... birth and up
WWW.GYMWORLDOFGA.COM
ALPHARETTA—5500 MCGINNIS FERRY RD (AT MCGINNIS VILLAGE PL); 770.751.9019; CHECK SCHEDULE ONLINE; FREE PARKING

Little Gym, The ★★★★☆

"...a well thought-out program of gym and tumbling geared toward different age groups... a clean facility, excellent and knowledgeable staff... we love the small-sized gym equipment and their willingness to work with kids with special needs... activities are fun and personalized to match the kids' age... great place for birthday parties with a nice party room—they'll organize and do everything for you..."

Customer service .... ❹ $$$ .... Prices
Age range .... 4 mths to 12 yrs
WWW.THELITTLEGYM.COM
ROSWELL—2000 HOLCOMB WOODS PKWY (AT ROYAL OAKS AVE); 770.640.0028; CALL FOR SCHEDULE; FREE PARKING

Little Moves ★★★★☆

"...moms will learn a lot about how to encourage their baby to do tummy time and other exercises... a great way for moms to get out of the house and see others moms and babies and compare notes... teaches exercises to help with rolling, crawling and walking... classes had fun songs and activities and brought up great discussions..."

Customer service .... ❺ $$$ .... Prices
Age range .... 3 mths to 12 mths
WWW.LITTLEMOVES.COM
DUNWOODY—404.277.3695; CHECK SCHEDULE ONLINE

Music Class, The ★★★★★

"...an excellent introduction to music for your children... you will sing the songs for years to come... we love the music pups program...

classes help children develop an ear for music... friendly and enthusiastic teachers... songs are great, easy to remember, and enjoyed by kids and parents alike... you get more out of the class if you listen to the CD/tape at home or in the car... the 45-minute class is the perfect length for kids to stay interested... ”

Customer service........................❺ $$$.......................................Prices

Age range................ 3 mths to 4 yrs

WWW.THEMUSICCLASS.COM

ROSWELL—2500 OLD ALABAMA RD (AT ROXBURGH DR); 770.645.5578; CHECK SCHEDULE ONLINE

Music Together ★★★★½

“*...the best mom and baby classes out there... music, singing, dancing—even instruments for tots to play with... liberal make-up policy, great venues, take home books, CDs and tapes which are different each semester... it's a national franchise so instructors vary and have their own style... different age groups get mixed up which makes it a good learning experience for all involved... the highlight of our week—grandma always comes along... be prepared to have your tot sing the songs at home, in the car—everywhere...* ”

Customer service........................❹ $$$.......................................Prices

Age range................ 2 mths to 5 yrs

WWW.MUSICTOGETHER.COM

ALPHARETTA—404.209.9953; CALL FOR SCHEDULE

DUNWOODY—404.209.9953; CALL FOR SCHEDULE

Naked Clay Studio ★★★★☆

“*...a paint-a-pottery and mosaic studio with classes, camps and parties for children and adults... the staff was very accommodating by allowing us (5 moms all with babies in strollers) to sit in the private room... the teacher helped us make our babies' foot and hand prints on tiles... can be pricey...* ”

Customer service........................❺ $$$$....................................Prices

WWW.NAKEDCLAY.COM

SANDY SPRINGS—227 SANDY SPRINGS PL (AT SANDY SPRINGS CIR NE); 404.252.9505; M-TU 11-5:30, W-SA 11-9, SU 11-4; STREET PARKING

Sophie Hirsh Srochi Jewish Discovery Museum ★★★★★

“*...this hidden secret is a perfect play area for toddlers... it provides several unique, well thought out and well-designed creative play centers... a wonderful way of introducing kids to Jewish culture...* ”

Customer service........................❹ $ ....Prices

Age range................3 mths to 11 yrs

WWW.ATLANTAJCC.ORG

DUNWOODY—5342 TILLY MILL RD (AT WESTOVER PLANTATION); 770.395.2553; SU 1-5, T 1-4, W 4-7, TH 11-4; FREE PARKING

Swim Atlanta ★★★½☆

“*...great staff and extremely safety oriented... they support and encourage children at various stages... the environment can be very competitive and fun at the same time... 3 locations offering classes from 6 months and up...* ”

Customer service........................❹ $$$.......................................Prices

Age range.................. 6 mths and up

WWW.SWIMATLANTA.COM

ROSWELL—795 OLD ROSWELL RD (AT COMMERCE PKWY); 770.992.1778; CHECK SCHEDULE ONLINE; FREE PARKING

YMCA

★★★★☆

"...most of the Ys in the area have classes and activities for kids... swimming, gym classes, dance—even play groups for the really little ones... ... some facilities are nicer than others, but in general their programs are worth checking out... prices are more than reasonable for what is offered... the best bang for your buck... they have it all—great programs that meet the needs of a diverse range of families... check out their camps during the summer and school breaks..."

Customer service .... ❹ $$ .... Prices

Age range ....3 mths and up

WWW.YMCAATLANTA.ORG

ALPHARETTA—3655 PRESTON RIDGE RD (AT NORTH POINT PKWY); 770.664.1220; M-F 5:30-9:30, SA 8-5, SU 1-5:30; PARKING LOT

South Fulton, Fayette & Clayton

Barnes & Noble ★★★★½

"...wonderful weekly story times for all ages and frequent author visits for older kids... lovely selection of books and the story times are fun and very well done... they have evening story times—we put our kids in their pjs and come here as a treat before bedtime... they read a story, and then usually have a little craft or related coloring project... times vary by location so give them a call..."

Customer service........................❹ $ .... Prices
Age range................ 6 mths to 6 yrs
WWW.BARNESANDNOBLE.COM

FAYETTEVILLE—1415 HWY 85 N (OFF FAYETTEVILLE RD); 770.716.7640; CALL FOR SCHEDULE

MORROW—1939 MT ZION RD (OFF MT ZION BLVD); 770.471.2227; CALL FOR SCHEDULE

Chuck E Cheese's ★★★☆☆

"...lots of games, rides, playrooms and very greasy food... the kids can play and eat and parents can unwind a little... a good rainy day activity... the kids love the food, but it's a bit greasy for adults... always crowded and crazy—but that's half the fun... can you ever go wrong with pizza, games and singing?.. although they do have a salad bar for adults, remember, you're not going for the food—you're going because your kids will love it... just about the easiest birthday party around—just pay money and show up..."

Customer service........................❷ $$.. Prices
Age range...............12 mths to 7 yrs
WWW.CHUCKECHEESE.COM

FAYETTEVILLE—786 GLYNN ST N (AT W FAYETTEVILLE RD); 770.461.7974; SU-TH 9-10, F-SA 9-11

Little Gym, The ★★★★☆

"...a well thought-out program of gym and tumbling geared toward different age groups... a clean facility, excellent and knowledgeable staff... we love the small-sized gym equipment and their willingness to work with kids with special needs... activities are fun and personalized to match the kids' age... great place for birthday parties with a nice party room—they'll organize and do everything for you..."

Customer service........................❹ $$$...................................... Prices
Age range...............4 mths to 12 yrs
WWW.THELITTLEGYM.COM

PEACHTREE CITY—2733 W HWY 54 (OFF RT 74); 770.631.3731; CALL FOR SCHEDULE

Music Together ★★★★½

"...the best mom and baby classes out there... music, singing, dancing—even instruments for tots to play with... liberal make-up policy, great venues, take home books, CDs and tapes which are different each semester... it's a national franchise so instructors vary and have their own style... different age groups get mixed up which makes it a good learning experience for all involved... the highlight of our week—grandma always comes along... be prepared to have your tot sing the songs at home, in the car—everywhere..."

Customer service........................❹ $$$...................................... Prices

Age range ....2 mths to 5 yrs

WWW.MUSICTOGETHER.COM

FAYETTEVILLE—404.209.9953; CALL FOR SCHEDULE

PEACHTREE CITY—404.209.9953; CALL FOR SCHEDULE

YMCA ★★★★☆

"...most of the Ys in the area have classes and activities for kids... swimming, gym classes, dance—even play groups for the really little ones... ... some facilities are nicer than others, but in general their programs are worth checking out... prices are more than reasonable for what is offered... the best bang for your buck... they have it all—great programs that meet the needs of a diverse range of families... check out their camps during the summer and school breaks..."

Customer service .... ❹ $$ .... Prices

Age range ....3 mths and up

WWW.YMCAATLANTA.ORG

FAYETTEVILLE—215 HUIET RD (AT LESTER RD); 770.719.9622; M-F 9-5:30; PARKING LOT

Dekalb

★★★★★

"lila picks"

- ★Build-A-Bear Workshop
- ★Miss Jamie's House
- ★Stone Mountain Park

Borders Books ★★★★☆

"...very popular weekly story time held in most branches (check the web site for locations and times)... call before you go since they are very popular and get extremely crowded... kids love the unique blend of songs, stories and dancing... Mr. Hatbox's appearances are a delight to everyone (unfortunately he doesn't make appearances at all locations)... large children's section is well categorized and well priced... they make it fun for young tots to browse through the board-book section by hanging toys around the shelves... the low-key cafe is a great place to have coffee with your baby and leaf through some magazines..."

Customer service........................❹ $ ....Prices

Age range................ 6 mths to 6 yrs

WWW.BORDERSSTORES.COM

LITHONIA—8000 MALL PKWY (AT TURNER HILL RD); 678.526.2550; CALL FOR SCHEDULE

Build-A-Bear Workshop ★★★★★

"...design and make your own bear—it's a dream come true... the most cherished toy my daughter owns... they even come with birth certificates... the staff is fun and knows how to play along with the kids' excitement... the basic stuffed animal is only about $15, but the extras add up quickly... great for field trips, birthdays and special occasions... how darling—my nephew is 8 years old now, and still sleeps with his favorite bear..."

Customer service........................❹ $$$....................................Prices

Age range....................3 yrs and up

WWW.BUILDABEAR.COM

LITHONIA—2929 TURNER HILL RD (AT MALL AT STONECREST); 770.482.9239; M-SA 10-9, SU 12-6; MALL PARKING

Little Shop Of Stories ★★★★½

"...a cute little space connected to Jake's Ice Cream... they offer several story times during the day, evening and weekends... stories are tailored to the age of the audience... a wonderful collection of books to purchase so you can recreate story time at home... sharing space with Jake's Ice Cream makes this a fantastic way to spend a rainy day..."

Customer service........................❹ $$.......................................Prices

Age range...............3 mths to 12 yrs

DECATUR—515 N MCDONOUGH ST (AT E TRINITY PL); 404.373.6300; M-W F-SA 10-6, TH 10-9, SU 1-5; GARAGE & STREET PARKING

Miss Jamie's House ★★★★★

"...this cute little 'house' is a fabulous place to play... lots of activities, you can't do them all in an single afternoon... take advantage of the babysitting services on weekday mornings and date nights on Fridays... birthday room available... outdoor bunny play area where kids can play with the bunnies... $3.50 per child; parents free..."

Customer service .... ❹ $ .... Prices
Age range .... 3 mths to 6 yrs
WWW.MISSJAMIESHOUSE.COM
TUCKER—2273 BROCKETT RD (AT BANCROFT CIR); 770.938.5108; T-F 10-5, SA 10-3; STREET PARKING

Music Together ★★★★½

"...the best mom and baby classes out there... music, singing, dancing—even instruments for tots to play with... liberal make-up policy, great venues, take home books, CDs and tapes which are different each semester... it's a national franchise so instructors vary and have their own style... different age groups get mixed up which makes it a good learning experience for all involved... the highlight of our week—grandma always comes along... be prepared to have your tot sing the songs at home, in the car—everywhere..."

Customer service .... ❹ $$$ .... Prices
Age range .... 2 mths to 5 yrs
WWW.MUSICTOGETHER.COM
DECATUR—404.288.5424; CALL FOR SCHEDULE

Stone Mountain Park ★★★★★

"...a wonderful place to take long walks and enjoy the scenery... plenty of playgrounds with lots of things to climb on and swing from... events are spectacular and generally baby-friendly, although the fireworks may scare some of the really little ones... with the children's barn, fishing, swimming and paddle boats, it's a great park for all ages..."

Customer service .... ❸ $$$ .... Prices
Age range .... 2 yrs and up
WWW.STONEMOUNTAINPARK.COM
STONE MOUNTAIN—STONE MOUNTAIN HWY 78 (AT W PARK PL BLVD SW); 770.498.5690; CALL FOR HOURS

Tucker Recreation Center ★★★★★

"...offers swim lessons at 12 pool locations... youth sports like soccer, baseball, softball, football and lacrosse... 8-week summer camps with crafts, field trips and nature activities... parks with playgrounds and picnic areas..."

Customer service .... ❺ $ .... Prices
Age range .... 6 mths and up
WWW.CO.DEKALB.GA.US
TUCKER—4898 LAVISTA RD (AT BROCKETT RD); 770.270.6226; CHECK SCHEDULE ONLINE; FREE PARKING

YMCA ★★★★☆

"...most of the Ys in the area have classes and activities for kids... swimming, gym classes, dance—even play groups for the really little ones... ... some facilities are nicer than others, but in general their programs are worth checking out... prices are more than reasonable for what is offered... the best bang for your buck... they have it all—great programs that meet the needs of a diverse range of families... check out their camps during the summer and school breaks..."

Customer service .... ❹ $$ .... Prices
Age range .... 3 mths and up

WWW.YMCAATLANTA.ORG

DECATUR—1100 CLAIREMONT AVE (AT N DECATUR RD); 404.377.0241; CALL FOR SCHEDULE; FREE PARKING

DECATUR—2565 SNAPFINGER RD (AT WESLEY CHAPEL RD); 770.987.3500; M-F 6-9:30, SA 9-6, SU 2-6; PARKING LOT

LITHONIA—1185 ROCK CHAPEL RD (AT STEPHENSON RD); 770.484.9622; M-F 9-5; PARKING LOT

LITHONIA—2924 EVANS MILL RD (AT WOODROW DR); 770.484.1625; CHECK SCHEDULE ONLINE

CUMMING—5920 ODELL ST (AT POST RD); 770.888.2788; M-F 8-5; PARKING LOT

Gwinnett

★★★★★

"lila picks"

- ★My Gym Children's Fitness Center
- ★The Music Class
- ★Yellow River Game Ranch

Barnes & Noble ★★★★½

"...wonderful weekly story times for all ages and frequent author visits for older kids... lovely selection of books and the story times are fun and very well done... they have evening story times—we put our kids in their pjs and come here as a treat before bedtime... they read a story, and then usually have a little craft or related coloring project... times vary by location so give them a call..."

Customer service .... ❹ $ .... Prices
Age range .... 6 mths to 6 yrs

WWW.BARNESANDNOBLE.COM

BUFORD 3333 BUFORD DR (AT MALL OF GEORGIA); 678.482.4150; CALL FOR SCHEDULE

DULUTH—2205 PLEASANT HILL RD (AT SATELLITE BLVD); 770.495.7200; CALL FOR SCHEDULE

NORCROSS—5141 PEACHTREE PKWY (AT PEACHTREE CORNERS CIR); 770.209.4244; CALL FOR SCHEDULE

Borders Books ★★★★☆

"...very popular weekly story time held in most branches (check the web site for locations and times)... call before you go since they are very popular and get extremely crowded... kids love the unique blend of songs, stories and dancing... Mr. Hatbox's appearances are a delight to everyone (unfortunately he doesn't make appearances at all locations)... large children's section is well categorized and well priced... they make it fun for young tots to browse through the board-book section by hanging toys around the shelves... the low-key cafe is a great place to have coffee with your baby and leaf through some magazines..."

Customer service .... ❹ $ .... Prices
Age range .... 6 mths to 6 yrs

WWW.BORDERSSTORES.COM

BUFORD—1705 MALL OF GEORGIA BLVD (AT BUFORD DR NE); 678.482.0872; CALL FOR SCHEDULE

SNELLVILLE—1929 SCENIC HWY (AT PINEHURST RD SW); 770.982.0454; CALL FOR SCHEDULE

SUWANEE—3630 PEACHTREE PKWY (AT JOHNS CREEK PKWY); CALL FOR SCHEDULE

Build-A-Bear Workshop ★★★½☆

"...design and make your own bear—it's a dream come true... the most cherished toy my daughter owns... they even come with birth certificates... the staff is fun and knows how to play along with the kids' excitement... the basic stuffed animal is only about $15, but the extras add up quickly... great for field trips, birthdays and special occasions... how darling—my nephew is 8 years old now, and still sleeps with his favorite bear..."

Customer service........................❹ $$$..Prices
Age range....................3 yrs and up
WWW.BUILDABEAR.COM

BUFORD—3333 BUFORD DR (AT MALL OF GEORGIA); 770.945.2990; M-SA 10-9, SU 11-6; MALL PARKING

Children's Arts Museum ★★★★☆

"...a thriving arts facility that houses galleries, a large education department, a world-class sculpture garden and a children's museum... the fine arts school offers children's classes in pottery, drawing and painting... a wonderful place for kids... staff is awesome..."

Customer service........................❹ $$..Prices
Age range.................3 mths and up
WWW.ARTSGWINNETT.ORG

DULUTH—6400 SUGARLOAF PKWY (AT SATELLITE BLVD NW); 770.623.6002; T-F 1-5, SA 10-3; FREE PARKING

Chuck E Cheese's ★★★☆☆

"...lots of games, rides, playrooms and very greasy food... the kids can play and eat and parents can unwind a little... a good rainy day activity... the kids love the food, but it's a bit greasy for adults... always crowded and crazy—but that's half the fun... can you ever go wrong with pizza, games and singing?.. although they do have a salad bar for adults, remember, you're not going for the food—you're going because your kids will love it... just about the easiest birthday party around—just pay money and show up..."

Customer service........................❸ $$..Prices
Age range...............12 mths to 7 yrs
WWW.CHUCKECHEESE.COM

BUFORD—1690 MALL OF GEORGIA BLVD (AT HWY 20); 770.614.5803; SU-TH 9-10, F-SA 9-11; MALL PARKING

NORCROSS—5019 JIMMY CARTER BLVD (AT ROCKBRIDGE RD NW); 770.449.1767; SU-TH 9-10, F-SA 9-11; FREE PARKING

Collins Hill Aquatic Center ★★★★☆

"...houses an indoor swimming and diving pool... offers swimming lessons and water aerobics... the outdoor kiddie pool has fun slides, squirt guns and sprinklers... toddler pool and 'lazy river' will help mom and dad relax... $1 for 3 and under, $3 for 4-10 yrs and $4 for adults..."

Customer service........................❺ $..Prices
Age range.................3 mths and up
WWW.CO.GWINNETT.GA.US

LAWRENCEVILLE—2000 COLLINS HILL RD (AT TAYLOR RD NW); 770.237.5647; CALL FOR SCHEDULE; FREE PARKING

Gymboree Play & Music ★★★★½

"...we've done several rounds of classes with our kids and they absolutely love it... colorful, padded environment with tons of things to climb and play on... a good indoor place to meet other families and for kids to learn how to play with each other... the equipment and play

areas are generally neat and clean... an easy birthday party spot... a guaranteed nap after class... costs vary, so call before showing up... ❞

Customer service .... ❹ $$$ .... Prices
Age range .... birth to 5 yrs
WWW.GYMBOREE.COM

BUFORD—1825 MALL OF GEORGIA BLVD NE (AT HWY 20); 678.482.4440; CHECK SCHEDULE ONLINE; FREE PARKING

Lake Lanier Islands ★★★★★

❝*...this family resort features a water park that has thrilling rides, slides and water attractions... has Georgia's largest wave pool... the little ones love the Kiddie Lagoon and Wiggle Waves... only 45 minutes from downtown Atlanta... luxury accommodations, golf, spa and horseback riding complete a vacation for families...* ❞

Customer service .... ❺ $$$ .... Prices
Age range .... 2 yrs and up
WWW.LAKELANIERISLANDS.COM

BUFORD—7000 HOLIDAY RD (AT CONVENTION CTR RD); 800.768.5253; CHECK SCHEDULE ONLINE

Little All Stars ★★★★☆

❝*...carefully designed classes for toddlers and young kids... focuses on one sport per class in a 6-week session... sessions teach football, basketball, soccer, golf and teeball and the 6th session is another sport such as bowling, hockey or tennis to name a few... allows kids under 5 to get an idea of what sports they like and dislike...* ❞

Customer service .... ❺ $$ .... Prices
Age range .... 18 mths to 5 yrs
WWW.LITTLEALLSTARS.COM

SUWANEE—3640 BURNETTE RD (AT MCGINNIS FERRY RD NW); 770.614.5252; CALL FOR SCHEDULE

Little Gym, The ★★★★☆

❝*...a well thought-out program of gym and tumbling geared toward different age groups... a clean facility, excellent and knowledgeable staff... we love the small-sized gym equipment and their willingness to work with kids with special needs... activities are fun and personalized to match the kids' age... great place for birthday parties with a nice party room—they'll organize and do everything for you...* ❞

Customer service .... ❹ $$$ .... Prices
Age range .... 4 mths to 12 yrs
WWW.THELITTLEGYM.COM

DULUTH—3170 PEACHTREE INDUSTRIAL BLVD (AT DULUTH HWY NW); 770.476.4400; CALL FOR SCHEDULE

LAWRENCEVILLE—1970 RIVERSIDE PKWY (AT DULUTH HWY NW); 770.822.5208; CALL FOR SCHEDULE

LILBURN—4051 E HWY 78 (AT KILLIAN HILL RD SW); 770.982.0901; CALL FOR SCHEDULE

Monkey Joe's Parties & Play ★★★½☆

❝*...a party and play center... indoor party areas have slides, jumps and obstacle courses... also rents out jumps and slides for parties at home... many parents say their kids are still talking about this place after attending my son's party... kids have lots of fun and are completely worn out at the end of the day... $8 per child...* ❞

Customer service .... ❹ $$ .... Prices
Age range .... 2 yrs to 12 yrs
WWW.MONKEYJOES.COM

NORCROSS—3190 REPS MILLER RD (AT PEACHTREE INDUSTRIAL BLVD); 770.734.9774; M-SA 10-6, SU 11-6

Mountain Park Aquatic Center ★★★★½

"...this facility houses a competition/lap pool and an instruction pool indoors and a terrific leisure pool outdoors... two giant slides, a rain bucket, water sprays, a bubble bench, a lazy river and other play features make the outdoor pool a children's paradise... activity building next door with lots to offer... great swim classes with very knowledgeable instructors... programs are popular and can be difficult to get into..."

Customer service........................❹ $ ....Prices
Age range.................8 mths and up

WWW.CO.GWINNETT.GA.US

LILBURN—1063 ROCKBRIDGE RD (AT POUNDS RD SW); 770.564.4650; CALL FOR SCHEDULE; FREE PARKING

Music Class, The ★★★★★

"...an excellent introduction to music for your children... you will sing the songs for years to come... we love the music pups program... classes help children develop an ear for music... friendly and enthusiastic teachers... songs are great, easy to remember, and enjoyed by kids and parents alike... you get more out of the class if you listen to the CD/tape at home or in the car... the 45-minute class is the perfect length for kids to stay interested..."

Customer service........................❺ $$$.....................................Prices
Age range................ 3 mths to 4 yrs

WWW.THEMUSICCLASS.COM

SUWANEE—3651 PEACHTREE PKWY (AT JOHNS CREEK PKWY); 770.645.5578; CHECK SCHEDULE ONLINE; FREE PARKING

My Gym Children's Fitness Center ★★★★★

"...a wonderful gym environment for parents with babies and older tots... classes range from tiny tots to school-aged children and the staff is great about making it fun for all ages... equipment and facilities are really neat—ropes, pulleys, swings, you name it... the kind of place your kids hate to leave... the staff's enthusiasm is contagious... great for memorable birthday parties... although it's a franchise, each gym seems to have its own individual feeling... awesome for meeting playmates and other parents..."

Customer service........................❹ $$$.....................................Prices
Age range................ 3 mths to 9 yrs

WWW.MY-GYM.COM

LAWRENCEVILLE—3521 SUGARLOAF PKWY (AT FIVE FORKS TRICKUM RD SW); 770.682.9802; CHECK SCHEDULE ONLINE; FREE PARKING

SUWANEE—4060 JOHNS CREEK PKWY (AT PEACHTREE PKWY); 770.814.2000; CHECK SCHEDULE ONLINE; STREET PARKING

North Georgia Dance & Music Factory ★★★★☆

"...a wonderful intro to dance—the instructors are great and know how to make it fun for the little ones... the little girls are adorable in their dance outfits... fun music and movement classes—great for coordination and socialization skills... this is a serious dance school so kids can keep learning once they get older..."

Customer service........................❸ $$$.....................................Prices
Age range.....................3 yrs and up

WWW.DANCEMUSICFACTORY.COM

BUFORD—2740 BRASELTON HWY (AT HWY 324); 678.546.8600; CHECK SCHEDULE ONLINE

Southeastern Railway Museum ★★★½☆

"...who doesn't love to ride a train?.. get on a restored caboose behind a steam or diesel train... features Pullman cars and steam locomotives... we have created many warm memories with our children here... watch your little ones carefully as some railcars are not 'childproofed'... $7 for adults; under 2 free..."

Customer service .... ❹ $ .... Prices
Age range .... 3 yrs and up

WWW.SRMDULUTH.ORG

DULUTH—3595 PEACHTREE RD NW (AT PLEASANT HILL RD NW); 770.476.2013; TH-SA 10-5; FREE PARKING

Swim Atlanta ★★★½☆

"...great staff and extremely safety oriented... they support and encourage children at various stages... the environment can be very competitive and fun at the same time... 3 locations offering classes from 6 months and up..."

Customer service .... ❹ $$$ .... Prices
Age range ....6 mths and up

WWW.SWIMATLANTA.COM

LAWRENCEVILLE—4850 SUGARLOAF PKWY NW (AT OLD NORCROSS RD NW); 678.442.7946; CHECK SCHEDULE ONLINE

SUWANEE—4050 JOHNS CREEK PKWY (AT MEDLOCK BRIDGE RD); 770.622.1735; CHECK SCHEDULE ONLINE

Yellow River Game Ranch ★★★★★

"...a wonderful ranch that allows you to feed the animals... deer walk right up to you and feed from your hands... kids get to be up close and personal with all kinds of animals—from chickens to buffalos... fun rural setting... great petting zoo..."

Customer service .... ❹ $$ .... Prices
Age range .... 2 yrs and up

WWW.YELLOWRIVERGAMERANCH.COM

LILBURN—4525 HWY 78 (AT STONE MOUNTAIN HWY); 770.972.6643; DAILY 9:30-6; FREE PARKING

YMCA ★★★★☆

"...most of the Ys in the area have classes and activities for kids... swimming, gym classes, dance—even play groups for the really little ones... ... some facilities are nicer than others, but in general their programs are worth checking out... prices are more than reasonable for what is offered... the best bang for your buck... they have it all—great programs that meet the needs of a diverse range of families... check out their camps during the summer and school breaks..."

Customer service .... ❹ $$ .... Prices
Age range ....3 mths and up

WWW.YMCAATLANTA.ORG

LAWRENCEVILLE—2985 SUGARLOAF PKWY (AT SCENIC HWY SW); 770.963.1313; M-TH 5:45-7:45, F 5:45-8:45, SA 8-5:45,SU 1-7:45; PARKING LOT

NORCROSS—5600 W JONES BRIDGE RD; 770.246.9622; CALL FOR SCHEDULE; FREE PARKING

Cobb & Douglas

★★★★★

"lila picks"

- ★American Adventures Park
- ★Gymboree Play & Music
- ★The Music Class

American Adventures Park ★★★★★

"...rides available for toddlers and up... some rides require an adult to ride with the child and rides have height requirements... my son really enjoyed himself... the indoor ball factory needs some work, but we love this place anyway... terrific birthday party venue... parents get in free..."

Customer service........................❸ $$$......................................Prices
Age range.................... 3 yrs to 8 yrs

WWW.SIXFLAGS.COM\GEORGIA

MARIETTA—250 COBB PKWY NE (AT N MARIETTA PKWY NE); 770.424.9283; CHECK SCHEDULE ONLINE; PARKING LOT

Barnes & Noble ★★★★½

"...wonderful weekly story times for all ages and frequent author visits for older kids... lovely selection of books and the story times are fun and very well done... they have evening story times—we put our kids in their pjs and come here as a treat before bedtime... they read a story, and then usually have a little craft or related coloring project... times vary by location so give them a call..."

Customer service........................❹ $ ....Prices
Age range................ 6 mths to 6 yrs

WWW.BARNESANDNOBLE.COM

MARIETTA—3625 DALLAS HWY SW (AT DUE WEST RD); 770.424.0511; CALL FOR SCHEDULE

MARIETTA—50 ERNEST W BARRETT PKWY (AT BELLS FERRY RD); 770.422.2261; CALL FOR SCHEDULE

Borders Books ★★★★☆

"...very popular weekly story time held in most branches (check the web site for locations and times)... call before you go since they are very popular and get extremely crowded... kids love the unique blend of songs, stories and dancing... Mr. Hatbox's appearances are a delight to everyone (unfortunately he doesn't make appearances at all locations)... large children's section is well categorized and well priced... they make it fun for young tots to browse through the board-book section by hanging toys around the shelves... the low-key cafe is a great place to have coffee with your baby and leaf through some magazines..."

Customer service........................❹ $ ....Prices
Age range................ 6 mths to 6 yrs

WWW.BORDERSSTORES.COM

AUSTELL—1605 EAST-WEST CONNECTOR RD (AT AUSTEL RD SW); 770.941.8740; CALL FOR SCHEDULE

DOUGLASVILLE—6594 DOUGLAS BLVD (AT ARBOR PL); 770.577.9787; CALL FOR SCHEDULE

KENNESAW—605 ERNEST W BARRETT PKWY (AT COBB PL BLVD NW); 678.581.1243; CALL FOR SCHEDULE

MARIETTA—THE AVENUE AT EAST COBB (ON ROSWELL RD NE); 770.565.0947; CALL FOR SCHEDULE

Build-A-Bear Workshop ★★★½☆

"...design and make your own bear—it's a dream come true... the most cherished toy my daughter owns... they even come with birth certificates... the staff is fun and knows how to play along with the kids' excitement... the basic stuffed animal is only about $15, but the extras add up quickly... great for field trips, birthdays and special occasions... how darling—my nephew is 8 years old now, and still sleeps with his favorite bear..."

Customer service .... ❹ $$$ .... Prices

Age range .... 3 yrs and up

WWW.BUILDABEAR.COM

DOUGLASVILLE—6700 DOUGLAS BLVD (AT ARBOR PLACE MALL); 678.838.4567; M-SA 10-9, SU 12-6

KENNESAW—400 ERNEST W BARRETT PKWY NW (AT TOWN CENTER AT COBB); 678.354.0603; M-SA 10-9, SU 11-6; FREE PARKING

Chattanooga School Of Gymnastics And Dance ★★★★☆

"...a non-profit dance organization with youth classes in tap, ballet, jazz and hip-hop for kids starting at 2 years of age... they work with all kinds of children, including those with special needs... be prepared to get a different instructor every week..."

Customer service .... ❸ $$ .... Prices

MARIETTA—4005 CANTON RD (AT HAWKINS STORE RD); 770.924.2832; CALL FOR SCHEDULE

Chuck E Cheese's ★★★☆☆

"...lots of games, rides, playrooms and very greasy food... the kids can play and eat and parents can unwind a little... a good rainy day activity... the kids love the food, but it's a bit greasy for adults... always crowded and crazy—but that's half the fun... can you ever go wrong with pizza, games and singing?.. although they do have a salad bar for adults, remember, you're not going for the food—you're going because your kids will love it... just about the easiest birthday party around—just pay money and show up..."

Customer service .... ❸ $$ .... Prices

Age range .... 12 mths to 7 yrs

WWW.CHUCKECHEESE.COM

DOUGLASVILLE—6890 DOUGLAS BLVD (AT ROSE AVE); 770.577.8951; SU-TH 9-10, F-SA 9-11; FREE PARKING

MARIETTA—4340 ROSWELL RD (AT JOHNSON FERRY RD NE); 770.971.0002; SU-TH 9-10, F-SA 9-11; FREE PARKING

Gymboree Play & Music ★★★★★

"...we've done several rounds of classes with our kids and they absolutely love it... colorful, padded environment with tons of things to climb and play on... a good indoor place to meet other families and for kids to learn how to play with each other... the equipment and play

areas are generally neat and clean... an easy birthday party spot... a guaranteed nap after class... costs vary, so call before showing up... ”

Customer service........................❹ $$$.......................................Prices
Age range....................birth to 5 yrs

WWW.GYMBOREE.COM

MARIETTA—1319 JOHNSON FERRY RD (AT E COBB DR NE); 770.579.0899; CHECK SCHEDULE ONLINE; FREE PARKING

MARIETTA—3718 DALLAS HWY (AT OLD HAMILTON RD NW); 770.499.0023; CHECK SCHEDULE ONLINE; FREE PARKING

Historic Village ★★★★☆

“*...located at Life University, this is a reconstruction of a 19th-century farming village... nice place to learn about nature... experience an older American village by walking through a 19th-century log cabin, corncrib, tobacco barn, animal barn and a working grist mill... see the changing of the leaves... great outdoor activities such as hiking and having a picnic...* ”

Customer service........................❸ $ ....Prices
Age range....................2 yrs and up

MARIETTA—1269 BARCLAY CIR (AT CHAMBLEE WAY SE); 770.794.3010; M-F 8-5, SA-SU 11-5; FREE PARKING

Jewish Community Center ★★★★☆

“*...programs vary from facility to facility, but most JCCs have outstanding early childhood programs... everything from mom and me music classes to arts and crafts for older kids... a wonderful place to meet other parents and make new friends... class fees are cheaper (if not free) for members, but still quite a good deal for nonmembers... a superb resource for new families looking for fun...* ”

Customer service........................❹ $$$.......................................Prices
Age range.................3 mths and up

WWW.ATLANTAJCC.ORG

MARIETTA—2509 POST OAK TRITT RD (AT HOLLY SPRINGS RD NE); 770.971.8901; CALL FOR SCHEDULE

JW Tumbles ★★★★☆

“*...a wonderful opportunity for meeting and playing with new kids... an okay play program... tots learn lots of fun things to do—my daughter is rolling and tumbling at home now too... a good alternative to Gymboree... great classes and some locations offer Friday night babysitting for a mom/dad only date night... some of the locations are a little small... my kids always have fun here...* ”

Customer service........................❹ $$$.......................................Prices
Age range................ 4 mths to 9 yrs

WWW.JWTUMBLES.COM

DOUGLASVILLE—2866 CHAPEL HILL RD (AT ARBOR PLACE BLVD); 770.949.5437; CHECK SCHEDULE ONLINE

Little Gym, The ★★★★☆

“*...a well thought-out program of gym and tumbling geared toward different age groups... a clean facility, excellent and knowledgeable staff... we love the small-sized gym equipment and their willingness to work with kids with special needs... activities are fun and personalized to match the kids' age... great place for birthday parties with a nice party room—they'll organize and do everything for you...* ”

Customer service........................❹ $$$.......................................Prices
Age range................4 mths to 12 yrs

WWW.THELITTLEGYM.COM

MARIETTA—3085 JOHNSON FERRY RD (AT WATERFRONT DR NE); 678.585.0002; CALL FOR SCHEDULE

POWDER SPRINGS—4150 MACLAND RD (AT LOST MOUNTAIN RD SW); 770.222.4444; CALL FOR SCHEDULE

Music Class, The ★★★★★

"...an excellent introduction to music for your children... you will sing the songs for years to come... we love the music pups program... classes help children develop an ear for music... friendly and enthusiastic teachers... songs are great, easy to remember, and enjoyed by kids and parents alike... you get more out of the class if you listen to the CD/tape at home or in the car... the 45-minute class is the perfect length for kids to stay interested..."

Customer service .... ❺ $$$ .... Prices

Age range .... 3 mths to 4 yrs

WWW.THEMUSICCLASS.COM

MARIETTA—3330 COBB PKWY (AT BLACKBERRY LN NE); 770.645.5578; CHECK SCHEDULE ONLINE; FREE PARKING

Music Together ★★★★½

"...the best mom and baby classes out there... music, singing, dancing—even instruments for tots to play with... liberal make-up policy, great venues, take home books, CDs and tapes which are different each semester... it's a national franchise so instructors vary and have their own style... different age groups get mixed up which makes it a good learning experience for all involved... the highlight of our week—grandma always comes along... be prepared to have your tot sing the songs at home, in the car—everywhere..."

Customer service .... ❹ $$$ .... Prices

Age range .... 2 mths to 5 yrs

WWW.MUSICTOGETHER.COM

DOUGLASVILLE—404.287.0087; CALL FOR SCHEDULE

KENNESAW—404.209.9953; CALL FOR SCHEDULE

MARIETTA—770.772.4844; CALL FOR SCHEDULE

My Gym Children's Fitness Center ★★★★☆

"...a wonderful gym environment for parents with babies and older tots... classes range from tiny tots to school-aged children and the staff is great about making it fun for all ages... equipment and facilities are really neat—ropes, pulleys, swings, you name it... the kind of place your kids hate to leave... the staff's enthusiasm is contagious... great for memorable birthday parties... although it's a franchise, each gym seems to have its own individual feeling... awesome for meeting playmates and other parents..."

Customer service .... ❹ $$$ .... Prices

Age range .... 3 mths to 9 yrs

WWW.MY-GYM.COM

MARIETTA—2965 JOHNSON FERRY RD (AT FREEMAN RD NE); 770.579.5496; CHECK SCHEDULE ONLINE; PARKING LOT

parks & playgrounds

City of Atlanta

★★★★★

"lila picks"

- ★Atlanta Botanical Garden
- ★Centennial Olympic Park
- ★Hastings Nature & Garden Center

Ardmore Park ★★★★☆

"...great small in-town park with new equipment... little boys will love the elevated train track behind the park... conveniently located near Piedmont Hospital for post-appointment visits... be prepared for mosquitoes in the summer... great place to spend an hour or two... also a nice place to have a party..."

Equipment/play structures........... ❹ ❺ .... Maintenance

WWW.BUCKHEAD.ORG/PARKS/ARDMORE/INDEX.HTML

ATLANTA—ARDMORE RD (TANYARD CREEK PK); 770.216.1662

Ashford Park ★★★★☆

"...something for everyone and easy to watch multiple kids... big sandbox, usually with toys... two play structures for both big and little kids, swings, grassy area, sidewalk for riding bikes, pushing toys, etc... no shade, so don't go on a hot sunny day, and no bathrooms unless the multipurpose building is open..."

Equipment/play structures........... ❹ ❹ .... Maintenance

ATLANTA—2980 REDDING RD NE (AT PEACHTREE RD NE)

Atlanta Botanical Garden ★★★★★

"...a wonderful children's garden... children's concerts, puppet shows, etc. offered on Saturday mornings during spring and summer... strollers work great on most of the grounds... bring swimsuits in the summer for playing in the water fountain... the butterfly garden is enchanting... parking can be a problem at peak times..."

Equipment/play structures........... ❹ ❹ .... Maintenance

WWW.ATLANTABOTANICALGARDEN.ORG

ATLANTA—1345 PIEDMONT (AT THE PRADO NE); 404.876.5859

Candler Park ★★★★☆

"...a fabulous new park with equipment for all ages... lots of shade and off-street parking... nice circular sidewalk for biking... picnic tables, benches, hills to climb, lots of swings, swimming pool and a nice golf course nearby... a very friendly atmosphere where there are always lots of children to play with... a beautiful walking trail for mom and dad... a great place to meet other moms..."

Equipment/play structures........... ❹ ❹ .... Maintenance

WWW.ATLANTA-MIDTOWN.COM/NEIGHBORHOODS/PARKS/ATLANTA/CANDLER/

ATLANTA—585 CANDLER PARK DR NE (AT NORTH AVE NE); 404.371.1260

Centennial Olympic Park ★★★★★

"...the water fountain, called the Fountain of Rings, gets my daughter cooing every time... a great way to spend a summer afternoon... fun and event-filled during the holidays... combine your trip with a visit to the Children's Museum... bring swimsuits for the fountain... lots and lots of room to run around..."

Equipment/play structures .... ❹ ❹.............................. Maintenance

WWW.CENTENNIALPARK.COM

ATLANTA—265 PARK AVE W (AT THURMOND ST NW); 404.222.7275

Charles McDaniel Park ★★★☆☆

"...a large round wheelchair-friendly cement path encloses a grass playing field, explaining why locals call it 'Circle Park'... the sandbox playground offers separate equipment for both toddlers and older children... a hike in fhe adjacent woods provides another alternative... no bathrooms..."

Equipment/play structures .... ❸ ❹.............................. Maintenance

ATLANTA—HERITAGE RD (AT BRIARCLIFF RD); 404.371.2631

Chastain Park Playground ★★★½☆

"...an average playground... not the best in terms of supervising kids play—the play structure is rather far from the stone wall where the seating area is, but the equipment itself is nice... great place to meet other parents, and a good amount of shade..."

Equipment/play structures .... ❹ ❹.............................. Maintenance

WWW.ATLANTAGA.GOV

ATLANTA—W WIEUCA RD (AT DUDLEY LANE); 404.817.6744; STREET PARKING

Ellsworth Park ★★★★☆

"...a pretty park tucked away and protected from its busy surroundings with a stone and iron fence... neat playground equipment... the wheelchair accessible rubberized floor feels much safer than the hard surfaces at other playgrounds... a great venue for birthday parties... always crowded, no bathrooms or water fountains..."

Equipment/play structures .... ❺ ❺.............................. Maintenance

WWW.ATLANTAGA.GOV

ATLANTA—HOWELL MILL RD (AT COLLIER RD NW); 404.817.6734

Garden Hills Park

WWW.GARDENHILLSPOOL.COM

ATLANTA—E WESLEY RD NE (AT RUMSON RD NE); 404.848.7220; CALL FOR HOURS; FREE PARKING

Glen Emerald Park ★★★☆☆

"...always packed with kids... great people-watching... we usually meet up with friends and switch off playing tennis at the courts and watching the kids... picturesque location, lots of playground equipment, nice nature trails and a beautiful lake..."

Equipment/play structures .... ❸ ❸.............................. Maintenance

WWW.ATLANTA-MIDTOWN.COM/NEIGHBORHOODS/PARKS/DEKALB_COUNTY/GLEN_EMERALD/

ATLANTA—1479 BOULDERCREST RD (AT CECILIA DR SE); 404.817.6744

Grant Park ★★★★☆

"...beautiful park in a historic neighborhood... playground is new and very nice... near zoo... the slides are fabulous and the climbing wall is

fun, too... also a community pool... small slides and hobbyhorses are great for tiny tots... easy access to zoo and ice cream parlor... ❞

Equipment/play structures........... ❹ ❹ .... Maintenance

HTTP://GPCONSERVANCY.ORG/

ATLANTA—404.817.6766

Hastings Nature & Garden Center ★★★★★

❝*...not a public park, but a 116-year-old garden center with a bird aviary, outdoor railroad garden, turtle pond and koi ponds... a beautiful place to walk around with kids... they also have 'just for kids' workshops...* ❞

Equipment/play structures........... ❹ ❺ .... Maintenance

WWW.HASTINGSGARDENCENTER.COM/INDEX.HTML

ATLANTA—3920 PEACHTREE RD (AT N DRUID HILLS); 404.869.7447; M-F 9-7, SA 8-6, SU 10-6

John Howell Memorial Park ★★★½☆

❝*...a fun neighborhood park... lots of families and their dogs... nice combination of shade and sun... divided roughly in half, the west side features a children's playscape next to the well maintained volleyball courts... ...* ❞

Equipment/play structures........... ❹ ❹ .... Maintenance

WWW.ATLANTA-MIDTOWN.COM/NONPROFIT/HOWELLPARK/

ATLANTA—869 VIRGINIA AVE NE (AT BARNETT ST NE); 404.817.6744

Lake Claire Park ★★★☆☆

❝*...lots of room for your kids to play and your dog to run... children's playscape with swings, a large multi-purpose sports field... the lightly wooded far end of the park provides shade...* ❞

Equipment/play structures........... ❹ ❸ .... Maintenance

WWW.ATLANTA-MIDTOWN.COM/NEIGHBORHOODS/PARKS/ATLANTA/LAKE_CLAIRE

ATLANTA—430 LAKESHORE DR NE (AT CLAIRE DR NE); 404.817.6744

Lenox-Wildwood Park ★★★☆☆

❝*...small, neighborhood park... two tennis courts, a wooden play area, a reasonably large green space (large enough for frisbee or a possibly a pick-up softball game—bring your own bases), with a few picnic tables and benches... the park is wooded and has no surfaced paths...* ❞

Equipment/play structures........... ❸ ❷ .... Maintenance

WWW.ATLANTA-MIDTOWN.COM/NEIGHBORHOODS/PARKS/ATLANTA/LENOX-WILDWOOD

ATLANTA—LENOX RD (AT WILDWOOD RD)

Murphy Candler Park ★★★☆☆

❝*...a wonderful park for older and younger children... has a lake, playground area, and plenty of tables for a picnic...* ❞

Equipment/play structures........... ❹ ❹ .... Maintenance

ATLANTA—1551 W NANCY CREEK DR (AT CANDLER LAKE WEST NE); 404.371.2631

Orme Park ★★★★½

❝*...always seems clean and has safe equipment for kids to play on... good place to meet other moms... small and well laid out so your kids are always close by... in a gorgeous neighborhood lined with beautiful architecture... plenty of shade in the playground area... swings, monkey bars and big sandbox... nice natural surroundings...* ❞

Equipment/play structures........... ❹ ❹ .... Maintenance

WWW.ATLANTAGA.GOV

ATLANTA—795 BROOKRIDGE DR NE (AT ELKMONT DR NE); 404.817.6752

Piedmont Park ★★★★★

"...playgrounds, ball fields, a swimming pool in the summer, hosts festivals throughout the year... great walking paths for strollers... nice pond for feeding ducks... the paved trails are excellent for bike riding, rollerblading or pulling your kids in a wagon..."

Equipment/play structures .... ❸ ❹ .... Maintenance

WWW.PIEDMONTPARK.ORG

ATLANTA—400 PARK DR NE (AT NORFOLK SOUTHERN); 404.875.7275

Sidney Marcus Park ★★★★☆

"...the best playground in intown (Atlanta (and we frequent them all)... small neighborhood park with new equipment, rubber surfacing, sandbox, and not too crowded... great for picnics with several tables and benches, and a fair amount of shade... a wonderful, popular park—parking can be a problem..."

Equipment/play structures .... ❹ ❹ .... Maintenance

WWW.ATLANTA-MIDTOWN.COM/NEIGHBORHOODS/PARKS/ATLANTA/SIDNEY_MARCUS/

ATLANTA—CUMBERLAND RD (AT CUMBERLAND CIR); 404.817.6744

Sunken Garden Park ★★★☆☆

"...a small, but quaint neighborhood park... perfect for the preschool-aged crowd, with a great toddler slide... nice grassy areas that are good for playing and impromptu picnics... not too crowded, with an open field for older kids to run around in..."

Equipment/play structures .... ❸ ❸ .... Maintenance

WWW.ATLANTA-MIDTOWN.COM/NEIGHBORHOODS/PARKS/ATLANTA/SUNKEN_GARDEN/

ATLANTA—1000 E ROCK SPRINGS RD NE (AT E SUSSEX RD NE); 404.817.6744

Wildwood Gardens Park ★★★☆☆

"...not exactly a park, rather a wild greenbelt spanning the undeveloped land between two streets... an awesome park for the little ones as well as the older kids, my child just loves their playground... very scenic with a steep grade... popular with squirrels... no amenities..."

Equipment/play structures .... ❹ ❹ .... Maintenance

WWW.ATLANTA-MIDTOWN.COM/NEIGHBORHOODS/PARKS/ATLANTA/WILDWOOD

ATLANTA—735 WILDWOOD RD NE (AT WINDMERE DR NE)

North Fulton

★★★★★

"lila picks"

- ★Riverside Park
- ★Webb Bridge Park
- ★Wills Park

Big Creek Greenway ★★★★☆

"...a gem in Alpharetta... paved and non-paved paths... beautiful area, I've seen deer there on multiple occasions... good path for biking, rollerblading or walking with a stroller... convenient... large and pleasant... tucked away from the hustle and bustle ..."

Equipment/play structures .... ❹ ❹ .... Maintenance

WWW.GEORGIATRAILS.COM/TRAILS/BIGCREEK.HTML

ALPHARETTA—NORTH POINT PKY

Chattahoochee River Park ★★★★½

"...a favorite when I was little, now I enjoy taking my daughter here... awesome for babies!... the river is so beautiful and always creates a wonderful atmosphere... the equipment is nice, but the park is usually crowded on weekends... come early... a nice place to introduce kids to the beauty of nature... perfect spot for picnicking and relaxing with the family..."

Equipment/play structures .... ❹ ❹ .... Maintenance

WWW.ROSWELLGOV.COM

ROSWELL—203 AZALEA DR (AT ROSWELL RD); 770.740.2416

Hammond Park ★★★★☆

"...two play ground areas quite far apart... the area for young walkers is fenced in with rubber matting for ground cover... nice park..."

Equipment/play structures .... ❹ ❹ .... Maintenance

WWW.CO.FULTON.GA.US/DEPARTMENTS/HAMMOND.HTML

SANDY SPRINGS—705 HAMMOND DR NE (AT GLENRIDGE); 404.303.6176

Newtown Park ★★★★½

"...the spongy floor prevents scrapes and bruises... generally clean, and socially active park... playground structures are age-appropriate and offer plenty for a variety of ages and skill sets... nice covered/shaded picnic areas, paved paths, plenty of grassy fields... well maintained restrooms..."

Equipment/play structures .... ❹ ❹ .... Maintenance

WWW.CO.FULTON.GA.US

ALPHARETTA—OLD ALABAMA RD AT NESBIT FERRY RD; 404.730.6200

North Park ★★★★☆

"...lots of options as far as playground settings... a fenced in area for the littler ones, which is adhered to, and other areas as well... nice, quiet and not too crowded... picnic pavilion, playground and walking trail..."

Equipment/play structures .... ❹ ❹.............................. Maintenance

WWW.ALPHARETTA.GA.US

ALPHARETTA—13450 COGBURN RD (AT BETHANY RD)

Northpoint Mall Children's Play Area ★★★★☆

"...convenient and fun indoor playground is good while shopping at this busy mall... good alternative on a rainy day... nice soft structures... age limits are not always enforced and older children can be intimidating, especially when it's crowded..."

Equipment/play structures .... ❹ ❹.............................. Maintenance

WWW.NORTHPOINTMALL.COM

ALPHARETTA—1000 NORTH POINT CIR (AT NORTH POINT MALL); 770.740.8636; MALL PARKING

Ocee Park ★★★★☆

"...pavilion, playground, three picnic shelters, walking/jogging track, picnic tables and grills... never too crowded, and a bit smaller than your typical park..."

Equipment/play structures .... ❹ ❺.............................. Maintenance

WWW.N-GEORGIA.COM/FULTON_CO.HTM

ALPHARETTA—10900 BUICE RD (BTWN PINECREST & KIMBALL BRIDGE RDS); 770.663.3500

Riverside Park ★★★★★

"...the best roswell park by far... great fun for all ages... a small playground for young tots, but older kids have fun, too... kids can ride their bikes in the huge grassy field... clean and safe... there is no shade and can be very hot in the summer... no changing stations in the bathrooms..."

Equipment/play structures .... ❺ ❹.............................. Maintenance

WWW.COLUMBIACOUNTYGA.GOV

ROSWELL —RIVERSIDE RD (AT RIVERSIDE ELEMENTARY); 404.352.0240

Roswell Area Park ★★★★½

"...huge sports and activity complex with some nice areas for toddlers... large playground... the lake is surrounded by tons of trails and good spots for picnics... the community buildings have lots of activities and classes that are inexpensive... lots of swings, a fenced play area for the real little ones, a nice trail that is good for strollers, even a duck pond... very spacious..."

Equipment/play structures .... ❹ ❹.............................. Maintenance

ROSWELL—10495 WOODSTOCK RD (AT OLD RIDGE RUN); 770.641.3706

Sweet Apple Park ★★★½☆

"...nicely arranged, newer equipment and variety of equipment to keep the children busy... i'm not a big fan of sand, so I didn't "dig" all the dirt... on school grounds, so always populated enough for socializing, but not too crowded..."

Equipment/play structures .... ❹ ❹.............................. Maintenance

WWW.ALPHARETTA.GA.US

ALPHARETTA—CRABAPPLE DR (OFF THOMPSON RD); 678.297.6100

Webb Bridge Park ★★★★★

"...good combination of hills and flat areas to make it a real work out... this place is so fun when the creek/stream is turned on... imaginative play areas for both younger and older children... soccer and baseball fields are very well maintained... play areas and swings always in good working order and are the latest in modern design..."

Equipment/play structures............❺ ❺..............................Maintenance

WWW.ALPHARETTA.GA.US

ALPHARETTA—4780 WEBB BRIDGE RD (AT KIMBBALL BRIDGE RD); 678.297.6150

Wills Park ★★★★★

"...a popular park for children in Alpharetta... wooden castle play structure is awesome... there's always a horse or dog show going on that kids love to watch... great tennis courts and baseball fields... fenced in playground is a bonus... bathrooms and water fountains available..."

Equipment/play structures............❹ ❹..............................Maintenance

WWW.ALPHARETTA.GA.US

ALPHARETTA—1825 OLD MILTON PKWY (AT WILLS DR); 678.297.6130

South Fulton, Fayette & Clayton

★★★★★

"lila picks"

★All Children's Playground

★Fayette Family Play Park

All Children's Playground ★★★★★

"...a special place for kids—including wheelchair-bound tots... nice and soft, rubbery bouncy floor... lots of shade... a true play haven for families with kids of all ages..."

Equipment/play structures .... ❺ ❺ .... Maintenance

PEACHTREE CITY—WILLOWBEND RD (OFF HWY 54); 770.631.2542; PARKING LOT AT PARK ENTRANCE

Fayette Family Play Park ★★★★★

"...I love the all wood construction... an awesome park maintained by the YMCA... it's in good condition and never seems too crowded even when the parking lot is full... it isn't fenced in so you need to keep a good eye on your child at all times..."

Equipment/play structures .... ❹ ❹ .... Maintenance

WWW.YMCAATLANTA.ORG

FAYETTEVILLE—215 HUIET RD (AT LESTER RD); 770.719.9622; DAILY 8-DUSK; PARKING LOT

Fayette Park ★★★☆☆

"...we had a lot of fun at this park... very big playground for the kids and very scenic for the adults..."

Equipment/play structures .... ❹ ❹ .... Maintenance

WWW.FAYETTEVILLE-GA-US.ORG/

FAYETTEVILLE—770.716.4320

Welcome All Park ★★★★★

"...lots of ducks at the lake... an excellent children's playground with age appropriated equipment... restrooms are nearby and the park building hosts all kinds of neat classes... indoor swimming pool, tennis courts, ball fields... always great people watching and socializing..."

Equipment/play structures .... ❺ ❺ .... Maintenance

WWW.CO.FULTON.GA.US

COLLEGE PARK—4255 WILL LEE RD (AT GRANADA DR); 404.762.4058

Dekalb

★★★★★

"lila picks"

★Glen Lake Park

★Stone Mountain Park

Dearborn Park 1.★★★★★

"...heavily shaded with a few walking trails and a picnic pavilion... great place for family barbecues or just to take a little nature break... there's also a bridge across a small stream..."

Equipment/play structures........... ❸ ❸ ....Maintenance

WWW.ATLANTA-MIDTOWN.COM/NEIGHBORHOODS/PARKS/DEKALB_COUNTY/DEARBORN/

DECATUR—DEARWOOD DR (CREEKWOOD TERR); 404.817.6744

Glen Lake Park ★★★★★

"...Decatur's largest park has much to offer... play structures are nice and new, there's swings and a creek to wade in... equipment for both toddlers and older kids... amenities include swimming pool, 5 lighted tennis courts, 2 sports fields, basketball court, picnic pavillion, picnic tables, children's play structures, swings... a good place to meet moms from Decatur... bathroom facilities and shelter available... can get crowded..."

Equipment/play structures........... ❺ ❹ ....Maintenance

WWW.ATLANTA-MIDTOWN.COM/NEIGHBORHOODS/PARKS/DECATUR/GLENLAKE/

DECATUR—1211 CHURCH ST (AT NORRIS ST); 404.377.7231

Keswick Park ★★★★☆

"...great park for the whole family... the 45 acre park features two wheelchair accessible playgrounds—one for toddlers, another for bigger kids... swings, picnic area, nice walking path... only downside, not much shade..."

Equipment/play structures........... ❺ ❺ ....Maintenance

WWW.CHAMBLEEGA.COM

CHAMBLEE—HILDON CIR (HILDON RD)

McKoy Park ★★★★☆

"...excellent park for parents with toddlers and preschool-aged children... play equipment is good for all ages... a small, toddler-sized area with a small slide, baby swings and a tube to crawl through... the larger structure has three slides, a rock climbing wall, monkey bars and various other fun features... also a skate park area... on a nice, quiet street..."

Equipment/play structures........... ❺ ❹ ....Maintenance

WWW.DECATUR-GA.COM

DECATUR—534 MCKOY ST (AT W HILL ST); 404.377.0494

Scott Park ★★★★☆

"...beautiful mature trees provide lots of shade... nice playground equipment... features a community garden, and we love going to see what nice flowers and vegetables people are growing... next to the Decatur Library and behind the Decatur Recreation Center..."

Equipment/play structures .... ❹ ❹.............................. Maintenance

WWW.DECATURGA.COM

DECATUR—231 SYCAMORE ST (AT CHURCH ST)

Stone Mountain Park ★★★★★

"...lots of fun for the kids with different play areas for different ages, shows and a train ride around the base of the mountain... putt putt golf, the children's barn, 4-D theater, walking and hiking trails, children's playground, fishing, swimming, paddle boats, etc... the playground area is fantastic... the sand area is similar to a beach... the hiking trails are shaded and brush free... the annual pass is a great value... always something new to explore..."

Equipment/play structures .... ❹ ❹.............................. Maintenance

WWW.STONEMOUNTAINPARK.COM

STONE MOUNTAIN—STONE MOUNTAIN HWY 78 (AT W PARK PL BLVD SW); 770.498.5690; CALL FOR HOURS

Gwinnett

★★★★★

"lila picks"

★Bogan Park

★Jones Bridge County Park

★Rhodes Jordan Park

Bogan Park ★★★★★

"...a wonderful family park... long paved trails that are good for walking with strollers or tots on bikes... a couple of nice playgrounds with age-appropriate equipment... the indoor pool costs a couple of dollars per child and is fantastic... with water guns, a water mushroom and a slide..."

Equipment/play structures........... ❺ ❺ .... Maintenance

WWW.GWINNETTCOUNTY.COM

BUFORD—2723 N BOGAN RD (AT SPRINGLAKE DR NE); 770.614.2060

Briscoe Park ★★★★☆

"...the playground is great, though it's on a hard surface... a short walk from the playground takes you to the lake where ducks will be more than happy to accept some bread crumbs... lots of shade... also features tennis and volleyball courts..."

Equipment/play structures........... ❹ ❸ .... Maintenance

WWW.SNELLVILLE.ORG

SNELLVILLE—2500 SAWYER PKWY (AT LENORA CHURCH RD SW); 770.985.3535

Collins Hill Park ★★★½☆

"...two large playgrounds in the midst of ball fields and tennis courts... the equipment is awesome and well maintained... the playground by the pavilion is good for the little ones—the one by the ball fields has two separate areas for toddlers and older kids... bathrooms on premises... great people-watching on the playground or near the volleyball and tennis courts..."

Equipment/play structures........... ❺ ❺ .... Maintenance

WWW.CO.GWINNETT.GA.US

LAWRENCEVILLE—2225 COLLINS HILL RD (AT TAYLOR RD NW); 770.614.2060

Grayson Park ★★★★☆

"...a great park... it's small, mostly consisting of two playgrounds, but very nice... lots of shade, some nice wooden bench swings, the equipment is new and safe... the younger kids play area is one of the best I've seen for the 2-5 year old set, with short slides, low, easy to climb steps, an nice teeter totter... this is our favorite park...."

Equipment/play structures........... ❺ ❹ .... Maintenance

WWW.CITYOFGRAYSON.ORG/PARKREC.HTM

GRAYSON—

Jones Bridge County Park ★★★★★

"...recently renovated... a cool playground with a twisty slide, swings and more... it's located near the river so you can walk down to see the water and the geese... two baby swings... benches and picnic tables are shaded, but the playground is not... the nearby pavilions can be rented out for parties..."

Equipment/play structures .... ❹ ❹.............................. Maintenance

WWW.CO.GWINNETT.GA.US

NORCROSS—4901 E JONES BRIDGE RD (AT JONES BRIDGE COUNTY PARK); 770.417.2257

Lenora Park ★★★★☆

"...beautiful park for walking, biking, etc... there is a nice lake, lots of ducks and geese, a huge field of open green space... playground is somewhat lacking, the equipment (small jungle gym and bucket swings) is old and there's no shade... disc golf course, 1.5 mile paved multipurpose path, gymnasium, pavilion, community room, fishing in the lake ..."

Equipment/play structures .... ❹ ❹.............................. Maintenance

WWW.CO.GWINNETT.GA.US

SNELLVILLE—4515 LENORA CHURCH RD (AT LEE RD SW); 770.978.5271

Mountain Park Park ★★★★½

"...a great park... the equipment on both playgrounds is relatively new and well maintained... a paved walking trail is perfect for pushing a stroller... my kids like to bring their bikes... nearby restrooms..."

Equipment/play structures .... ❹ ❺.............................. Maintenance

WWW.CO.GWINNETT.GA.US

LILBURN—5050 FIVE FORKS TRICKUM RD (AT SYCAMORE DR); 770.822.8840

PlayTown Suwanee ★★★★½

"...great trails and beautiful forestry... hard and soft surface area, picnic tables, grills, pavilions, public restrooms... great playground including a magical bus, castle, log cabin, boat, elephant, rocket, climbing wall, bridges, slides and swing sets... one of the best free parks for any child aged one and up..."

Equipment/play structures .... ❹ ❹.............................. Maintenance

WWW.SUWANEE.COM

SUWANEE—425 MAIN ST (AT BUFORD HWY); 770.945.8996

Rhodes Jordan Park ★★★★★

"...nice walking trails, a large pond with lots of ducks and geese to feed, and a great playground with a pool setting... the playground is a little old, but the pool slides and squirt guns are awesome... enough shade for hot summer days..."

Equipment/play structures .... ❹ ❹.............................. Maintenance

WWW.CO.GWINNETT.GA.US

LAWRENCEVILLE—HWY 29 (AT BUFORD DR N); 770.822.5414

Thrasher Park ★★★☆☆

"...sandbox and plenty of fun playground equipment to keep the kids busy... my kids enjoy the firetruck activity... small, so it is easy to keep a close eye on your kids... convenient, downtown location..."

Equipment/play structures .... ❹ ❸.............................. Maintenance

WWW.PATSABIN.COM/GWINNETT/INDEX.HTM

NORCROSS—THRASHER ST (AT PARK DR NW); 770.822.8875

Tribble Mill Park ★★★★★

"...beautiful setting!.. love the large playground and the "seat" swings for the little ones... tons of trails... it's always fun to watch the birds down by the lake... perfect for a leisurely walk with the stroller... picnic areas and bathrooms make this an easy outing..."

Equipment/play structures .... ❺ ❺ .... Maintenance

WWW.CO.GWINNETT.GA.US

GRAYSON—2125 TRIBBLE MILL PKWY (AT GRAYSON NEW HOPE RD SE); 770.822.5414

Vines Botanical Garden ★★★★☆

"...lush gardens and a gorgeous, relaxing atmosphere... perfect for long walks while pushing a stroller with a sleeping baby... the manor house is neat, but I go for the fountains and birds, especially the swans... no playgrounds, but a nice place for new walkers to practice..."

Equipment/play structures .... ❹ ❹ .... Maintenance

WWW.VINESBOTANICALGARDENS.COM

LOGANVILLE—3500 OAK GROVE RD (AT HOKE O'KELLY MILL RD SW); 770.466.7532

Cobb & Douglas

★★★★★

"lila picks"

★Lake Acworth Beach at Cauble Park

★Laurel Park

Adams Park ★★★★☆

"...we really enjoy this playground—it has a lot of equipment for both toddlers and older children... it's located right next to the bathrooms... it also offers tennis courts and numerous baseball fields..."

Equipment/play structures .... ❹ ❹ .... Maintenance

WWW.KENNESAW.GA.US

KENNESAW—2600 PARK DR (AT N MAIN ST NW); 770.422.9714

Cobb Park ★★★★☆

"...this park is great!... not a lot to do for the young toddlers—the equipment is a little too big -, but there are two baby swings... picnic and playground areas, nature trails, a gazebo and fountain, an area for outdoor concerts and exhibits, as well as areas devoted to outdoor environmental education opportunities... newly renovated..."

Equipment/play structures .... ❹ ❺ .... Maintenance

WWW.EASTCOBBPARK.ORG/ABOUTUS.HTM

SMYRNA—2776 SANFORD PL (AT WARD ST SE); 770.591.3160

East Cobb Park ★★★★★

"...a great park for kids in East Cobb... one of the best parks in Atlanta... plenty of equipment, fields, bike paths and picnic areas... wonderfully cared for... clean and safe... the swings and the parking lot can be very crowded on weekends..."

Equipment/play structures .... ❺ ❺ .... Maintenance

WWW.EASTCOBBPARK.ORG

MARIETTA—3322 ROSWELL RD (AT MURDOCK RD NE); 770.591.3160

Hunter Memorial Park ★★★☆☆

"...nice walking path... a partially fenced-in playground with all the usual equipment—swings, slides, monkey bars, etc... the mini train costs a couple of bucks and is always a crowd pleaser... sometimes crowded, but a fun place to meet new playmates..."

Equipment/play structures .... ❸ ❶ .... Maintenance

WWW.CI.DOUGLASVILLE.GA.US

DOUGLASVILLE—8830 GURLEY RD (AT HIGHWAY 5); 770.920.3007

Lake Acworth Beach at Cauble Park ★★★★★

"...from swimming to outdoor games this park has it all... very scenic, with a large play area and a nice variety of equipment... play area is

very close to the beach as well as picnic pavilions and restrooms... lots of open lawn to run and play on... bring your own toilet paper, parking is more difficult on weekends... ❞

Equipment/play structures........... ❹ ❹ .... Maintenance

WWW.ACWORTH.ORG

ACWORTH—BEACH ST; 770.974.3112

Laurel Park ★★★★★

❝*...a great park with new equipment, a paved walking trail and pond with ducks and geese... lots of climbing things, slides and bridges, all in primary colors... huge tennis center... big field for kite flying... no gate between the playground and the busy parking lot... you can spend a whole day here... our favorite park!...* ❞

Equipment/play structures........... ❹ ❹ .... Maintenance

WWW.CITY.MARIETTA.GA.US/PARKS_REC/REC_CENTERS.HTM

MARIETTA—151 MANNING RD (AT HERITAGE DR SW); 770.794.5634

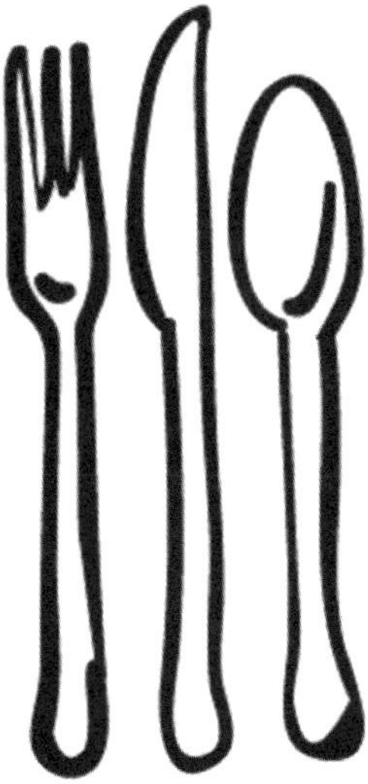

restaurants

City of Atlanta

★★★★★

"lila picks"

- ★Benihana
- ★California Pizza Kitchen
- ★Ippolito's Family Style Italian
- ★Jake's Ice Cream
- ★Johnny Rockets

American Roadhouse ★★★½☆

"...great kids' menu and very kid-friendly... restaurant always has a lot going on—TVs, music, video games—so it is easy to distract a child... delicious breakfast served all day long... friendly staff is sensitive to challenges of dining out with children... reasonable prices..."

Children's menu	✓	$$	Prices
Changing station	✗	❹	Customer service
Highchairs/boosters	✓	❹	Stroller access

ATLANTA—842 N HIGHLAND AVE (AT DREWRY ST NE); 404.872.2822; M-F 7-3, F-SA 7-4

Atkins Park Restaurant ★★★★☆

"...upscale cuisine in a historic setting... a surprisingly good spot for kids... dining room has a little play area for children... terrific menus for both adults and kids... who would have thought such a nice restaurant would cater to kids so well?.. don't miss the spectacular Sunday brunch... service is friendly and efficient... the chef frequently comes out of the kitchen to make sure guests are enjoying their food..."

Children's menu	✓	$$$	Prices
Changing station	✗	❹	Customer service
Highchairs/boosters	✓	❸	Stroller access

WWW.ATKINSPARK.COM

ATLANTA—794 N HIGHLAND (AT ST LOUIS PL NE); 404.876.7249; M-SA 11-2:30AM, SU 11-12AM; STREET PARKING

Bambinelli's Italian Restaurant ★★★★☆

"...we really love this neighborhood restaurant... prices are reasonable and stroller access is decent... the speed of service is variable... waitstaff is always very friendly... food is delicious..."

Children's menu	✓	$$$	Prices
Changing station	✓	❹	Customer service
Highchairs/boosters	✓	❹	Stroller access

WWW.BAMBINELLIS.HOMESTEAD.COM

ATLANTA—3202 NORTHLAKE PKWY NE (BEHIND NORTHLAKE SHOPPING MALL); 770.493.1311; M-TH 11-3 5-10, F 11-3 5-11, SA 4-11, SU 4-10; STREET PARKING

Benihana ★★★★★

"...stir-fry meals are always prepared in front of you—it keeps everyone entertained, parents and kids alike... chefs often perform especially for the little ones... tables sit about 10 people, so it encourages talking with other diners... tend to be pretty loud so it's pretty family friendly... delicious for adults and fun for kids..."

Children's menu .... ✗ | $$$ .... Prices
Changing station .... ✓ | ❹ .... Customer service
Highchairs/boosters .... ✓ | ❸ .... Stroller access

WWW.BENIHANA.COM

ATLANTA—2143 PEACHTREE RD NE (AT BENNETT ST NW); 404.355.8565; M-TH 11-1:45, 5-10, F 11-1:45, 4-10, SA 4-10, SU 3-9

ATLANTA—229 PEACHTREE ST NE (AT HARRIS ST NE); 404.522.9629; M-F 11-1:45, M-TH 5-9:30, F-SA 5-10:30, SU 1:30-9

Burrito Art ★★★☆☆

"...they have tasty burritos and they go a step beyond most burrito places as far as the quality of ingredients and the creativity of the menu... fun and quick... always tasty..."

Children's menu .... ✗ | $$ .... Prices
Changing station .... ✗ | ❸ .... Customer service
Highchairs/boosters .... ✓ | ❹ .... Stroller access

ATLANTA—1451 OXFORD RD NE (AT N DECATUR RD NE); 404.377.7786; M-F 11:30-10, SA 12-10, SU 4-10

Cafe At The Corner

Children's menu .... ✓ | ✗ .... Changing station
Highchairs/boosters .... ✓

ATLANTA—636 S CENTRAL AV (AT DOGWOOD DR); 404.766.1155; DAILY LUNCH

California Pizza Kitchen ★★★★★

"...you can't go wrong with their fabulous pizza... always clean... the food's great, the kids drinks all come with a lid... the staff is super friendly to kids... crayons and coloring books keep little minds busy... most locations have a place for strollers at the front... no funny looks or attitude when breastfeeding... open atmosphere with friendly service... tables are well spaced so you don't feel like your kid is annoying the diners nearby (it's usually full of kids anyway)..."

Children's menu .... ✓ | $$ .... Prices
Changing station .... ✓ | ❹ .... Customer service
Highchairs/boosters .... ✓ | ❹ .... Stroller access

WWW.CPK.COM

ATLANTA—3393 PEACHTREE RD NE (AT LENOX SQ MALL); 404.262.9221; M-TH 11:30-9, F-SA 11:30-10, SU 12-7; MALL PARKING

ATLANTA—4600 ASHFORD DUNWOODY RD NE (AT PERIMETER CTR N); 770.393.0390; M-TH 11-10, F 10:30-10:30, SA11:30-10:30, SU 11:30-9

Cheesecake Factory, The ★★★★☆

"...although their cheesecake is good, we come here for the kid-friendly atmosphere and selection of good food... eclectic menu has something for everyone... they will bring your tot a plate of yogurt, cheese, bananas and bread free of charge... we love how flexible they are—they'll make whatever my kids want... lots of mommies here... always fun and always crazy... no real kids menu, but the pizza is great to share... waits can be really long..."

Children's menu .... ✗ | $$$ .... Prices
Changing station .... ✓ | ❹ .... Customer service
Highchairs/boosters .... ✓ | ❸ .... Stroller access

restaurants

WWW.THECHEESECAKEFACTORY.COM

ATLANTA—3024 PEACHTREE RD NW (AT PIEDMONT RD); 404.816.2555; M-TH 10:30-11, F-SA 10:30-12:30AM, SU 10-11

ATLANTA—4400 ASHFORD DUNWOODY RD NE (AT PERIMETER MALL); 678.320.0201; M-TH 11-11, F-SA 11-12:30, SU 10-11

Cici's Pizza ★★★★☆

"...a great buffet for easy dining with kids... pizza at the right price... kids 3 and under eat free... very crowded during lunch and dinner rushes... not much room for strollers, but they'll help you find a place to stash it... they always have birthday parties and it's usually very crowded and noisy... pizza, pasta and salad buffet for under $10..."

Children's menu	✓	$	Prices
Changing station	✓	❹	Customer service
Highchairs/boosters	✓	❹	Stroller access

WWW.CICISPIZZA.COM

ATLANTA—6050 PEACHTREE PKWY NW (AT PEACHTREE INDUSTRIAL BLVD); 770.300.0535; SU-TH 9-10, F-SA 11-11

ATLANTA—6690 ROSWELL RD NE (AT ABERNATHY RD NW); 404.257.9944; DAILY 10-10

Crescent Moon ★★★★☆

"...kid-friendly... they provide crayons and color sheet... waitstaff is extremely patient with the little ones .. they will also put in an order for the little ones separately... would not recommend going on a Sunday morning—it's way packed... the best brunch in town..."

Children's menu	✓	$$	Prices
Changing station	✗	❹	Customer service
Highchairs/boosters	✓	❸	Stroller access

WWW.CRESCENTMOONEATERY.COM

ATLANTA—4800 BRIARCLIFF RD (AT NORTHLAKE SHOPPING MALL); 678.937.9020; DAILY 8-9

Don Pablo's ★★★★☆

"...yummy Mexican dishes... spacious and super kid-friendly—we've been coming here since our baby was 2 weeks old... kid's meals are inexpensive and plentiful... my son loves playing with the dough and the meal arrives in no time... fun, boisterous setting... can get busy, but you generally get a table with little delay..."

Children's menu	✓	$$	Prices
Changing station	✓	❹	Customer service
Highchairs/boosters	✓	❹	Stroller access

WWW.DONPABLOS.COM

ATLANTA—3131 COBB PKWY SE (AT CUMBERLAND BLVD SE); 770.955.5929; SU-TH 11-10, F-SA 11-11

Down The Hatch

Children's menu	✗	✗	Changing station
Highchairs/boosters	✓		

WWW.DANTESDOWNTHEHATCH.COM

ATLANTA—3380 PEACHTREE RD NE (AT STRATFORD RD); 404.266.1600; M 4-11, T-TH 4-11:30, F-SA 4-12:30, SU 5-11

ESPN Zone ★★★☆☆

"...loud and crazy with average food... kids like to play the arcade games and carry the beeper, which alerts diners when their table is ready... we avoid it during big sporting events... lots of room for strollers... staff is friendly and accommodating..."

Children's menu	✓	$$$	Prices
Changing station	✓	❹	Customer service

Highchairs/boosters ✓	❸ Stroller access

WWW.ESPNZONE.COM

ATLANTA—3030 PEACHTREE RD NW (AT PIEDMONT RD NE); 404.682.3776; M-TH 11:30-12, F 11:30-1:30, SA 11 1:30, SU 11:30 11

Everybody's Pizza ★★★½☆

"...great pizza... a very pleasant patio to hang out on—it's stroller accessible and kids love watching the fountain... our play group meets here for early dinners... huge menu with lots of pizza and non-pizza options..."

Children's menu ✓	$$ Prices
Changing station ✗	❸ Customer service
Highchairs/boosters ✓	❸ Stroller access

WWW.EVERYBODYSPIZZA.COM

ATLANTA—1040 N HIGHLAND AVE NE (AT VIRGINIA AVE); 404.873.4545; M-T 11:30-10, W-TH 11:30-10:30, F-SA 11:30-12, SU 12-10; DRIVE-UP

ATLANTA—1593 N DECATUR RD NE (AT OXFORD RD); 404.377.7766; M-TH 11:30-11, F-SA 11:30-12, SU 12-11; DRIVE-UP

Fellini's Pizza ★★★★☆

"...by far the best pizza restaurant in Atlanta—we're from New York and they make me feel as though I were back home... excellent food—you can even sneak some veggies into your kid's diets with the toppings... friendly staff... it's so noisy, no one minds if your child is making noise... casual environment where kids can be kids... great salads, fast service and low prices..."

Children's menu ✗	$$ Prices
Changing station ✗	❹ Customer service
Highchairs/boosters ✗	❹ Stroller access

ATLANTA—1634 MCLENDON AVE (AT PAGE AVE NE); 404.687.9190; M-SA 11-12, SU 12-12

ATLANTA—1991 HOWELL MILL RD NW (AT COLLIER RD NW); 404.352.0799; M-SA 11-2, SU 12-12

ATLANTA—4429 ROSWELL RD NE (AT WIEUCA RD NE); 404.303.8248; M-SA 11-2, SU 12:30-12

ATLANTA—909 PONCE DE LEON AV NE (AT LINWOOD AVE NE); 404.873.3088; M-SA 11-2, SU 12-12

Frontera Mex Grill ★★★★☆

"...incredibly kid-friendly... kids love celebrating birthdays here because they get to wear a special hat and the waitstaff sings 'Happy Birthday'... lovely outdoor patio for warm nights... live music on the weekend is a big draw... a very popular weekend spot for families... free ice cream for kids is a big hit..."

Children's menu ✓	$$ Prices
Changing station ✗	❹ Customer service
Highchairs/boosters ✓	❹ Stroller access

WWW.NORSANGROUP.COM

ATLANTA—4279 ROSWELL RD NE (AT PIEDMONT RD); 404.236.0777; M-SA 11-10:30, SU 11-10

Fuddruckers ★★★★☆

"...a super burger chain with fresh and tasty food... colorful and noisy with lots of distraction until the food arrives... loads of fresh toppings so that you can make your perfectly cooked burger even better... great kids deals that come with a free treat... noise not a problem in this super casual atmosphere... some locations have video games in the back which will buy you an extra half hour if you need it... low-key and very family friendly..."

Children's menu	✓	$$	Prices
Changing station	✓	❹	Customer service
Highchairs/boosters	✓	❹	Stroller access

WWW.FUDDRUCKERS.COM

ATLANTA—240 PERIMETER CTR PKWY NE (AT HAMMOND DR NE); 770.399.6641; DAILY 7-9

ATLANTA—815 SYDNEY MARCUS BLVD NE (AT PIEDMONT RD NE); 404.264.0079; DAILY 7-9

Gordon Biersch ★★★★☆

"...a fantastic brewery that serves delicious food... awesome beer that is brewed onsite... fun atmosphere that works well for kids... high-end bar food... staff seems to adore babies... server was very doting and attentive to my family's needs... best to go early before the after work scene gets going... the big vats and pipes provide for a fun walk-around with my tot..."

Children's menu	✓	$$$	Prices
Changing station	✓	❹	Customer service
Highchairs/boosters	✓	❹	Stroller access

WWW.GORDONBIERSCH.COM

ATLANTA—3242 PEACHTREE RD NE (AT PIEDMONT RD); 404.264.0253; DAILY 11:30-1AM

ATLANTA—848 PEACHTREE ST NE (AT 6TH ST NE); 404.870.0805; SU-TH 11:30-12, F-SA 11:30-2

Grant Central Pizza ★★★★☆

"...great pizza in a very family friendly setting... noisy and inexpensive—perfect for my little boisterous gang of tots... Thursday nights are family nights and the restaurant is completely packed with kids..."

Children's menu	✓	$	Prices
Changing station	✓	❺	Customer service
Highchairs/boosters	✓	❺	Stroller access

ATLANTA—1279 GLENWOOD AVE SE (AT FLAT SHOALS AVE SE); 404.627.0007; M-F 11-11, F-SA 11-12, SU 12-11

Hard Rock Cafe ★★★½☆

"...fun and tasty if you can get in... the lines can be horrendous so be sure to check in with them first... a good spot if you have tots in tow—food tastes good and the staff is clearly used to messy eaters... hectic and loud... fun for adults as well as kids..."

Children's menu	✓	$$$	Prices
Changing station	✓	❹	Customer service
Highchairs/boosters	✓	❸	Stroller access

WWW.HARDROCK.COM

ATLANTA—215 PEACHTREE ST NE (AT JILES RD NW); 404.688.7625; SU-TH 11-12AM, F-SA 11-1AM

IKEA ★★★★☆

"...Swedish meatballs and funny berry drinks—all yummy and cheap... a clean, comfortable place to eat... the restaurant sells baby food and has bottle/jar warmers... worth visiting even if you aren't shopping—the food is cheap, but good... totally kid-friendly... lines can sometimes be long, especially during peak shopping hours..."

Children's menu	✓	$$	Prices
Changing station	✓	❹	Customer service
Highchairs/boosters	✓	❹	Stroller access

WWW.IKEA.COM

ATLANTA—441 16TH ST (OFF MECASLIN ST); 404.745.4532; DAILY 10-9

Ippolito's Family Style Italian Restaurant ★★★★★

"...a great neighborhood 'joint' with a welcoming ambiance... they even give kids pizza dough to play with while they are waiting... varied menu and fast service... although it doesn't look like a classic baby-friendly place, the staff is fantastic with kids and the food is awesome... good food for adults and easy atmosphere for kids..."

Children's menu ✓ | $$ Prices
Changing station ✓ | ❹ Customer service
Highchairs/boosters ✓ | ❸ Stroller access

WWW.IPPOLITOS.NET

ATLANTA—6623 ROSWELL RD NE (AT ABERNATHY RD NE); 404.256.3546; SU-TH 11-10, F-SA 11-11

Jake's Ice Cream & Muncheteria ★★★★★

"...the only way ice cream should be done—these guys know what they're doing... luscious ice cream and a bunch of locations make this a winner... there is plenty of room for kids to play while you dine or hangout... I like that they have a sign on the door saying they support breastfeeding moms... something for everyone to eat—soups, salads and sandwiches and of course, ice cream..."

Children's menu ✗ | $$ Prices
Changing station ✗ | ❸ Customer service
Highchairs/boosters ✓ | ❹ Stroller access

ATLANTA—8 KING'S CIR (AT PEACHTREE HILLS AVE); 404.869.9002; SU-TH 11-10, F-SA 11-11

Jake's Ice Cream & Sorbets ★★★★★

"...the only way ice cream should be done—these guys know what they're doing... luscious ice cream and a bunch of locations make this a winner... there is plenty of room for kids to play while you dine or hangout... I like that they have a sign on the door saying they support breastfeeding moms... something for everyone to eat—soups, salads and sandwiches and of course, ice cream..."

Children's menu ✗ | $$ Prices
Changing station ✗ | ❺ Customer service
Highchairs/boosters ✓ | ❹ Stroller access

ATLANTA—3232 PEACHTREE RD NE (AT PIEDMONT RD NE); 404.816.8696; M F-SA 10-12AM, T-TH SU 10-10

ATLANTA—970 PIEDMONT AVE (AT 10TH ST NE); 404.685.3101; SU-TH 11-10, F-SA 11-11

Jason's Deli ★★★½☆

"...sandwiches and tasty soup... a good counter restaurant with an inexpensive kids menu... cheap prices for kids and decent food—you can get fruit instead of chips... free ice cream after their meal... lots of choices for all family members... the staff is always helping out with highchairs and everything else..."

Children's menu ✓ | $$ Prices
Changing station ✗ | ❹ Customer service
Highchairs/boosters ✓ | ❹ Stroller access

WWW.JASONSDELI.COM

ATLANTA—1109 CUMBERLAND MALL (AT RT 407); 770.432.4414; M-SA 10-7; MALL PARKING

ATLANTA—3330 PIEDMONT RD NE (AT STATE ROUTE 147 CONN E); 404.231.3333; DAILY 10-10

ATLANTA—4705 ASHFORD DUNWOODY RD (AT ASHWOOD PKWY); 770.671.1555; DAILY 10-10

ATLANTA—5975 ROSWELL RD NE (AT HAMMOND DR NE); 404.843.8212; DAILY 10-10

Jocks & Jills Sports Bar ★★★★☆

"...when we want to have an adult conversation over dinner, this is where we take our kids... there is plenty there to amuse them whether it's the tons of TVs or sports jerseys... food is surprisingly good and diverse and before 6:30, the dinning area is virtually all families with kids..."

Children's menu	✓	$$	Prices
Changing station	✓	5	Customer service
Highchairs/boosters	✓	5	Stroller access

WWW.JOCKS-FRANKIES.COM

ATLANTA—4046 PEACHTREE RD NE (AT DRESDEN DR NE); 404.816.2801; M-TH 11-1, F-SA 11-2, SU 11-12; FREE PARKING

Joe's Crab Shack ★★★★☆

"...for the young and the young at heart... newspaper lined tables, crabs done every which way... the staff sings and dances and so do my kids... dining inside and out... this is a kick back place where we always have a good time and a good crab... plenty for the kids to choose from even if they're not into crab... lots of fun items on the walls and ceilings—keeps kids entertained until the food comes... perfect for appetizers and beer when you need a break..."

Children's menu	✓	$$$	Prices
Changing station	✓	4	Customer service
Highchairs/boosters	✓	3	Stroller access

WWW.JOESCRABSHACK.COM

ATLANTA—3013 PEACHTREE RD NE (AT PHARR RD); 404.869.0500; SU-TH 11-10, F-SA 11-11

Johnny Rockets ★★★★★

"...burgers, fries and a shake served up in a 50's style diner... we love the singing waiters—they're always good for a giggle... my daughter is enthralled with the juke box and straw dispenser... sit at the counter and watch the cooks prepare the food... simple, satisfying and always a hit with the little ones..."

Children's menu	✓	$$	Prices
Changing station	✗	4	Customer service
Highchairs/boosters	✓	3	Stroller access

WWW.JOHNNYROCKETS.COM

ATLANTA—2970 COBB PKWY (AT CUMBERLAND); 770.955.6068; SU-TH 11-10 F-SA 11-11; FREE PARKING

ATLANTA—3500 PEACHTREE RD (AT PHIPPS PLAZA); 404.233.9867; M-TH 9-10, F-SA 9-11, SU 9-9

ATLANTA—5 W PACES FERRY RD (AT EARLY ST NW); 404.231.5555; SU-TH 11-10, F-SA 11-1

ATLANTA—50 UPPER ALABAMA ST (AT MARTIN LUTHER KING JR DR); 404.525.7117; M-SA 11-11; FREE PARKING

Lil Azio ★★★☆☆

"...great atmosphere for when you are tired of the completely family oriented restaurant .. feels a little more upscale, but you order at the counter and they deliver it to the table... Brusters is next store and you can get a free baby cone for the kids..."

Children's menu	✗	$$	Prices
Changing station	✗	3	Customer service
Highchairs/boosters	✓	5	Stroller access

ATLANTA—903 PEACHTREE ST NE (AT 8TH ST NE); 404.876.7711; M-TH 11-10, F-SA 11-11, SU 11-10; PARKING LOT

Longhorn Steakhouse ★★★★☆

"...for meat and seafood lovers... the staff totally gets 'the kid thing' here... they bring out snacks, get the orders going quickly, and frequently check back for things like new spoons and napkins... lots of things for baby to look at... get there early or call ahead to avoid the wait..."

Children's menu ✓ | $$$ Prices
Changing station ✓ | ❹ Customer service
Highchairs/boosters ✓ | ❸ Stroller access

WWW.LONGHORNSTEAKHOUSE.COM

ATLANTA—2973 COBB PKWY (AT PROFESSIONAL PKWY SE); 770.859.0341; SU-TH 11-10, F-SA 11-11

Maggiano's Little Italy ★★★½☆

"...Southern Italian cuisine served in huge, family-style portions... so much food, we didn't even need a kid's meal... yummy for both adults and kids... fun atmosphere and friendly staff... not the easiest place with a baby, but servers are helpful... they will help you store your stroller... where else can I eat with my kids and listen to Sinatra playing... rather noisy which is great if baby gets fussy... kids love all the activity..."

Children's menu ✓ | $$$ Prices
Changing station ✓ | ❹ Customer service
Highchairs/boosters ✓ | ❸ Stroller access

WWW.MAGGIANOS.COM

ATLANTA—4400 ASHFORD DUNWOODY RD NE (AT PERIMETER CTR E); 770.804.3313; SU-TH 11-10, F-SA 11-11

Mary Mac's Tea Room

Children's menu ✓ | ✓ Changing station
Highchairs/boosters ✓

WWW.MARYMACS.COM

ATLANTA—224 PONCE DE LEON AVE NE (AT MYRTLE ST NE); 404.876.1800; DAILY 11-9

McCormick & Schmicks ★★★★☆

"...steak and seafood are the mainstay but the menu is broad... terrific happy-hour menu... a little more formal than your regular 'tot-friendly' restaurant, but the staff is great and goes out of their way to make sure you're comfortable... try to get one of the banquet rooms—it makes breastfeeding much easier... good food for adults and more than enough for the little ones too..."

Children's menu ✓ | $$$ Prices
Changing station ✓ | ❹ Customer service
Highchairs/boosters ✓ | ❹ Stroller access

WWW.MCCORMICKANDSCHMICKS.COM

ATLANTA—190 MARIETTA ST NW (AT CNN CTR); 404.521.1236; M-F 11-12, SA 12-12, SU 4-10

ATLANTA—600 ASHWOOD PKWY (OFF MEADOW LN RD); 770.399.9900; M-TH 11-10 F-SA 11-11 SU 4-10

Mellow Mushroom ★★★★☆

"...pizzas, salads, calzones and hoagies... simply delicious laid back atmosphere with a nice mellow vibe... amusing characters and fun setting... always a hit with my kids... friendly, efficient service... our mom's group meets here every week and the staff is terrific... kids love looking at the fun decor..."

Children's menu	✓	$$	Prices
Changing station	×	❹	Customer service
Highchairs/boosters	✓	❸	Stroller access

WWW.MELLOWMUSHROOM.COM

ATLANTA—1770 PEACHTREE ST NW (AT HIGHWAY 85); 404.815.8730; DAILY 11-12

ATLANTA—4058 PEACHTREE RD NE (AT DRESDEN DR NE); 404.266.1661; DAILY 11-12

ATLANTA—5575 CHAMBLEE DUNWOODY RD (AT ROBERTS DR); 770.396.1393; DAILY 11-12AM

ATLANTA—6218 ROSWELL RD NE (AT JOHNSON FERRY RD NE); 404.252.5560; DAILY 11-12; FREE PARKING

Moe's Southwest Grill ★★★½☆

"...fresh Mex food—burritos, quesedillas and tacos... there always are a ton of babies and kids there... if you want a drink other than juice or soda, bring your own sippy cup... tasty, good quality, cheap chow that satisfies both young and old... kids' meals for less than $3 and free on Monday nights... they only serve sodas and fruit punch for the kids..."

Children's menu	✓	$$	Prices
Changing station	✓	❹	Customer service
Highchairs/boosters	✓	❹	Stroller access

WWW.MOES.COM

ATLANTA—1544 PIEDMONT AV NE (AT MONROE DR NE); 404.879.9663; DAILY 11-10

ATLANTA—2915 PEACHTREE RD NE (AT PEACHTREE AVE NE); 404.442.8932; DAILY 11-10

ATLANTA—3722 ROSWELL RD NE (AT POWERS FERRY RD NW); 404.231.1690; DAILY 11-10

ATLANTA—5562 CHAMBLEE DUNWOODY RD (AT DOWNWOODY VILLAGE PKWY); 678.320.0360; DAILY 11-10

ATLANTA—70 PEACHTREE ST SW (AT MARTIN LUTHER KING JR DR); 404.688.4288; DAILY 11-10

ATLANTA—8290 ROSWELL RD (AT NORTHRIDGE RD); 678.585.7573; DAILY 11-10

ATLANTA—863 PONCE DE LEON AVE NE (AT FREEDOM PKY); 404.607.7892; DAILY 11-10

My Friend's Place ★★★★☆

"...would be nice to have some more kid-friendly options... wonderful, fresh deli food... all of the 'My Friend's Places' are impeccably clean and score a perfect rating with the health department..."

Children's menu	×	$	Prices
Changing station	×	❹	Customer service
Highchairs/boosters	×	❹	Stroller access

WWW.MYFRIENDSPLACEDELI.COM

ATLANTA—4400 ASHFORD DUNWOODY RD NE (AT PERIMETER MALL); 770.399.5794; M-SA 10-9, SU 10-6

ATLANTA—5533 CHAMBLEE DUNWOODY RD (AT MT VERNON RD); 770.396.1128; M-F 10-3, SA 11-3

Old Spaghetti Factory, The ★★★½☆

"...good for a fast, cheap meal if the place isn't too packed... apple sauce for kids... fun for the whole family and easy to eat for under $25 (family of four)... if you've got a hankering for spaghetti and meatballs, look no further... relatively inexpensive and you get big portions for your money... a place with a relaxed feel... it is usually so busy that no one will notice if your toddler is crying... the staff makes it easy to hang out and have a good time..."

Children's menu ✓ | $$ Prices
Changing station ✓ | ❹ Customer service
Highchairs/boosters ✓ | ❹ Stroller access

WWW.OLDSPAGHETTIFACTORY.COM

ATLANTA—249 PONCE DE LEON AVE NE (AT PENN AVE); 404.872.2841; M-TH 11:30-9:30, F 5-10, SA 11:30-10, SU 11:30-9:30; PARKING IN FRONT OF BLDG

Original Pancake House ★★★★½

"...consistently the best breakfast around... great flapjacks and appropriately-sized kids meals... food comes quickly... the most amazing apple pancakes ever... service is always friendly, but sometimes it can take a while to actually get the food... the highlight for my daughter is the free balloon when we leave... always a lot of families here with small children on the weekends, so you don't have to worry about being the only one..."

Children's menu ✓ | $$ Prices
Changing station ✓ | ❹ Customer service
Highchairs/boosters ✓ | ❸ Stroller access

WWW.ORIGINALPANCAKEHOUSE.COM

ATLANTA—2321 CHESHIRE BRIDGE RD (AT RT 236); 404.633.5677; M-F 7-3, SA-SU 7-4

Osteria 832 ★★★★☆

"...a great place to take kids... lots of young families here, great community atmosphere and best of all tasty, cheap food... one of the best places in town for wonderful Italian pastas and pizzas... very kid-friendly, but sophisticated enough for adults-only as well... great outdoor patio..."

Children's menu ✓ | $$ Prices
Changing station ✓ | ❹ Customer service
Highchairs/boosters ✓ | ❹ Stroller access

WWW.OSTERIA832.COM

ATLANTA—832 N HIGHLAND (AT ST LOUIS PL NE); 404.897.1414; M 5-10, T-TH SU 11:30-10, F-SA 11:30-11

Piccadilly Cafeteria

Children's menu ✓ | × Changing station
Highchairs/boosters ✓

WWW.PICCADILLY.COM

ATLANTA—1544 PIEDMONT (AT MONROE DR NE); 404.872.8091; DAILY 11-8:30

Roasters Rotisserie ★★★★☆

"...great kid menu... wonderful family feeling and the staff is very friendly... delicious grilled corn and fresh food... reasonable prices..."

Children's menu ✓ | $$ Prices
Changing station × | ❹ Customer service
Highchairs/boosters ✓ | ❸ Stroller access

WWW.ROASTERSFRESH.COM

ATLANTA—2770 LENOX RD (OFF BUFORD HWY); 404.237.1122; SU-TH 11-9, F-SA 11-9:30

ATLANTA—2997 CUMBERLAND BLVD (AT CUMBERLAND MALL); 770.333.6222; SU-TH 11-9, F-SA 11-9:30

ATLANTA—6225-B ROSWELL RD (AT MT VERNON HWY); 678.701.1100; SU-TH 11-9, F-SA 11-9:30

Ruby Tuesday ★★★½☆

"...nice variety of healthy choices on the kids' menu—turkey, spaghetti, chicken tenders... you can definitely find something healthy

here... prices are on the high side, but at least everyone can find something they like... service is fast and efficient... my daughter makes a mess and they never let me clean it up... your typical chain, but it works—you'll be happy to see ample aisle space, storage for your stroller, and attentive staff... ❞

Children's menu	✓	$$	Prices
Changing station	✓	❹	Customer service
Highchairs/boosters	✓	❸	Stroller access

WWW.RUBYTUESDAY.COM

ATLANTA—3345 LENOX RD NE (AT LENOX SQ MALL); 404.364.9050; SU-TH 11-11, F-SA 11-12AM

Six Feet Under ★★★½☆

❝*...Southern-style fish house... catfish and oysters are a mainstay... extremely friendly staff... if you can find a seat upstairs on the outside deck, it's a great place for the kids to watch cars and people... inside, the music absorbs the sounds of an unhappy child...* ❞

Children's menu	✓	$$	Prices
Changing station	✗	❹	Customer service
Highchairs/boosters	✓	❸	Stroller access

WWW.SIXFEETUNDERATLANTA.COM

ATLANTA—415 MEMORIAL DR (AT CHEROKEE AVE SE); 404.523.6664; M-TH 11-1, F-SA 11-2, SU 11-12

Sonny's Real Pit Bar-B-Q ★★★½☆

❝*...big BBQ chain with a small town feel... slow cooked meats, coleslaw and beans... finger lickin' good for the kids... dependable, fast and easy...* ❞

Children's menu	✓	$$	Prices
Changing station	✓	❸	Customer service
Highchairs/boosters	✓	❸	Stroller access

WWW.SONNYSBBQ.COM

ATLANTA—2350 CHESHIRE BRIDGE RD (AT LAVISTA RD); 404.929.0404; SU-TH 11-10, F-SA 11-10:30

Souplantation/Sweet Tomatoes ★★★★☆

❝*...you can't beat the price and selection of healthy foods... all you can eat—serve yourself soup and salad bar... lots of healthy choices plus pizza and pasta... great for picky eaters... free for 2 and under and only $3 for kids under 5... booths for comfy seating and discreet breastfeeding... helps to have another adult along since it is self serve... they always bring fresh cookies to the table and offer to refill drinks...* ❞

Children's menu	✓	$$	Prices
Changing station	✓	❹	Customer service
Highchairs/boosters	✓	❹	Stroller access

WWW.SOUPLANTATION.COM

ATLANTA—6350 PEACHTREE DUNWOODY RD (AT CRESTLINE PKY); 770.913.0203; F-SA 10:30-10, SU-TH 10:30-9

Taco Mac ★★★½☆

❝*...popular northern cuisine in the sunny South... tiny taco shack at the corner of Virginia and Highland Avenues—now known as 'The Virginia-Highlands'... quiet, tucked away, well-kept secret that might welcome a neighborhood pub...* ❞

Children's menu	✓	$$	Prices
Changing station	✗	❹	Customer service
Highchairs/boosters	✓	❸	Stroller access

WWW.TACOMAC.COM

ATLANTA—1006 N HIGHLAND AVE (AT VIRGINIA AVE); 404.873.6529; M-TH 11-2, F-SA 11-3, SU 11:30-12

TGI Friday's ★★★★☆

"...good old American bar food with a reasonable selection for the healthier set as well... I love that the kids meal includes salad... my daughter requests the potato skins on a regular basis (which is good because they are also my favorite)... moderately priced... cheerful servers are used to the mess my kids leave behind... relaxed scene... I'd steer clear on a Friday night unless you don't mind waiting and watching the singles scene..."

Children's menu .... ✓ | $$ .... Prices
Changing station .... ✓ | ❹ .... Customer service
Highchairs/boosters .... ✓ | ❸ .... Stroller access

WWW.TGIFRIDAYS.COM

ATLANTA—1925 POWERS FERRY RD (AT WINDY HILL RD); 770.951.0821; M-SA 11-2, SU 11-12

ATLANTA—2061 PEACHTREE RD NE (AT SEABOARD COAST LINE); 404.350.0199; M-TH 11-12, F-SA 11-1, SU 11-11

ATLANTA—INTL AIRPORT (OFF INTL AIRPORT); 404.763.3420; DAILY 7-10

Varsity, The ★★★½☆

"...an Atlanta institution since 1928... great food and fun for all ages... chili dogs, chili steaks, fries, onion rings and frosted oranges... not a lot of healthy options... yummy, fun and fattening... there are classroom-style seats and desks and TV's in many of the rooms... drive-in is a lot of fun, too... best to go early before the crowds arrive..."

Children's menu .... ✓ | $$ .... Prices
Changing station .... ✗ | ❹ .... Customer service
Highchairs/boosters .... ✓ | ❸ .... Stroller access

WWW.THEVARSITY.COM

ATLANTA—61 NORTH AVE (AT SPRING ST); 404.881.1706; SU-TH 10-11:30, F-SA 11:30-12:30AM

Villa Christina ★★★★☆

"...a taste of Italy... too fancy for the little ones, but every third Friday of the month, you can have a date night while they babysit your kids for only $10... a brilliant night out..."

Children's menu .... ✗ | $$$ .... Prices
Changing station .... ✗ | ❹ .... Customer service
Highchairs/boosters .... ✗ | ❹ .... Stroller access

WWW.VILLACHRISTINA.COM

ATLANTA—4000 SUMMIT BLVD (AT ASHFORD DUNWOODY RD); 404.303.0133; M-F 11:30-2:30 6-9, SA 6-9; PARKING BEHIND BLDG

Willy's Mexicana Grill ★★★★☆

"...Willy's has several booths and tables to accommodate a baby car seat... laid back place with yummy food..."

Children's menu .... ✓ | $ .... Prices
Changing station .... ✗ | ❹ .... Customer service
Highchairs/boosters .... ✓ | ❹ .... Stroller access

WWW.WILLYS.COM

ATLANTA—2460 CUMBERLAND PKWY SE (AT CRESTLANE DR); 770.801.8633; DAILY 11-10

ATLANTA—333 BUFORD DR NE (AT MALL OF GEORGIA); 404.422.7107; M-SA 11-9, SU 11-7

North Fulton

★★★★★

"lila picks"

- ★Benihana
- ★Bugaboo Creek Steak House
- ★California Pizza Kitchen
- ★Ippolito's Family Style Italian

Alessio's Restaurant & Pizzeria

Children's menu........................... ✓ ✗ .... Changing station
Highchairs/boosters..................... ✓
WWW.ALESSIOSRESTAURANT.COM
ALPHARETTA—3005 OLD ALABAMA RD (AT HAYNES BRIDGE RD); 770.751.0300; M-TH 11-10, F-SA 11-10:30, SU 4:30-9:30

Alpha Soda Restaurant

Children's menu........................... ✗ ✗ .... Changing station
Highchairs/boosters..................... ✓
WWW.ALPHASODA.COM
ALPHARETTA—11760 HAYNES BRIDGE RD (AT OLD MILTON PKY); 770.442.3102; SU-TH 7-10, F-SA 7-11

Benihana ★★★★★

"...stir-fry meals are always prepared in front of you—it keeps everyone entertained, parents and kids alike... chefs often perform especially for the little ones... tables sit about 10 people, so it encourages talking with other diners... tend to be pretty loud so it's pretty family friendly... delicious for adults and fun for kids..."

Children's menu........................... ✗ $$$.. Prices
Changing station .... ✓ ❹ ....Customer service
Highchairs/boosters..................... ✓ ❸ .... Stroller access
WWW.BENIHANA.COM
ALPHARETTA—2365 MANSELL RD (AT NORTH PT PKY); 678.4618440; M-TH 5-10, F 4:30-10, SA-SU 3:30-10

Buffalo Wild Wings

Children's menu........................... ✓ ✓........................... Changing station
Highchairs/boosters..................... ✓
WWW.BUFFALOWILDWINGS.COM
ALPHARETTA—2375 MANSELL RD (OFF TURNER MCDONALD PKY); 678.352.4599; M-SA 11-2, SU 11-12

Bugaboo Creek Steak House ★★★★★

"...a definite must-go place for families with children... delicious food for grown-ups and a nice selection of food on the kids' menu... all kids' meals come with ice cream... all the hustle and bustle around us kept my son entertained while we waited for our meal... the singing tree (and Moose) will either delight your child or scare the bejesus out of him... terrific service—the staff goes out of their way to cater to families... fun for birthdays—staff sings and brings out the birthday moose, which the honored one is supposed to kiss..."

Children's menu ✓ | $$$ Prices
Changing station ✓ | ❹ Customer service
Highchairs/boosters ✓ | ❹ Stroller access

WWW.BUGABOOCREEKSTEAKHOUSE.COM

ALPHARETTA—10890 HAYNES BRIDGE RD (AT NORTH POINT DR); 770.667.2188; M-TH 11:30-10, F-SA 11:30-10:30, SU 12-9

Calico Cow Creamery ★★★☆☆

"...friendly family-run dessert shop and cafe specializing in homemade ice cream... fabulous cheesecakes and specialty coffees... a super neighborhood kind of place where the owners know people's names..."

Children's menu ✓ | $$$ Prices
Changing station ✗ | ❸ Customer service
Highchairs/boosters ✓ | ❸ Stroller access

WWW.CALICOCOW.COM

ROSWELL—4401 SHALLOWFORD RD (AT JOHNSON FERRY RD); 678.205.3647; M-TH 11-9, F-SA 11-10, SU 2-8

California Pizza Kitchen ★★★★★

"...you can't go wrong with their fabulous pizza... always clean... the food's great, the kids drinks all come with a lid... the staff is super friendly to kids... crayons and coloring books keep little minds busy... most locations have a place for strollers at the front... no funny looks or attitude when breastfeeding... open atmosphere with friendly service... tables are well spaced so you don't feel like your kid is annoying the diners nearby (it's usually full of kids anyway)..."

Children's menu ✓ | $$ Prices
Changing station ✓ | ❹ Customer service
Highchairs/boosters ✓ | ❹ Stroller access

WWW.CPK.COM

ALPHARETTA—6301 NORTH POINT PKWY (AT N POINT CT); 770.664.8246; M-TH 11:30-9:30, F-SA 11:30-10, SU 11:30-9

Carmine's Restaurant & Pizzeria ★★★★½

"...pizza by the slice so everyone can have what they want... the even give pizza dough to kids to entertain them while they wait... staff is patient with kids... we always leave happy and well-fed... our two year old twin boys love it, and always get lots of attention from the staff... my kids love to watch the pizza man throw the dough up in the air..."

Children's menu ✓ | $$ Prices
Changing station ✗ | ❺ Customer service
Highchairs/boosters ✓ | ❺ Stroller access

ALPHARETTA—11875 JONES BRIDGE RD (AT SARGENT RD); 678.624.0009; DAILY 11-10

ALPHARETTA—4055 OLD MILTON PKWY (AT ALEXANDER DR); 770.772.3644; DAILY 11-10

Cheeburger Cheeburger ★★★½☆

"...old time feel... classic 50's and 60's rock and roll on the radio... big, big burgers—salads too... you can choose whatever topping you want for your burgers and salads... great shakes... don't miss the clown on Friday nights—free face painting and my kids love it... good food and a very relaxed environment..."

Children's menu ✓ | $$ Prices
Changing station ✓ | ❹ Customer service
Highchairs/boosters ✓ | ❸ Stroller access

WWW.CHEEBURGER.COM

ROSWELL—2300 HOLCOMB BRIDGE RD (AT FOUTS RD); 770.645.4702; M-TH 11-9, F-SA 11-11, SU 12-9; STREET PARKING

Cheesecake Factory, The ★★★★☆

"...although their cheesecake is good, we come here for the kid-friendly atmosphere and selection of good food... eclectic menu has something for everyone... they will bring your tot a plate of yogurt, cheese, bananas and bread free of charge... we love how flexible they are—they'll make whatever my kids want... lots of mommies here... always fun and always crazy... no real kids menu, but the pizza is great to share... waits can be really long..."

Children's menu ✗ | $$$ Prices
Changing station ✓ | ❹ Customer service
Highchairs/boosters ✓ | ❸ Stroller access

WWW.THECHEESECAKEFACTORY.COM

ALPHARETTA—2075 N POINT CIR (AT N POINT MALL); 770.751.7011; M-TH 11-11, F-SA 11-12:30, SU 11-11

Chili's Grill & Bar ★★★½☆

"...family-friendly, mild Mexican fare... delicious ribs, soups, salads... kids' menu and crayons as you sit down... on the noisy side, so you don't mind if your kids talk in their usual loud voices... service is excellent... fun night out with the family... a wide variety of menu selections for kids and their parents—all at a reasonable price... best chicken fingers on any kids' menu..."

Children's menu ✓ | $$ Prices
Changing station ✓ | ❹ Customer service
Highchairs/boosters ✓ | ❹ Stroller access

WWW.CHILIS.COM

ALPHARETTA—7800 NORTH POINT PKWY (AT MANSELL RD); 770.594.9063; SU-TH 11-11, F-SA 11-12AM

Cici's Pizza ★★★★☆

"...a great buffet for easy dining with kids... pizza at the right price... kids 3 and under eat free... very crowded during lunch and dinner rushes... not much room for strollers, but they'll help you find a place to stash it... they always have birthday parties and it's usually very crowded and noisy... pizza, pasta and salad buffet for under $10..."

Children's menu ✓ | $ Prices
Changing station ✓ | ❹ Customer service
Highchairs/boosters ✓ | ❹ Stroller access

WWW.CICISPIZZA.COM

ROSWELL—10516 ALPHARETTA HWY (AT ROSWELL MALL); 770.645.1550; DAILY 11-10; MALL PARKING

El Azteca Mexican Restaurant ★★★½☆

"...super friendly and accommodating—hot water for bottles, extra chips for fussy kids and food all over the floor is almost expected... we always enjoy the food at this Mexican restaurant... super family friendly and easy..."

Children's menu	×	$$	Prices
Changing station	×	❹	Customer service
Highchairs/boosters	✓	❸	Stroller access

ALPHARETTA—9925 HAYNES BRIDGE RD (AT OLD ALABAMA RD), 770.569.5234; DAILY 10-10:30

El Porton Mexican Restaurant ★★★½☆

"...friendly service and servers are very welcoming toward kids... enjoyable low-key atmosphere... don't worry about disturbing the other diners, many have small kids with them, too... great prices and decent portion sizes ..."

Children's menu	✓	$$	Prices
Changing station	×	❹	Customer service
Highchairs/boosters	✓	❹	Stroller access

ALPHARETTA—11190 ALPHARETTA HWY (AT UPPER HEMBREE RD); 678.393.0101; DAILY 10-10:30

ALPHARETTA—11950 JONES BRIDGE RD (AT SARGENT RD); 770.569.1775; DAILY 10-10:30

ROSWELL—910 MARIETTA HWY (AT COLEMAN RD); 770.552.1613; DAILY 10-10:30

El Torero Mexican Restaurant ★★★★★

"...this Mexican restaurant has become a favorite since our son was born... it is very casual... no carpet on the floor to destroy when your child throws food on the floor... waitstaff makes faces at our son to make him laugh... very quick and pretty inexpensive..."

Children's menu	✓	$	Prices
Changing station	×	❺	Customer service
Highchairs/boosters	✓	❹	Stroller access

ROSWELL—625 W CROSSVILLE RD (AT HACKETT RD); 770.640.1603; DAILY 10:30-10

Fuddruckers ★★★★☆

"...a super burger chain with fresh and tasty food... colorful and noisy with lots of distraction until the food arrives... loads of fresh toppings so that you can make your perfectly cooked burger even better... great kids deals that come with a free treat... noise not a problem in this super casual atmosphere... some locations have video games in the back which will buy you an extra half hour if you need it... low-key and very family friendly..."

Children's menu	✓	$$	Prices
Changing station	✓	❹	Customer service
Highchairs/boosters	✓	❹	Stroller access

WWW.FUDDRUCKERS.COM

ALPHARETTA—6360 NORTH POINT PKWY (AT HAYNES BRIDGE RD); 770.475.3338; SU-TH 11-9, F-SA 11-10

ROSWELL—11000 ALPHARETTA HWY (AT HOUZE WAY); 678.352.3290; DAILY 11-9; FREE PARKING

Golden Corral ★★★½☆

"...terrific place for new parents and kids of all ages... huge buffet and kids under 3 eat free... a great place for little eaters to try a lot of new foods... perfect for picky eaters... friendly, relaxed atmosphere... okay for kids to run around a little... reasonable prices..."

Children's menu	✓	$$	Prices
Changing station	✓	❹	Customer service
Highchairs/boosters	✓	❹	Stroller access

WWW.GOLDENCORRAL.COM

ALPHARETTA—915 NORTH POINT DR (AT NORTH POINT PKY); 678.867.2881; M-F 10:45-10, F 10:45-10:30 SA-SU 7:30-10:30

Ippolito's Family Style Italian Restaurant ★★★★★

"...a great neighborhood 'joint' with a welcoming ambiance... they even give kids pizza dough to play with while they are waiting... varied menu and fast service... although it doesn't look like a classic baby-friendly place, the staff is fantastic with kids and the food is awesome... good food for adults and easy atmosphere for kids..."

Children's menu .... ✓ $$ .... Prices
Changing station .... × ❹ .... Customer service
Highchairs/boosters .... ✓ ❸ .... Stroller access

WWW.IPPOLITOS.NET

ROSWELL—2270 HOLCOMB BRIDGE RD (NEAR OLD SCOTT RD); 770.992.0781; M-TH 11-10, F-SA 11-11, SU 12:30-10

Jason's Deli ★★★½☆

"...sandwiches and tasty soup... a good counter restaurant with an inexpensive kids menu... cheap prices for kids and decent food—you can get fruit instead of chips... free ice cream after their meal... lots of choices for all family members... the staff is always helping out with highchairs and everything else..."

Children's menu .... ✓ $$ .... Prices
Changing station .... × ❹ .... Customer service
Highchairs/boosters .... ✓ ❹ .... Stroller access

WWW.JASONSDELI.COM

ALPHARETTA—3070 WINDWARD PLZ (AT WINDWARD PKWY); 770.619.2300; DAILY 10-10

ALPHARETTA—7300 NORTH POINT PKY (AT CTR BRIDGE RD); 770.664.5002; DAILY 10-10

Olive Garden ★★★★☆

"...finally a place that is both kid and adult friendly... tasty Italian chain with lot's of convenient locations... the staff consistently attends to the details of dining with babies and toddlers—minimizing wait time, highchairs offered spontaneously, bread sticks brought immediately... food is served as quickly as possible... happy to create special orders... our waitress even acted as our family photographer..."

Children's menu .... ✓ $$ .... Prices
Changing station .... ✓ ❹ .... Customer service
Highchairs/boosters .... ✓ ❹ .... Stroller access

WWW.OLIVEGARDEN.COM

ROSWELL—905 HOLCOMB BRIDGE RD (AT WARSAW RD); 770.642.0395; SU-TH 11-10, F-SA 11-11

Roasters Rotisserie ★★★★☆

"...great kid menu... wonderful family feeling and the staff is very friendly... delicious grilled corn and fresh food... reasonable prices..."

Children's menu .... ✓ $$ .... Prices
Changing station .... × ❹ .... Customer service
Highchairs/boosters .... × ❸ .... Stroller access

WWW.ROASTERSFRESH.COM

ALPHARETTA—11585 JONES BRIDGE RD (AT ABBOTTS BRIDGE RD); 770.753.0055; SU-TH 11-9, F-SA 11-9:30

Ruby Tuesday ★★★½☆

"...nice variety of healthy choices on the kids' menu—turkey, spaghetti, chicken tenders... you can definitely find something healthy here... prices are on the high side, but at least everyone can find something they like... service is fast and efficient... my daughter makes a mess and they never let me clean it up... your typical chain, but it

works—you'll be happy to see ample aisle space, storage for your stroller, and attentive staff... ”

Children's menu .... ✓	$$ .... Prices
Changing station .... ✓	❹ .... Customer service
Highchairs/boosters .... ✓	❸ .... Stroller access

WWW.RUBYTUESDAY.COM

ALPHARETTA—6055 NORTH POINT PKWY (AT HAYNES BRIDGE RD); 770.667.5776; M-TH 10:30-11, F-SA 10:30-12, SU 10:30-10

Smokey Bones BBQ ★★★★☆

“*...reasonably healthy food for kids—not fried chicken fingers and fries... lots of TVs to entertain kids so adults can have a little time to talk... volume control at each table, stations often set to Nickelodeon... unique holders for car seats that cradle the seats...* ”

Children's menu .... ✓	$$$ .... Prices
Changing station .... ✓	❹ .... Customer service
Highchairs/boosters .... ✓	❹ .... Stroller access

WWW.SMOKEYBONES.COM

ALPHARETTA—7900 NORTH POINT PKWY (AT MANSELL RD); 770.518.5588; SU-TH 11-10, F-SA 11-11

DUNWOODY—4764 ASHFORD DUNWOODY RD (OFF VALLEY VIEW RD); 678.587.9087; SU-TH 11-10, F-SA 11-11

Souplantation/Sweet Tomatoes ★★★★☆

“*...you can't beat the price and selection of healthy foods... all you can eat—serve yourself soup and salad bar... lots of healthy choices plus pizza and pasta... great for picky eaters... free for 2 and under and only $3 for kids under 5... booths for comfy seating and discreet breastfeeding... helps to have another adult along since it is self serve... they always bring fresh cookies to the table and offer to refill drinks...* ”

Children's menu .... ✓	$$ .... Prices
Changing station .... ✓	❹ .... Customer service
Highchairs/boosters .... ✓	❹ .... Stroller access

WWW.SOUPLANTATION.COM

ALPHARETTA—950 NORTH POINT DR (AT NORTH POINT PKWY); 770.777.9500; SU-TH 11-9, F-SA 11-10

Taco Mac

Children's menu .... ✗	✗ .... Changing station
Highchairs/boosters .... ✗	

ALPHARETTA—8440 HOLCOMB BRIDGE RD (AT BARNWELL RD); 770.518.5565; M-SA 11-2, SU 11:30-12

TGI Friday's ★★★★☆

“*...good old American bar food with a reasonable selection for the healthier set as well... I love that the kids meal includes salad... my daughter requests the potato skins on a regular basis (which is good because they are also my favorite)... moderately priced... cheerful servers are used to the mess my kids leave behind... relaxed scene... I'd steer clear on a Friday night unless you don't mind waiting and watching the singles scene...* ”

Children's menu .... ✓	$$ .... Prices
Changing station .... ✓	❹ .... Customer service
Highchairs/boosters .... ✓	❸ .... Stroller access

WWW.TGIFRIDAYS.COM

ALPHARETTA—6250 NORTH POINT PKWY (AT NORTH POINT PL); 770.667.6010; DAILY 11:30-1:30

Village Tavern ★★★★☆

"...great food and nice patio during the warm months... excellent food... some of the staff are a little baby shy, while others go nuts of the little ones... huge menu with variety..."

Children's menu .... ✓ $$$ .... Prices
Changing station .... ✓ ❹ .... Customer service
Highchairs/boosters .... ✓ ❸ .... Stroller access

WWW.VILLAGETAVERN.COM

ALPHARETTA—11555 RAINWATER DR (AT MORRISON PKY); 770.777.6490; SU 10-11, M-TH 11-10, F-SA 11-11

South Fulton, Fayette & Clayton

★★★★★

"lila picks"

★Bugabook Creek Steak House

restaurants

Bugaboo Creek Steak House ★★★★★

"...a definite must-go place for families with children... delicious food for grown-ups and a nice selection of food on the kids' menu... all kids' meals come with ice cream... all the hustle and bustle around us kept my son entertained while we waited for our meal... the singing tree (and Moose) will either delight your child or scare the bejesus out of him... terrific service—the staff goes out of their way to cater to families... fun for birthdays—staff sings and brings out the birthday moose, which the honored one is supposed to kiss..."

Children's menu .... ✓ $$$ .... Prices
Changing station .... ✓ ❹ .... Customer service
Highchairs/boosters .... ✓ ❹ .... Stroller access

WWW.BUGABOOCREEKSTEAKHOUSE.COM

FAYETTEVILLE—1380 HWY 85 S (AT HARP RD); 770.461.2240; M-TH 11:30-10, F-SA 11:30-10:30, SU 12-9

Cracker Barrel Old Country Store ★☆☆☆☆

"...a bit on the cheesy side, but the food is surprisingly good... good old homestyle cooking... don't worry if your kids are noisy, the whole place is loud... service is quick and generally baby-friendly... very affordable... you can browse the store while you are waiting for your food... often crowded... great highchairs..."

Children's menu .... ✓ $$ .... Prices
Changing station .... ✓ ❹ .... Customer service
Highchairs/boosters .... ✓ ❸ .... Stroller access

WWW.CRACKERBARREL.COM

MORROW—1458 SOUTHLAKE PLZ DR (AT S LEE ST); 770.961.4533; SU-TH 6-10PM, F-SA 6-11PM

UNION CITY—4540 JONESBORO RD (AT SHANNON WY); 770.964.9996; SU-TH 6-10PM, F-SA 6-11PM

Folks Southern Kitchen ★★★★½

"...speedy service... busy atmosphere to drown out shrieking kids... large portions at small prices... Kids' 99 cent menu all day, everyday..."

Children's menu .... ✓ $ .... Prices
Changing station .... × ❺ .... Customer service
Highchairs/boosters .... ✓ ❹ .... Stroller access

WWW.FOLKSKITCHEN.COM

JONESBORO—6564 TARA BLVD (AT MORROW INDUSTRIAL BLVD); 770.968.8965; DAILY 11-10

Fuddruckers ★★★★☆

“...a super burger chain with fresh and tasty food... colorful and noisy with lots of distraction until the food arrives... loads of fresh toppings so that you can make your perfectly cooked burger even better... great kids deals that come with a free treat... noise not a problem in this super casual atmosphere... some locations have video games in the back which will buy you an extra half hour if you need it... low-key and very family friendly...”

Children's menu ✓ | $$ Prices
Changing station ✓ | ❹ Customer service
Highchairs/boosters ✓ | ❹ Stroller access

WWW.FUDDRUCKERS.COM

PEACHTREE CITY—200 PEACHTREE E SHOPPING CTR (AT SMOKERISE TRCE); 770.486.8841; DAILY 11-9; FREE PARKING

Italian Oven Restaurant

Children's menu ✗ | ✗ Changing station
Highchairs/boosters ✓

WWW.THEITALIANOVEN.COM

PEACHTREE CITY—100 PEACHTREE CITY E SHOPPING CTR (OFF HWY 54); 770.486.9642; SU-TH 11-10, F-SA 11-11

Joe's Crab Shack ★★★★☆

“...for the young and the young at heart... newspaper lined tables, crabs done every which way... the staff sings and dances and so do my kids... dining inside and out... this is a kick back place where we always have a good time and a good crab... plenty for the kids to choose from even if they're not into crab... lots of fun items on the walls and ceilings—keeps kids entertained until the food comes... perfect for appetizers and beer when you need a break...”

Children's menu ✓ | $$$ Prices
Changing station ✓ | ❹ Customer service
Highchairs/boosters ✓ | ❸ Stroller access

WWW.JOESCRABSHACK.COM

MORROW—1965 MT ZION RD (AT MT ZION BLVD); 770.472.0024; M-SA 11-11; FREE PARKING

La Fiesta Bar & Grill

Children's menu ✓ | ✗ Changing station
Highchairs/boosters ✓

COLLEGE PARK—1808 PHOENIX BLVD (AT W FAYETTEVILLE RD); 770.907.9691; SU-TH 5-12, F-SA 5-2

Mike & C's Family Sports Grill ★★★½☆

“...excellent food... very reasonable prices... a great kids menu... lots of TV's tuned to a variety of sports and cartoon programs... a game room for big and little kids...”

Children's menu ✓ | $$ Prices
Changing station ✓ | ❺ Customer service
Highchairs/boosters ✓ | ❸ Stroller access

PEACHTREE CITY—1200 S HWY 74 (AT DIVIDEND DR); 770.486.1982; SU-TH 7-10, F-SA 7-11

Olive Garden ★★★★☆

“...finally a place that is both kid and adult friendly... tasty Italian chain with lot's of convenient locations... the staff consistently attends to the details of dining with babies and toddlers—minimizing wait time,

highchairs offered spontaneously, bread sticks brought immediately... food is served as quickly as possible... happy to create special orders... our waitress even acted as our family photographer... ”

Children's menu ✓ — $$ Prices
Changing station ✓ — ❹ Customer service
Highchairs/boosters ✓ — ❹ Stroller access

WWW.OLIVEGARDEN.COM

MORROW—1176 MT ZION RD (AT SOUTH LAKE MALL); 770.968.4800; SU-TH 11-10, F-SA 11-11

Original Pancake House ★★★★½

“...consistently the best breakfast around... great flapjacks and appropriately-sized kids meals... food comes quickly... the most amazing apple pancakes ever... service is always friendly, but sometimes it can take a while to actually get the food... the highlight for my daughter is the free balloon when we leave... always a lot of families here with small children on the weekends, so you don't have to worry about being the only one... ”

Children's menu ✓ — $$ Prices
Changing station ✓ — ❹ Customer service
Highchairs/boosters ✓ — ❸ Stroller access

WWW.ORIGINALPANCAKEHOUSE.COM

PEACHTREE CITY—239-243 MARKETPLACE CONNECTOR (BETWEEN RT 54 AND 74); 770.486.7634; M-F 7-3, SA-SU 7-4

Roadhouse Grill ★★★★☆

“...delicious grilled steak, chicken and shrimp... pasta too... my kids love that you can throw peanut shells on the floor... nice, simple children's' menu... they also give your child a balloon when you walk in... reasonable prices and nice atmosphere—an easy choice for when you want to take a break from cooking... ”

Children's menu ✓ — $$ Prices
Changing station ✓ — ❹ Customer service
Highchairs/boosters ✓ — ❹ Stroller access

WWW.ROADHOUSEGRILL.COM

MORROW—1869 MT ZION RD (AT ALMA CT); 770.960.2526; SU-TH 11-10, F-SA 11-11

Romano's Macaroni Grill ★★★★☆

“...family oriented and tasty... noisy so nobody cares if your kids make noise... the staff goes out of their way to make families feel welcome... they even provide slings by the table for infant carriers... the noise level is pretty constant so it's not too loud, but loud enough so that crying babies don't disturb the other patrons... good kids' menu with somewhat healthy items... crayons for kids to color on the paper tablecloths... ”

Children's menu ✓ — $$$ Prices
Changing station ✓ — ❹ Customer service
Highchairs/boosters ✓ — ❹ Stroller access

WWW.MACARONIGRILL.COM

PEACHTREE CITY—200 MARKET PLACE CONNECTOR (AT HWY 54); 770.487.0379; SU-TH 11-10, F-SA 11-11

Ruby Tuesday ★★★½☆

“...nice variety of healthy choices on the kids' menu—turkey, spaghetti, chicken tenders... you can definitely find something healthy here... prices are on the high side, but at least everyone can find something they like... service is fast and efficient... my daughter makes a mess and they never let me clean it up... your typical chain, but it *works—you'll be happy to see ample aisle space, storage for your stroller, and attentive staff...*"

Children's menu ✓	$$ Prices
Changing station ✓	❹ Customer service
Highchairs/boosters ✓	❸ Stroller access

WWW.RUBYTUESDAY.COM

COLLEGE PARK—1925 SULLIVAN RD (AT AIRPORT VIEW DR); 770.994.1122; M-TH 11-11, F-SA 11-12, SU 11-10

EAST POINT—3390 CAMP CREEK PKWY (OFF N DESERT DR); 404.344.0221; M-TH 10:30-11, F-SA 10:30-12AM, SU 10:30-10

FAYETTEVILLE—1405 HWY 85 N (AT W FAYETTEVILLE RD); 770.716.6801; M-TH 10:30-11, F-SA 10:30-12, SU 10:30-10

PEACHTREE CITY—100 S PEACHTREE PKY (AT FLOY FARR PKWY); 770.487.0909; M-TH 10:30-11, F-SA 10:30-12, SU 10:30-10

Smokey Bones BBQ ★★★★☆

"*...reasonably healthy food for kids—not fried chicken fingers and fries... lots of TVs to entertain kids so adults can have a little time to talk... volume control at each table, stations often set to Nickelodeon... unique holders for car seats that cradle the seats...*"

Children's menu ✓	$$$ Prices
Changing station ✓	❹ Customer service
Highchairs/boosters ✓	❹ Stroller access

WWW.SMOKEYBONES.COM

MORROW—2971 MT ZION RD (OFF FIELDER RD); 678.479.9909; SU-TH 11-10, F-SA 11-11

PEACHTREE CITY—100 MARKET PLACE BLVD (OFF RT 54); 678.364.8460; SU-TH 11-10, F-SA 11-11

TGI Friday's ★★★★☆

"*...good old American bar food with a reasonable selection for the healthier set as well... I love that the kids meal includes salad... my daughter requests the potato skins on a regular basis (which is good because they are also my favorite)... moderately priced... cheerful servers are used to the mess my kids leave behind... relaxed scene... I'd steer clear on a Friday night unless you don't mind waiting and watching the singles scene...*"

Children's menu ✓	$$ Prices
Changing station ✓	❹ Customer service
Highchairs/boosters ✓	❸ Stroller access

WWW.TGIFRIDAYS.COM

MORROW—1881 MT ZION RD (OFF MT ZION BLVD); 770.968.3303; SU-TH 11-12, F-SA 11-1; PARKING LOT

Dekalb

★★★★★

"lila picks"

★Bugaboo Creek Steak House

★Jake's Ice Cream

★Johnny Rockets

Bugaboo Creek Steak House ★★★★★

❝*...a definite must-go place for families with children... delicious food for grown-ups and a nice selection of food on the kids' menu... all kids' meals come with ice cream... all the hustle and bustle around us kept my son entertained while we waited for our meal... the singing tree (and Moose) will either delight your child or scare the bejesus out of him... terrific service—the staff goes out of their way to cater to families... fun for birthdays—staff sings and brings out the birthday moose, which the honored one is supposed to kiss...*❞

Children's menu .... ✓ $$$ .... Prices
Changing station........................... ✓ ❹........................... Customer service
Highchairs/boosters .... ✓ ❹................................Stroller access

WWW.BUGABOOCREEKSTEAKHOUSE.COM

LITHONIA—2965 TURNER HILL RD (AT STONECREST PKWY); 678.526.5000; M-TH 11:30-10, F-SA 11:30-10:30, SU 12-9

Cici's Pizza ★★★★☆

❝*...a great buffet for easy dining with kids... pizza at the right price... kids 3 and under eat free... very crowded during lunch and dinner rushes... not much room for strollers, but they'll help you find a place to stash it... they always have birthday parties and it's usually very crowded and noisy... pizza, pasta and salad buffet for under $10...*❞

Children's menu .... ✓ $.. Prices
Changing station........................... ✓ ❹........................... Customer service
Highchairs/boosters .... ✓ ❹................................Stroller access

WWW.CICISPIZZA.COM

DECATUR—3912 N DRUID HILLS RD (AT HIGHWAY 29); 404.329.1535; SU-TH 11-10, F-SA 11-11

Crescent Moon ★★★★☆

❝*...kid-friendly... they provide crayons and color sheet... waitstaff is extremely patient with the little ones .. they will also put in an order for the little ones separately... would not recommend going on a Sunday morning—it's way packed... the best brunch in town...*❞

Children's menu .... ✓ $$ .... Prices
Changing station........................... × ❹........................... Customer service
Highchairs/boosters .... ✓ ❸................................Stroller access

WWW.CRESCENTMOONEATERY.COM

DECATUR—174 W PONCE DE LEON AVE (AT COMMERCE DR); 404.377.5623; SU-M 7:30-3, T-F 7:30-9, SA 7:30-3 5:30-9:30

Fuddruckers ★★★★☆

"...a super burger chain with fresh and tasty food... colorful and noisy with lots of distraction until the food arrives... loads of fresh toppings so that you can make your perfectly cooked burger even better... great kids deals that come with a free treat... noise not a problem in this super casual atmosphere... some locations have video games in the back which will buy you an extra half hour if you need it... low-key and very family friendly..."

Children's menu	✓	$$	Prices
Changing station	✓	❹	Customer service
Highchairs/boosters	✓	❹	Stroller access

WWW.FUDDRUCKERS.COM

TUCKER—3953 LAVISTA RD (AT EVELYN ST); 770.493.4014; SU-TH 11-9, F-SA 11-10; FREE PARKING

Jake's Ice Cream & Coffeteria ★★★★★

"...the only way ice cream should be done—these guys know what they're doing... luscious ice cream and a bunch of locations make this a winner... there is plenty of room for kids to play while you dine or hangout... I like that they have a sign on the door saying they support breastfeeding moms... something for everyone to eat—soups, salads and sandwiches and of course, ice cream..."

Children's menu	×	$$$	Prices
Changing station	×	❸	Customer service
Highchairs/boosters	✓	❸	Stroller access

DECATUR—2144 N DECATUR RD (AT CLAIREMONT AVE); 404.633.4066; M-TH 7-10, F 7-11, SA 12-11, SU 12-10

Jake's Ice Cream ★★★★★

"...the only way ice cream should be done—these guys know what they're doing... luscious ice cream and a bunch of locations make this a winner... there is plenty of room for kids to play while you dine or hangout... I like that they have a sign on the door saying they support breastfeeding moms... something for everyone to eat—soups, salads and sandwiches and of course, ice cream..."

Children's menu	×	$$	Prices
Changing station	×	❹	Customer service
Highchairs/boosters	✓	❹	Stroller access

DECATUR—129 CHURCH ST (AT W HOWARD AVE); 404.377.9300; SU-TH 11-10, F-SA 11-11

Jason's Deli ★★★½☆

"...sandwiches and tasty soup... a good counter restaurant with an inexpensive kids menu... cheap prices for kids and decent food—you can get fruit instead of chips... free ice cream after their meal... lots of choices for all family members... the staff is always helping out with highchairs and everything else..."

Children's menu	✓	$$	Prices
Changing station	×	❹	Customer service
Highchairs/boosters	✓	❹	Stroller access

WWW.JASONSDELI.COM

TUCKER—4073 LAVISTA RD (AT WEEMS RD); 770.493.4020; DAILY 10-10

Johnny Rockets ★★★★★

"...burgers, fries and a shake served up in a 50's style diner... we love the singing waiters—they're always good for a giggle... my daughter is enthralled with the juke box and straw dispenser... sit at the counter

and watch the cooks prepare the food... simple, satisfying and always a hit with the little ones... ”*

Children's menu ✓	$$ Prices
Changing station ×	❹ Customer service
Highchairs/boosters ✓	❸ Stroller access

WWW.JOHNNYROCKETS.COM

LITHONIA—2929 TURNER HILL RD (THE MALL AT STONE CREST); 770.484.3843; M-SA 11-9, SU 12-6; FREE PARKING

Mama Mia's Pasta & Pizza

Children's menu ×	× Changing station
Highchairs/boosters ✓	

WWW.RESTAURANT.COM

STONE MOUNTAIN—961 MAIN ST (AT JAMES B RIVERS MEM DR); 770.469.1199; M-TH 5-9, F-SA 5-9:30, SU 12:30-4, TH-F11:30-2, SA 12-3

Mellow Mushroom ★★★★☆

“...pizzas, salads, calzones and hoagies... simply delicious laidback atmosphere with a nice mellow vibe... amusing characters and fun setting... always a hit with my kids... friendly, efficient service... our mom's group meets here every week and the staff is terrific... kids love looking at the fun decor... ”

Children's menu ✓	$$ Prices
Changing station ×	❹ Customer service
Highchairs/boosters ✓	❸ Stroller access

WWW.MELLOWMUSHROOM.COM

DECATUR—265 PONCE DE LEON PL (AT W PONCE DE LEON AVE); 404.370.0008; SU-TH 11-11, F-SA 11-12

Melton's App & Tap

Children's menu ✓	× Changing station
Highchairs/boosters ✓	

DECATUR—2500 N DECATUR RD (AT SCOTT BLVD); 404.634.9112; M-W 11:30-12, TH-SA 11:30-1, SU 11:30-11

Mexico City Gourmet ★★★☆☆

“...a cut above the usual Mexican restaurant... very personalized feeling—there are pictures of customers all over the walls... very tasty rice and beans as well as food for adults... ”

Children's menu ✓	$$ Prices
Changing station ×	❹ Customer service
Highchairs/boosters ✓	❹ Stroller access

WWW.MEXICOCITYGOURMET.COM

DECATUR—2134 N DECATUR RD (AT CLAIRMONT RD); 404.634.1128; M-TH 11-10, F-SA 11-10:30, SU 10:30-9

Moe's Southwest Grill ★★★½☆

“...fresh Mex food—burritos, quesedillas and tacos... there always are a ton of babies and kids there... if you want a drink other than juice or soda, bring your own sippy cup... tasty, good quality, cheap chow that satisfies both young and old... kids' meals for less than $3 and free on Monday nights... they only serve sodas and fruit punch for the kids... ”

Children's menu ✓	$$ Prices
Changing station ✓	❹ Customer service
Highchairs/boosters ✓	❹ Stroller access

WWW.MOES.COM

TUCKER—4450 HUGH HOWELL RD (AT FULLER WAY); 770.934.5555; DAILY 11-9

Olive Garden ★★★★☆

"...finally a place that is both kid and adult friendly... tasty Italian chain with lot's of convenient locations... the staff consistently attends to the details of dining with babies and toddlers—minimizing wait time, highchairs offered spontaneously, bread sticks brought immediately... food is served as quickly as possible... happy to create special orders... our waitress even acted as our family photographer..."

Children's menu .... ✓ $$ .... Prices
Changing station .... ✓ ❹ .... Customer service
Highchairs/boosters .... ✓ ❹ .... Stroller access

WWW.OLIVEGARDEN.COM

LITHONIA—3011 TURNER HILL RD (AT THE MALL AT STONECREST); 770.482.4600; SU-TH 11-10, F-SA 11-11; MALL PARKING

TUCKER—2077 NORTHLAKE PKWY (AT E EXCHANGE PL); 770.938.6904; SU-TH 11-10, F-SA 11-11

Original Pancake House ★★★★½

"...consistently the best breakfast around... great flapjacks and appropriately-sized kids meals... food comes quickly... the most amazing apple pancakes ever... service is always friendly, but sometimes it can take a while to actually get the food... the highlight for my daughter is the free balloon when we leave... always a lot of families here with small children on the weekends, so you don't have to worry about being the only one..."

Children's menu .... ✓ $$ .... Prices
Changing station .... ✓ ❹ .... Customer service
Highchairs/boosters .... ✓ ❸ .... Stroller access

WWW.ORIGINALPANCAKEHOUSE.COM

STONE MOUNTAIN—5099 MEMORIAL DR (OFF RAYS RD); 404.292.6914; M-F 7-3, SA-SU 7-4

Ruby Tuesday ★★★½☆

"...nice variety of healthy choices on the kids' menu—turkey, spaghetti, chicken tenders... you can definitely find something healthy here... prices are on the high side, but at least everyone can find something they like... service is fast and efficient... my daughter makes a mess and they never let me clean it up... your typical chain, but it works—you'll be happy to see ample aisle space, storage for your stroller, and attentive staff..."

Children's menu .... ✓ $$ .... Prices
Changing station .... ✓ ❹ .... Customer service
Highchairs/boosters .... ✓ ❸ .... Stroller access

WWW.RUBYTUESDAY.COM

DECATUR—158 W PONCE DE LEON AVE (OFF CLAIREMONT AVE); 404.687.3389; M-TH 11-10, F-SA 11-11, SU 11-9

LITHONIA—3010 PANOLA RD (AT THOMPSON MILL RD); 678.418.0847; SU-TH 11-11, F-SA 11-12AM

Smokey Bones BBQ ★★★★☆

"...reasonably healthy food for kids—not fried chicken fingers and fries... lots of TVs to entertain kids so adults can have a little time to talk... volume control at each table, stations often set to Nickelodeon... unique holders for car seats that cradle the seats..."

Children's menu .... ✓ $$$ .... Prices
Changing station .... ✓ ❹ .... Customer service
Highchairs/boosters .... ✓ ❹ .... Stroller access

WWW.SMOKEYBONES.COM

LITHONIA—2930 STONECREST CIR (OFF PURPLE HEART HWY); 770.484.0020; SU-TH 11-10, F-SA 11-11

Sushi Avenue

Children's menu .... ✗ ✗ .... Changing station
Highchairs/boosters .... ✓

DECATUR—308 W PONCE DE LEON AV (AT TRINITIY PL); 404.378.8448; M-F 10-10, SA 5-10:30, SU 5-9:30

Gwinnett

★★★★★

"lila picks"

★Bugabook Creek Steak House

★Johnny Rockets

Barnacle's Seafood Oysters & Sports ★★★½☆

"...a fun sports bar with good prices for kids meal... plenty of beer and sports for adults, while tots can run around... each child leaves with a Frisbee... games and coloring books for children help to pass the waiting time..."

Children's menu .... ✓ | $$ .... Prices
Changing station .... ✓ | ❺ .... Customer service
Highchairs/boosters .... ✓ | ❹ .... Stroller access

WWW.BARNACLES.NET

DULUTH—2125 MARKET ST NW (AT GWINNETT PL MALL); 770.418.9510; M-SA 11-2, SU 12-12; MALL PARKING

Buffalo's Cafe

Children's menu .... ✓ | ✓ .... Changing station
Highchairs/boosters .... ✓

WWW.BUFFALOSSOUTHWESTCAFE.COM

BUFORD—3333 BUFORD DR NE (AT WOODWARD CROSSING BLVD); 678.482.0398; SU-TH 11-10, F-SA 11-11

Bugaboo Creek Steak House ★★★★★

"...a definite must-go place for families with children... delicious food for grown-ups and a nice selection of food on the kids' menu... all kids' meals come with ice cream... all the hustle and bustle around us kept my son entertained while we waited for our meal... the singing tree (and Moose) will either delight your child or scare the bejesus out of him... terrific service—the staff goes out of their way to cater to families... fun for birthdays—staff sings and brings out the birthday moose, which the honored one is supposed to kiss..."

Children's menu .... ✓ | $$$ .... Prices
Changing station .... ✓ | ❹ .... Customer service
Highchairs/boosters .... ✓ | ❹ .... Stroller access

WWW.BUGABOOCREEKSTEAKHOUSE.COM

DULUTH—3505 SATELLITE BLVD (AT GWINNETT PL MALL); 770.476.1500; M-TH 11:30-10, F-SA 11:30-10:30, SU 12-9; MALL PARKING

Caribbean Kitchen

Children's menu .... × | × .... Changing station
Highchairs/boosters .... ✓

NORCROSS—5675 JIMMY CARTER BLVD NW (OFF VETERANS PKY); 770.582.1791; DAILY 10-10

Cracker Barrel Old Country Store ★★★★½

"...a bit on the cheesy side, but the food is surprisingly good... good old homestyle cooking... don't worry if your kids are noisy, the whole place is loud... service is quick and generally baby-friendly... very affordable... you can browse the store while you are waiting for your food... often crowded... great highchairs..."

Children's menu	✓	$$	Prices
Changing station	✓	4	Customer service
Highchairs/boosters	✓	3	Stroller access

WWW.CRACKERBARREL.COM

NORCROSS—6175 MCDONOUGH DR (OFF JIMMY CARTER BLVD); 770.446.1313; SU-TH 6-10, F-SA 6-11

SUWANEE—75 GWINCO BLVD (AT LAWENCEVILLE SUWANEE RD); 770.932.5692; SU-TH 6-10, F-SA 6-11

El Jinete Mexican Restaurant ★★★☆☆

"...customer service is great... they always talk to my son, and try to get him to laugh... they will fill his sippy cup, bring extra plates and napkins with out any fuss... they are just so sweet to the children, I have no worries taking my son there..."

Children's menu	×	$	Prices
Changing station	×	5	Customer service
Highchairs/boosters	✓	4	Stroller access

SNELLVILLE—3303 CENTERVILLE HWY (AT ZOAR RD SW); 770.982.1539; DAILY 10-11

El Porton Mexican Restaurant ★☆☆☆☆

"...friendly service and servers are very welcoming toward kids... enjoyable low-key atmosphere... don't worry about disturbing the other diners, many have small kids with them, too... great prices and decent portion sizes ..."

Children's menu	✓	$$	Prices
Changing station	×	4	Customer service
Highchairs/boosters	✓	4	Stroller access

DULUTH—2640 OLD PEACHTREE RD (AT PEACHTREE WALK); 678.205.5042; M-SA 11-10; FREE PARKING

Fazoli's ★★★½☆

"...quick, easy and satisfying Italian food... spacious and comfortable... free breadsticks to keep little minds in check before the meatballs and pasta arrive... a nice step up from the easy fast-food trap... service is quick and the food is good..."

Children's menu	✓	$$	Prices
Changing station	✓	4	Customer service
Highchairs/boosters	✓	3	Stroller access

WWW.FAZOLIS.COM

DULUTH—5970 STATE BRIDGE RD (AT MEDLOCK BRIDGE RD); 770.495.2438; SU-TH 10:30-10, F-SA 10:30-11; FREE PARKING

LAWRENCEVILLE—890 LAWRENCEVILLE-SUWANEE RD (BTWN DULUTH HWY & GREENVALE RD); 770.513.8444; SU-TH 10:30-10, F-SA 10:30-11; FREE PARKING

SNELLVILLE—1895 SCENIC HWY (AT TREE LN SW); 770.736.5041; SU-TH 10:30-10, F-SA 10:30-11; FREE PARKING

Flying Machine ★★★★★

"...watch the airplanes land... eat a burger... accomodating for small children... a bit slow with large groups... eat outside on the patio for the best view..."

Children's menu	✓	$	Prices
Changing station	✗	❹	Customer service
Highchairs/boosters	✓	❺	Stroller access

WWW.THEFLYINGMACHINE.COM

LAWRENCEVILLE—510 BRISCOE BLVD (AT GWINNETT CNTY AIRPORT); 770.962.2262; M-SA 11-10, SU 11-3

Fuddruckers ★★★★☆

"...a super burger chain with fresh and tasty food... colorful and noisy with lots of distraction until the food arrives... loads of fresh toppings so that you can make your perfectly cooked burger even better... great kids deals that come with a free treat... noise not a problem in this super casual atmosphere... some locations have video games in the back which will buy you an extra half hour if you need it... low-key and very family friendly..."

Children's menu	✓	$$	Prices
Changing station	✓	❹	Customer service
Highchairs/boosters	✓	❹	Stroller access

WWW.FUDDRUCKERS.COM

DULUTH—2180 MERCHANTS WY (AT MARKET ST); 770.497.9190; SU-TH 11-9, F-SA 11-10

SNELLVILLE—1915 SCENIC HWY SW (AT RONALD REGAN PKWY); 770.978.9951; SU-TH 11-9, F-SA 11-10:30

Golden Corral ★★★½☆

"...terrific place for new parents and kids of all ages... huge buffet and kids under 3 eat free... a great place for little eaters to try a lot of new foods... perfect for picky eaters... friendly, relaxed atmosphere... okay for kids to run around a little... reasonable prices..."

Children's menu	✓	$$	Prices
Changing station	✓	❹	Customer service
Highchairs/boosters	✓	❹	Stroller access

WWW.GOLDENCORRAL.COM

BUFORD—4020 BUFORD DR (AT HORIZON PKY); 770.831.3500; M-TH 11-10, F-SU 7:30-10:30

DULUTH—3270 SATELLITE BLVD (AT GWINNETT PL DR); 770.495.7999; M-TH 11-10, F-SU 7:30-10:30

LAWRENCEVILLE—2155 RIVERSIDE PKY (AT OX BRIDGE WAY); 678.442.8677; M-TH 11-10, F-SU 7:30-10:30

LOGANVILLE—3888 STONE MOUNTAIN HWY (AT MCDANIEL BRIDGE RD); 770.985.9700; M-SA 10-9; FREE PARKING

Jason's Deli ★★★½☆

"...sandwiches and tasty soup... a good counter restaurant with an inexpensive kids menu... cheap prices for kids and decent food—you can get fruit instead of chips... free ice cream after their meal... lots of choices for all family members... the staff is always helping out with highchairs and everything else..."

Children's menu	✓	$$	Prices
Changing station	✗	❹	Customer service
Highchairs/boosters	✓	❹	Stroller access

WWW.JASONSDELI.COM

NORCROSS—5131 PEACHTREE PKWY (AT WINDWARD PKWY); 770.368.9440; DAILY 10-10

Joe's Crab Shack ★★★★☆

"...for the young and the young at heart... newspaper lined tables, crabs done every which way... the staff sings and dances and so do my kids... dining inside and out... this is a kick back place where we always

have a good time and a good crab... plenty for the kids to choose from even if they're not into crab... lots of fun items on the walls and ceilings—keeps kids entertained until the food comes... perfect for appetizers and beer when you need a break... ”

Children's menu ✓ | $$$ Prices
Changing station ✓ | ❹ Customer service
Highchairs/boosters ✓ | ❸ Stroller access

WWW.JOESCRABSHACK.COM

DULUTH—1590 PLEASANT HILL RD (AT ROGER BLVD NW); 770.381.6333; SU-TH 11-10, F-SA 11-11

LILBURN—4300 US HWY 78 (AT ROSE RD NW); 770.736.2900; M-SA 11-11; FREE PARKING

Johnny Rockets ★★★★★

“...burgers, fries and a shake served up in a 50's style diner... we love the singing waiters—they're always good for a giggle... my daughter is enthralled with the juke box and straw dispenser... sit at the counter and watch the cooks prepare the food... simple, satisfying and always a hit with the little ones... ”

Children's menu ✓ | $$ Prices
Changing station × | ❹ Customer service
Highchairs/boosters ✓ | ❸ Stroller access

WWW.JOHNNYROCKETS.COM

DULUTH—2100 PLEASANT HILL RD (AT GWINNETT MALL); 770.622.4478; M-SA 11-11; FREE PARKING

LAWRENCEVILLE—5900 SUGARLOAF PKWY (AT DISCOVER MILLS); 678.847.5800; M-SA 11-11; FREE PARKING

Longhorn Steakhouse ★★★★☆

“...for meat and seafood lovers... the staff totally gets 'the kid thing' here... they bring out snacks, get the orders going quickly, and frequently check back for things like new spoons and napkins... lots of things for baby to look at... get there early or call ahead to avoid the wait... ”

Children's menu ✓ | $$$ Prices
Changing station ✓ | ❹ Customer service
Highchairs/boosters ✓ | ❸ Stroller access

WWW.LONGHORNSTEAKHOUSE.COM

BUFORD—1800 MALL OF GEORGIA BLVD (AT MALL OF GEORGIA); 678.482.7750; SU-TH 11-10, F-SA 11-11

Olive Garden ★★★★☆

“...finally a place that is both kid and adult friendly... tasty Italian chain with lot's of convenient locations... the staff consistently attends to the details of dining with babies and toddlers—minimizing wait time, highchairs offered spontaneously, bread sticks brought immediately... food is served as quickly as possible... happy to create special orders... our waitress even acted as our family photographer... ”

Children's menu ✓ | $$ Prices
Changing station ✓ | ❹ Customer service
Highchairs/boosters ✓ | ❹ Stroller access

WWW.OLIVEGARDEN.COM

BUFORD—3220 BUFORD DR (AT MALL OF GEORGIA); 678.546.1778; SU-TH 11-10, F-SA 11-11; MALL PARKING

DULUTH—3565 MALL BLVD (AT GWINNETT PL MALL); 770.497.0594; SU-TH 11-10, F-SA 11-11; MALL PARKING

Original Pancake House ★★★★½

“...consistently the best breakfast around... great flapjacks and appropriately-sized kids meals... food comes quickly... the most *amazing apple pancakes ever... service is always friendly, but sometimes it can take a while to actually get the food... the highlight for my daughter is the free balloon when we leave... always a lot of families here with small children on the weekends, so you don't have to worry about being the only one...* ”

Children's menu ✓ — $$ Prices
Changing station ✓ — ❹ Customer service
Highchairs/boosters ✓ — ❸ Stroller access

WWW.ORIGINALPANCAKEHOUSE.COM

DULUTH—3665 CLUB DR (AT PLEASANT HILL RD); 770.925.0065

Patio Cafe & Bakery

Children's menu ✗ — ✗ Changing station
Highchairs/boosters ✓

DULUTH—5950 STATE BRIDGE RD (AT MEDLOCK BRIDGE RD); 770.418.9300; M-F 8:30AM-8PM, SA 10AM-3PM

PF Chang's China Bistro ★★★★☆

“*...unique combination of Chinese cuisine, attentive service, wine, and tempting desserts all served in a stylish, high-energy bistro... waiters serve custom sauces table side, guiding us through the menu or suggesting dishes to enhance our meal... friendly, knowledgeable service staff and attention to detail are a winning combination...*”

Children's menu ✗ — $$$ Prices
Changing station ✗ — ❹ Customer service
Highchairs/boosters ✓ — ❸ Stroller access

WWW.PFCHANGS.COM

BUFORD—3333 BUFORD DR (AT MALL OF GEORGIA); 678.546.9005; SU-TH 11-10, F-SA 11-12

Roadhouse Grill ★★★★☆

“*...delicious grilled steak, chicken and shrimp... pasta too... my kids love that you can throw peanut shells on the floor... nice, simple childrens' menu... they also give your child a balloon when you walk in... reasonable prices and nice atmosphere—an easy choice for when you want to take a break from cooking...*”

Children's menu ✓ — $$ Prices
Changing station ✓ — ❹ Customer service
Highchairs/boosters ✓ — ❹ Stroller access

WWW.ROADHOUSEGRILL.COM

DULUTH—2000 SATELLITE BLVD (AT SUGARLOAF PKY); 770.476.0420; SU-TH 11-10, F-SA 11-11

DULUTH—3740 SHACKLEFORD RD (AT PINELAND RD); 770.935.5801; SU-TH 11-10, F-SA 11-11

Romano's Macaroni Grill ★★★★☆

“*...family oriented and tasty... noisy so nobody cares if your kids make noise... the staff goes out of their way to make families feel welcome... they even provide slings by the table for infant carriers... the noise level is pretty constant so it's not too loud, but loud enough so that crying babies don't disturb the other patrons... good kids' menu with somewhat healthy items... crayons for kids to color on the paper tablecloths...*”

Children's menu ✓ — $$$ Prices
Changing station ✓ — ❹ Customer service
Highchairs/boosters ✓ — ❹ Stroller access

WWW.MACARONIGRILL.COM

BUFORD—3226 BUFORD DR (AT MALL OF GEORGIA); 678.714.0049; SU-TH 11-10, F-SA 11-11

DULUTH—9700 MEDLOCK BRIDGE RD (AT STATE BRIDGE RD); 770.495.7855; SU-TH 11-10, F-SA 11-11

Ruby Tuesday ★★★½☆

"...nice variety of healthy choices on the kids' menu—turkey, spaghetti, chicken tenders... you can definitely find something healthy here... prices are on the high side, but at least everyone can find something they like... service is fast and efficient... my daughter makes a mess and they never let me clean it up... your typical chain, but it works—you'll be happy to see ample aisle space, storage for your stroller, and attentive staff..."

Children's menu ✓	$$ Prices
Changing station ✓	4 Customer service
Highchairs/boosters ✓	3 Stroller access

WWW.RUBYTUESDAY.COM

BUFORD—3333 BUFORD DR (AT MALL OF GEORGIA); 770.271.0932; M-TH 10:30-11, F-SA 10:30-12, SU 10:30-10

DULUTH—2100 PLEASANT HILL RD (AT GWINNETT PL MALL); 770.476.0388; M-TH 10:30-10, F-SA 10:30-11, SU 10:30-9

DULUTH—3580 PEACHTREE INDUSTRIAL BLVD (OFF HOWELL FERRY RD); 770.623.4467; M-TH 10:30-10, F-SA 10:30-11

LAWRENCEVILLE—1455 PLEASANT HILL RD (AT CLUB DR); 770.921.0507; SU-TH 11-11, F-SA 11-12

LOGANVILLE—4121 ATLANTA HWY (AT THERESA LN SW); 678.957.6243; M-TH 10:30-11, F-SA 10:30-12, SU 10:30-10

SNELLVILLE—3090 HWY 78 (AT HIGHPOINT RD); 770.979.7181; M-TH 10:30-11, F-SA 10:30-12, SU 10:30-10

Ryan's Family Steakhouse ★★½☆☆

"...great location, terrific selection and great food, especially those steaks..."

Children's menu ✓	$ Prices
Changing station ✓	1 Customer service
Highchairs/boosters ✓	3 Stroller access

WWW.RYANS.COM

BUFORD—3843 BUFORD DR (AT PLUNKETTS RD); 770.831.1066; SU-TH 10:30-9:30, F-SA 10:45-10:30

Smokey Bones BBQ ★★★★☆

"...reasonably healthy food for kids—not fried chicken fingers and fries... lots of TVs to entertain kids so adults can have a little time to talk... volume control at each table, stations often set to Nickelodeon... unique holders for car seats that cradle the seats..."

Children's menu ✓	$$$ Prices
Changing station ✓	4 Customer service
Highchairs/boosters ✓	4 Stroller access

WWW.SMOKEYBONES.COM

DULUTH—1555 PLEASANT HILL RD (OFF CLUB DR); 678.380.9002; SU-TH 11-10, F-SA 11-11

Souplantation/Sweet Tomatoes ★★★★☆

"...you can't beat the price and selection of healthy foods... all you can eat—serve yourself soup and salad bar... lots of healthy choices plus pizza and pasta... great for picky eaters... free for 2 and under and only $3 for kids under 5... booths for comfy seating and discreet breastfeeding... helps to have another adult along since it is self serve... they always bring fresh cookies to the table and offer to refill drinks..."

Children's menu .... ✓ $$ .... Prices
Changing station .... ✓ ❹ .... Customer service
Highchairs/boosters .... ✓ ❹ .... Stroller access

WWW.SOUPLANTATION.COM

DULUTH—3505 MALL BLVD (AT RING RD); 770.418.1148; SU-TH 11-9, F-SA 11-10; MALL PARKING

Stevi B's Pizza ★★★★★

"...better pizza than other buffet places... be adventurous and try the unusual flavors, i.e. Baked Potato, BLT, Taco—they are the best... fresh salad bar... great game room complete with tickets and prizes..."

Children's menu .... ✓ $ .... Prices
Changing station .... ✓ ❺ .... Customer service
Highchairs/boosters .... ✓ ❺ .... Stroller access

DULUTH—1500 PLEASANT HILL RD NW (AT CLUB DR); 770.935.0735; M-TH 11-9, F-SA 11-10, SU 11-9; PARKING IN FRONT OF BLDG

TGI Friday's ★★★★☆

"...good old American bar food with a reasonable selection for the healthier set as well... I love that the kids meal includes salad... my daughter requests the potato skins on a regular basis (which is good because they are also my favorite)... moderately priced... cheerful servers are used to the mess my kids leave behind... relaxed scene... I'd steer clear on a Friday night unless you don't mind waiting and watching the singles scene..."

Children's menu .... ✓ $$ .... Prices
Changing station .... ✓ ❹ .... Customer service
Highchairs/boosters .... ✓ ❸ .... Stroller access

WWW.TGIFRIDAYS.COM

BUFORD—1795 MALL OF GEORGIA BLVD (AT BUFORD DR); 678.482.1800; M-TH 11-1, F-SA 11-2, SU 11-12; MALL PARKING

DULUTH—1695 PLEASANT HILL RD (AT CLUB DR NW); 770.381.8342; DAILY 11:30-1:30

Wild Wing Cafe

Children's menu .... ✓ ✓ .... Changing station
Highchairs/boosters .... ✓

WWW.WILDWINGCAFE.COM

SUWANEE—3265 LAWRENCEVILLE SUWANEE RD (AT SATELITE BLVD NE); 770.945.9090; M-SA 11-2, SU 11-12

Cobb & Douglas

★★★★★

"lila picks"

- ★Bugabook Creek Steak House
- ★Ippolito's Family Style Italian
- ★Johnny Rockets

Bugaboo Creek Steak House ★★★★★

"...a definite must-go place for families with children... delicious food for grown-ups and a nice selection of food on the kids' menu... all kids' meals come with ice cream... all the hustle and bustle around us kept my son entertained while we waited for our meal... the singing tree (and Moose) will either delight your child or scare the bejesus out of him... terrific service—the staff goes out of their way to cater to families... fun for birthdays—staff sings and brings out the birthday moose, which the honored one is supposed to kiss..."

Children's menu ✓ | $$$ Prices
Changing station ✓ | 4 Customer service
Highchairs/boosters ✓ | 4 Stroller access

WWW.BUGABOOCREEKSTEAKHOUSE.COM

KENNESAW—840 ERNEST BARRETT PKWY (AT COBB PLACE PKWY); 770.919.2200; M-TH 11-10, F-SA 11-11, SU 11-9; PARKING LOT

Cici's Pizza ★★★★☆

"...a great buffet for easy dining with kids... pizza at the right price... kids 3 and under eat free... very crowded during lunch and dinner rushes... not much room for strollers, but they'll help you find a place to stash it... they always have birthday parties and it's usually very crowded and noisy... pizza, pasta and salad buffet for under $10..."

Children's menu ✓ | $ Prices
Changing station ✓ | 4 Customer service
Highchairs/boosters ✓ | 4 Stroller access

WWW.CICISPIZZA.COM

AUSTELL—3999 AUSTELL RD SW (AT EAST-WEST CONNECTOR); 770.745.9779; SU-TH 11-10, F-SA 11-11

KENNESAW—3161 COBB PKWY NW (AT PARK FOREST DR NW); 770.529.0900; SU-TH 11-9, F-SA 11-10

Cracker Barrel Old Country Store ★★★½☆

"...a bit on the cheesy side, but the food is surprisingly good... good old home style cooking... don't worry if your kids are noisy, the whole place is loud... service is quick and generally baby-friendly... very affordable... you can browse the store while you are waiting for your food... often crowded... great highchairs..."

Children's menu ✓ | $$ Prices

Changing station ✓ | ❹ Customer service
Highchairs/boosters ✓ | ❸ Stroller access

WWW.CRACKERBARREL.COM

DOUGLASVILLE—5483 WESTMORELAND PLZ (AT FAIRBURN RD); 770.949.0999; SU-TH 6-10, F-SA 6-11

KENNESAW—3389 GEORGE BUSBEE PKWY NW (AT CHASTAIN RD NW); 770.429.1524; SU-TH 6-10, F-SA 6-11

MARIETTA—2150 DELK RD SE (AT FRANKLIN RD SE); 770.951.2602; SU-TH 6-10, F-SA 6-11

Dave & Buster's ★★★☆☆

"...lively bar and dining room paired with an adult style arcade... games and television throughout the restaurant give you plenty to keep your eyes on... decent food... can get a little loud and smoky for your average tot... most games are geared for adults... keep your eyes on your kids—it gets crowded..."

Children's menu ✓ | $$$ Prices
Changing station ✓ | ❹ Customer service
Highchairs/boosters ✓ | ❹ Stroller access

WWW.DAVEANDBUSTERS.COM

MARIETTA—2215 D & B DR (AT DALLAS RD); 770.951.5554; SU-TH 11:30-12, F-SA 11:30-2

Fuddruckers ★★★★☆

"...a super burger chain with fresh and tasty food... colorful and noisy with lots of distraction until the food arrives... loads of fresh toppings so that you can make your perfectly cooked burger even better... great kids deals that come with a free treat... noise not a problem in this super casual atmosphere... some locations have video games in the back which will buy you an extra half hour if you need it... low-key and very family friendly..."

Children's menu ✓ | $$ Prices
Changing station ✓ | ❹ Customer service
Highchairs/boosters ✓ | ❹ Stroller access

WWW.FUDDRUCKERS.COM

KENNESAW—2708 TOWN CTR DR (AT BUSBEE PKY); 770.424.8423; SU-TH 11-9, F-SA 11-10

MARIETTA—3000 WINDY HILL RD SE (AT SPECTRUM CIR SE); 770.980.9863; SU-TH 11-9, F-SA 11-10

Golden Corral ★★★½☆

"...terrific place for new parents and kids of all ages... huge buffet and kids under 3 eat free... a great place for little eaters to try a lot of new foods... perfect for picky eaters... friendly, relaxed atmosphere... okay for kids to run around a little... reasonable prices..."

Children's menu ✓ | $$ Prices
Changing station ✓ | ❹ Customer service
Highchairs/boosters ✓ | ❹ Stroller access

WWW.GOLDENCORRAL.COM

KENNESAW—700 ERNEST W BARRETT PKY (AT COBB PLACE BLVD); 770.428.6770; M-TH 11-10, F-SU 7:30-10:30

International House Of Pancakes ★★★½☆

"...perfect for a Sunday morning pancake feast... pancakes of all types and flavors, not to mention the variety of syrups... they love the babies and are quick with the juice and food... kids' menu with crayons... you may have to wait for a table... some locations are open 24 hours, which is convenient when my baby wakes up at ridiculous hours..."

Children's menu	✓	$$	Prices
Changing station	✓	❹	Customer service
Highchairs/boosters	✓	❹	Stroller access

WWW.IHOP.COM

AUSTELL—1870 E W CONNECTOR (AT CHAMPION DR); 678.945.4311; OPEN 24 HRS

Ippolito's Family Style Italian Restaurant ★★★★★

"...a great neighborhood 'joint' with a welcoming ambiance... they even give kids pizza dough to play with while they are waiting... varied menu and fast service... although it doesn't look like a classic baby-friendly place, the staff is fantastic with kids and the food is awesome... good food for adults and easy atmosphere for kids..."

Children's menu	✓	$$	Prices
Changing station	×	❹	Customer service
Highchairs/boosters	✓	❸	Stroller access

WWW.IPPOLITOS.NET

KENNESAW—425 BARRETT PKWY NW (AT TOWN CTR AT COBB); 770.514.8500; M-TH 11-10, F-SA 11-11, SU 11-10

Italian Oven Restaurant

Children's menu	✓	×	Changing station
Highchairs/boosters	✓		

WWW.THEITALIANOVEN.COM

AUSTELL—1355 EAST WEST CONNECTOR (OFF FLOYD RD); 770.948.5777; SU-TH 11-10, F-SA 11-11

Joe's Crab Shack ★★★★☆

"...for the young and the young at heart... newspaper lined tables, crabs done every which way... the staff sings and dances and so do my kids... dining inside and out... this is a kick back place where we always have a good time and a good crab... plenty for the kids to choose from even if they're not into crab... lots of fun items on the walls and ceilings—keeps kids entertained until the food comes... perfect for appetizers and beer when you need a break..."

Children's menu	✓	$$$	Prices
Changing station	✓	❹	Customer service
Highchairs/boosters	✓	❸	Stroller access

WWW.JOESCRABSHACK.COM

DOUGLASVILLE—2868 CHAPEL HILL RD (AT ARBOR PLACE BLVD); 770.947.5990; SU-TH 11-10, F-SA 11-11; FREE PARKING

KENNESAW—2501 COBB PLACE LN NW (AT COBB PLACE BLVD NW); 770.429.7703; SU-TH 11-10, F-SA 11-11

Johnny Rockets ★★★★★

"...burgers, fries and a shake served up in a 50's style diner... we love the singing waiters—they're always good for a giggle... my daughter is enthralled with the juke box and straw dispenser... sit at the counter and watch the cooks prepare the food... simple, satisfying and always a hit with the little ones..."

Children's menu	✓	$$	Prices
Changing station	×	❹	Customer service
Highchairs/boosters	✓	❸	Stroller access

WWW.JOHNNYROCKETS.COM

DOUGLASVILLE—6700 DOUGLAS BLVD (AT ARBOR PLACE); 770.577.2636; M-TH 11-9, F-SA 11-10, SU 11-8; FREE PARKING

MARIETTA—4475 ROSWELL RD (AT E COBB DR); 770.509.0377; M-TH 9-10, F-SA 9-11, SU 9-9

Life Grocery And Cafe

Children's menu .... ✗   ✗ .... Changing station
Highchairs/boosters .... ✗

WWW.LIFEGROCERY.COM

MARIETTA—1453 ROSWELL RD (AT POWERS FERRY RD SE); 770.977.9583; M-SA 9-8, SU 11-6

Olive Garden ★★★★☆

"...finally a place that is both kid and adult friendly... tasty Italian chain with lot's of convenient locations... the staff consistently attends to the details of dining with babies and toddlers—minimizing wait time, highchairs offered spontaneously, bread sticks brought immediately... food is served as quickly as possible... happy to create special orders... our waitress even acted as our family photographer..."

Children's menu .... ✓ $$ .... Prices
Changing station .... ✓   ❹ .... Customer service
Highchairs/boosters .... ✓   ❹ .... Stroller access

WWW.OLIVEGARDEN.COM

DOUGLASVILLE—6710 DOUGLAS BLVD (AT ARBOR PL BLVD); 770.577.5858; M-TH 11-10, F-SA 11-11, SU 11-10; MALL PARKING

KENNESAW—429 ERNEST W BARRETT PKY (AT TOWN CTR AT COBB); 770.424.3668; SU-TH 11-10, F-SA 11-11

SMYRNA—2467 COBB PKY (AT HERODIAN WY); 770.933.8971; SU-TH 11-10, F-SA 11-11

Roadhouse Grill ★★★★☆

"...delicious grilled steak, chicken and shrimp... pasta too... my kids love that you can throw peanut shells on the floor... nice, simple children's' menu... they also give your child a balloon when you walk in... reasonable prices and nice atmosphere—an easy choice for when you want to take a break from cooking..."

Children's menu .... ✓ $$ .... Prices
Changing station .... ✓   ❹ .... Customer service
Highchairs/boosters .... ✓   ❹ .... Stroller access

WWW.ROADHOUSEGRILL.COM

KENNESAW—905 ERNEST BARRETT PKY (AT COBB PL SHOPPING CTR); 770.422.3351; SU-TH 11-10, F-SA 11-11

POWDER SPRINGS—2810 E W CONNECTOR (OFF POWDER SPRINGS RD); 770.222.0749; SU-TH 11-10, F-SA 11-11

Romano's Macaroni Grill ★★★★☆

"...family oriented and tasty... noisy so nobody cares if your kids make noise... the staff goes out of their way to make families feel welcome... they even provide slings by the table for infant carriers... the noise level is pretty constant so it's not too loud, but loud enough so that crying babies don't disturb the other patrons... good kids' menu with somewhat healthy items... crayons for kids to color on the paper tablecloths..."

Children's menu .... ✓ $$$ .... Prices
Changing station .... ✓   ❹ .... Customer service
Highchairs/boosters .... ✓   ❹ .... Stroller access

WWW.MACARONIGRILL.COM

MARIETTA—3625 DALLAS RD (AT CASTEEL RD); 678.581.5624; SU-TH 11-10, F-SA 11-11

Ruby Tuesday ★★★½☆

"...nice variety of healthy choices on the kids' menu—turkey, spaghetti, chicken tenders... you can definitely find something healthy here... prices are on the high side, but at least everyone can find

something they like... service is fast and efficient... my daughter makes a mess and they never let me clean it up... your typical chain, but it works—you'll be happy to see ample aisle space, storage for your stroller, and attentive staff... ❞

Children's menu	✓	$$	Prices
Changing station	✓	❹	Customer service
Highchairs/boosters	✓	❸	Stroller access

WWW.RUBYTUESDAY.COM

ACWORTH—3338 COBB PKWY (OFF ACWORTH DUE W RD); 678.574.4550; SU-TH 11-11, F-SA 11-12

DOUGLASVILLE—9579 HWY 5 (OFF ARBOR PKWY); 770.942.8522; M-TH 10:30-11, F-SA 10:30-12

KENNESAW—400 BARRETT PKWY (AT TOWN CTR AT COBB); 770.426.8061; M-TH 10:30-10, F-SA 10:30-11, SU 10:30-9

LITHIA SPRINGS—642 THORNTON RD (AT MAXHAM RD); 770.948.3707; M-TH 10:30-10, F-SA 10:30-11, SU 10:30-10

MARIETTA—2435 DELK RD (OFF RT 75); 770.933.9050; M-TH 11-11, F-SA 11-12, SU 11-10

SMYRNA—3197 S COBB DR (AT CONCORD RD); 770.333.0781; SU-TH 11-11, F-SA 11-12

restaurants

Ryan's Family Steak House ★★★★☆

❝*...our family loves this place... it is mostly buffet style, offering delicious 'down-home' comfort foods... there are generous choices of any meat, potato, salad and side dishes... a dessert bar to die for... the staff here is wonderful and extremely personable and attentive-making you feel like family... great family and kids place...* ❞

Children's menu	✓	$$	Prices
Changing station	✗	❺	Customer service
Highchairs/boosters	✓	❹	Stroller access

WWW.RYANSINC.COM

MARIETTA—680 MARIETTA PKY (AT FAIRGROUNDS ST); 770.429.0551; SU-TH 11-9, F-SA 11-10; PARKING LOT

Smokey Bones BBQ ★★★★☆

❝*...reasonably healthy food for kids—not fried chicken fingers and fries... lots of TVs to entertain kids so adults can have a little time to talk... volume control at each table, stations often set to Nickelodeon... unique holders for car seats that cradle the seats...* ❞

Children's menu	✓	$$$	Prices
Changing station	✓	❹	Customer service
Highchairs/boosters	✓	❹	Stroller access

WWW.SMOKEYBONES.COM

DOUGLASVILLE—6855 DOUGLAS BLVD (OFF RT 402); 678.838.7779; SU-TH 11-10, F-SA 11-11

KENNESAW—2475 GEORGE BUSBEE PKWY (OFF ERNEST BARRETT PKWY); 678.290.7771

Souplantation/Sweet Tomatoes ★★★★☆

❝*...you can't beat the price and selection of healthy foods... all you can eat—serve yourself soup and salad bar... lots of healthy choices plus pizza and pasta... great for picky eaters... free for 2 and under and only $3 for kids under 5... booths for comfy seating and discreet breastfeeding... helps to have another adult along since it is self serve... they always bring fresh cookies to the table and offer to refill drinks...* ❞

Children's menu	✓	$$	Prices
Changing station	✓	❹	Customer service

Highchairs/boosters .... ✓ ❹ .... Stroller access

WWW.SOUPLANTATION.COM

KENNESAW—1125 ERNEST BARRETT PKWY NW (AT ROBERTS BLVD NW); 770.429.5522; SU-TH 11-9, F-SA 11-10

Spaghetti Warehouse ★★★½☆

"...lots of Italian choices... we never go wrong with their delicious pasta... large portions, so I can get away with ordering one dish and sharing it with my tot... they have a kids-eat-free night, which is great with multiple kids... prices are reasonable..."

Children's menu .... ✓ $$ .... Prices
Changing station .... ✓ ❹ .... Customer service
Highchairs/boosters .... ✓ ❹ .... Stroller access

WWW.MEATBALLS.COM

MARIETTA—2475 DELK RD SE (AT COLLINGWOOD DR SE); 770.953.1175; SU-TH 11-10, F-SA 11-11

TGI Friday's ★★★★☆

"...good old American bar food with a reasonable selection for the healthier set as well... I love that the kids meal includes salad... my daughter requests the potato skins on a regular basis (which is good because they are also my favorite)... moderately priced... cheerful servers are used to the mess my kids leave behind... relaxed scene... I'd steer clear on a Friday night unless you don't mind waiting and watching the singles scene..."

Children's menu .... ✓ $$ .... Prices
Changing station .... ✓ ❹ .... Customer service
Highchairs/boosters .... ✓ ❸ .... Stroller access

WWW.TGIFRIDAYS.COM

DOUGLASVILLE—9300 LANDING DR (OFF DOUGLAS BLVD); 770.920.1667; M-SA 11-12, SU 11-10

KENNESAW—840 COBB PL BLVD (OFF COBB PL SHOPPING CTR); 770.419.0228; M-SA 11-1, SU 11-11

Wild Wing Cafe

Children's menu .... ✓ ✓ .... Changing station
Highchairs/boosters .... ✓

WWW.WILDWINGCAFE.COM

MARIETTA—2145 ROSWELL RD NE (AT ROBINSON RD NE); 770.509.9464; M-SA 11:30-11, SU 12-11

Yummy European Cafe & Deli ★★★½☆

"...amazing food cooked in a kitchen that you can see... wonderful staff that go out of their way to make it comfortable for me (and my baby)... relaxed atmosphere with delicious food and coffee..."

Children's menu .... ✓ $ .... Prices
Changing station .... ✕ ❺ .... Customer service
Highchairs/boosters .... ✓ ❺ .... Stroller access

WWW.YUMMYEUROPEANCAFE.COM

DOUGLASVILLE—4900 STEWART MILL RD (AT CHAPEL RD); 770.489.8747; T-SA 9:30-9, SU 9:30-5

doulas & lactation consultants

Editor's Note: Doulas and lactation consultants provide a wide range of services and are very difficult to classify, let alone rate. In fact the terms 'doula' and 'lactation consultant' have very specific industry definitions that are far more complex than we are able to cover in this brief guide. For this reason we have decided to list only those businesses and individuals who received overwhelmingly positive reviews, without listing the reviewers' comments.

Greater Atlanta Area

Association of Labor Assistants & Childbirth Educators (ALACE)

Labor doula .... ✓ ✗ .... Postpartum doula
Pre & post natal massage .... ✗ ✗ .... Lactation consultant

WWW.ALACE.ORG

ATLANTA—617.441.2500

Doulas of North America (DONA)

Labor doula .... ✓ ✓ .... Postpartum doula
Pre & post natal massage .... ✗ ✗ .... Lactation consultant

WWW.DONA.ORG

ATLANTA—888.788.3662

La Leche League

Labor doula .... ✗ ✗ .... Postpartum doula
Pre & post natal massage .... ✗ ✓ .... Lactation consultant

WWW.LALECHELEAGUE.ORG

ATLANTA—VARIOUS LOCATIONS; 847.519.7730

Lactation Consultants of Atlanta

Labor doula .... ✗ ✗ .... Postpartum doula
Pre & post natal massage .... ✗ ✓ .... Lactation consultant

WWW.BREASTFEEDINGATLANTA.COM

MARIETTA—1950 SPECTRUM CIR (AT WINDY HILL RD SE); 678.921.2838; M-F 9-4 BY APPT; FREE PARKING AT BLDG

Northside Hospital (Women's Place)

Labor doula .... ✗ ✗ .... Postpartum doula
Pre & post natal massage .... ✗ ✓ .... Lactation consultant

WWW.NORTHSIDE.COM/AWOMANSPLACE/MAIN.HTM

ATLANTA—1000 JOHNSON FERRY RD NE (AT MERIDIAN MARK RD NE); 404.845.5555; M-F 9-5; PARKING LOT AT HOSPITAL

exercise

City of Atlanta

★★★★★

"lila picks"

- ★Baby Boot Camp
- ★Pierce Yoga
- ★Stroller Strides

Atlanta Yoga ★★★☆☆

"...a great Ashtanga studio... day, evening and weekend classes... classes for all levels...clinics and workshops... no specific pre or postnatal classes, but they are very good about helping everyone at whatever level they are at... good vibes at this studio..."

Prenatal	×	$$$	Prices
Mommy & me	×	❸	Decor
Child care available	×	❸	Customer service

WWW.ATLANTAYOGA.COM

ATLANTA—660 9TH ST NW (AT WATKINS ST); 404.892.7797; CHECK SCHEDULE ONLINE

Baby Boot Camp ★★★★★

"...a great, low-cost, outdoor mom and baby workout... I've met some really fun moms and babies at these classes... not only fun, but more importantly I got results... the first class is free so there's no excuse not to give it a try... instructors are well-trained physical therapists that really know their stuff... class sizes are limited... it's like a personal trainer and motivational system all in one... I do their exercises even when I'm on my own with my baby..."

Prenatal	×	$$$	Prices
Mommy & me	✓	❹	Decor
Child care available	×	❷	Customer service

WWW.BABYBOOTCAMP.COM

ATLANTA—VARIOUS LOCATIONS; 770.444.9419; CHECK SCHEDULE ONLINE

Eclipse One On One ★★★★★

"...probably the best facility in Atlanta—if you can afford it... the owner, Steve Uria, is outstanding!.. simply the best—they got me in great shape for my wedding... now I will go back post-baby..."

Prenatal	×	$$$$	Prices
Mommy & me	×	❺	Decor
Child care available	✓	❺	Customer service

WWW.ECLIPSE1ON1.COM

ATLANTA—295 W WIEUCA RD NW (OFF POWERS FERRY RD); 404.843.2663; CHECK SCHEDULE ONLINE

Ellen Sichel's Yoga Studio ★★★★★

"...excellent prenatal class... the instructor has a wonderful calming presence and teaches a great class... she helped me take care of my backaches so I was able to stop going to the chiropractor... great way

to meet other new moms as well—everyone there seems to be really mellow and fun... ”

Prenatal ✓	$$ Prices
Mommy & me ✗	❹ Decor
Child care available ✗	❹ Customer service

WWW.ELLENSICHELYOGA.COM

ATLANTA—7878 ROSWELL RD (OFF PITTS RD); 770.313.6162; CHECK SCHEDULE ONLINE

Fit For 2 ★★★★☆

“*...a great step aerobics class for expectant and new moms... you can bring your baby to class and use him in your workout or simply let them hang out in the stroller... pretty casual and you can make the workouts as light or hard as you want... the best program for new and expecting moms in the area... the instructors are knowledgeable, committed, energetic and caring...* ”

Prenatal ✓	$ Prices
Mommy & me ✓	❹ Decor
Child care available ✓	❺ Customer service

WWW.FITFOR2.COM

ATLANTA—2001 PEACHTREE RD NE (AT PIEDMONT HOSPITAL); 404.605.1967; CHECK SCHEDULE ONLINE

ATLANTA—6335 ROSWELL RD NE (AT JOHNSON FERRY RD NE); 770.509.8078; CHECK SCHEDULE ONLINE

LA Fitness ★★★☆☆

“*...although they don't have any specific pre and postnatal programs I always felt safe and well guided by my aerobics instructor... most facilities have a Kids Klub—only $3 for up to 2 hours... great classes with excellent child care available... they have everything you need to get a great workout... the child care facilities are a lifesaver...* ”

Prenatal ✗	$$$ Prices
Mommy & me ✗	❸ Decor
Child care available ✓	❸ Customer service

WWW.LAFITNESS.COM

ATLANTA—1155 MT VERNON HWY NE (OFF ABERNATHY RD NE); 770.350.2470; CHECK SCHEDULE ONLINE

ATLANTA—2880 N DRUID HILLS RD NE (AT N TOCO HILLS SHOPPING CTR); 404.321.2330; CHECK SCHEDULE ONLINE; PARKING LOT

ATLANTA—3232 PEACHTREE RD NE (AT PIEDMONT RD NE); 404.233.8311; CHECK SCHEDULE ONLINE; GARAGE

ATLANTA—4200 PACES FERRY RD SE (AT PACES FERRY DR); 770.436.1557; CHECK SCHEDULE ONLINE

ATLANTA—75 5TH ST NW (AT 10TH ST); 404.249.6404; CHECK SCHEDULE ONLINE

Peachtree Yoga Center ★★★★☆

“*...a gentle class focusing on aiding the adjustment of the body as your belly grows, as well as techniques to ease the strenuous process of labor... includes yoga postures and breath work for each trimester... reasonable prices... their kids yoga classes are very popular too...* ”

Prenatal ✓	$$$ Prices
Mommy & me ✗	❸ Decor
Child care available ✗	❹ Customer service

WWW.PEACHTREEYOGA.COM

ATLANTA—6050 SANDY SPRINGS CIR NW (AT HAMMOND DR NE); 404.847.9642; CHECK SCHEDULE ONLINE

Piedmont Health & Fitness

Prenatal .... ✓ ✗ .... Mommy & me
Child care available .... ✗

ATLANTA—2001 PEACHTREE RD NE (AT PIEDMONT HOSPITAL); 404.605.1965; CALL FOR SCHEDULE

Pierce Yoga ★★★★★

"...wonderful pregnancy yoga classes... a terrific place to meet other pregnant women and learn about the birthing experience at the same time... I suffered a lot less aches and pains during pregnancy due to the yoga and it was a huge help during labor... they also provide a one-day labor and delivery class that is useful and supportive if you plan on attempting a drug-free childbirth... the stretching and poses helped soothe me back into a somewhat normal routine... fantastic instructors..."

Prenatal .... ✓ $$... Prices
Mommy & me .... ✓ ❹ .... Decor
Child care available .... ✗ ❹ ....Customer service

WWW.PIERCEYOGA.COM

ATLANTA—1164 N HIGHLAND (AT BELLEVUE DR NE); 404.875.7110; CHECK SCHEDULE ONLINE

Stillwater Yoga Studio ★★★★☆

"...I took their prenatal yoga during my pregnancy and was absolutely thrilled... good one-on-one attention... apparatus allows you to do poses on the wall instead of on the floor... they adapt to students of all levels... I felt fit even though my body was changing wildly..."

Prenatal .... ✓ $$$....................................... Prices
Mommy & me .... ✗ ❸ .... Decor
Child care available .... ✗ ❹ ....Customer service

WWW.STILLYOGA.COM

ATLANTA—931 MONROE DR (AT 8TH ST NE); 404.874.7813; CHECK SCHEDULE ONLINE

Stress Management Resources ★★★★★

"...the prenatal yoga class is really great and taught by a wonderful instructor... it was a great way to stretch and relax each week throughout my pregnancy... several different locations..."

Prenatal .... ✓ $$... Prices
Mommy & me .... ✗ ❹ .... Decor
Child care available .... ✗ ❺ ....Customer service

WWW.STRESSRESOURCES.ORG

ATLANTA—4477 JETT RD NW (AT BY CHASTAIN); 404.843.9997; CHECK SCHEDULE ONLINE

Stroller Fit ★★★★☆

"...a great workout for parents and the kids are entertained the whole time... a great way to ease back into exercise after your baby's birth... the instructor is knowledgeable about fitness and keeping babies happy... motivating, supportive, and fun for kids and moms... sometimes they even set up a play group for after class... not just a good workout, but also a great chance to meet other moms and kids..."

Prenatal .... ✗ $$$....................................... Prices
Mommy & me .... ✓ ❸ .... Decor
Child care available .... ✗ ❸ ....Customer service

WWW.STROLLERFIT.COM

ATLANTA—VARIOUS LOCATIONS; 678.463.3008

Stroller Strides ★★★★★

"...fantastic fun and very effective for losing those post-baby pounds... this is the greatest way to stay in shape as a mom—you have your baby in the stroller with you the whole time... the instructors are very professional, knowledgeable and motivating... beautiful, outdoor locations... classes consist of power walking combined with body toning exercises using exercise tubing and strollers... a great way to bond with my baby and other moms..."

Prenatal	✗	$$$	Prices
Mommy & me	✓	❹	Decor
Child care available	✗	❺	Customer service

WWW.STROLLERSTRIDES.NET

ATLANTA—VARIOUS LOCATIONS; 888.232.2397; CHECK SCHEDULE ONLINE

Studio Lotus ★★★★½

"...pilates, yoga and massage... super-friendly staff... great workout, and I am definitely seeing an improvement in my body and strength... wonderful for getting back into shape after pregnancy..."

Prenatal	✗	$$	Prices
Mommy & me	✗	❺	Decor
Child care available	✗	❺	Customer service

WWW.STUDIOLOTUS.COM

ATLANTA—1145 ZONOLITE RD NE (AT JOHNSON RD NE); 404.817.0900; CALL FOR SCHEDULE

YMCA ★★★★☆

"...the variety of fitness programs offered is astounding... class types and quality vary from facility to facility, but it's a must for new moms to check out... most facilities offer some kind of kids' activities or childcare so you can time your workouts around the classes... aerobics, yoga, pool—our Y even offers Pilates now... my favorite classes are the mom & baby yoga... the best bang for your buck... they have it all—great programs that meet the needs of a diverse range of families..."

Prenatal	✓	$$$	Prices
Mommy & me	✓	❸	Decor
Child care available	✓	❸	Customer service

WWW.YMCAATLANTA.ORG

ATLANTA—1160 MOORES MILL RD NW (AT MILMAR DR NW); 404.350.9292; CHECK SCHEDULE ONLINE

ATLANTA—2220 CAMPBELLTON RD SW (AT DELOWE DR SW); 404.753.4169; M-F 5-9:45, SA 8-6, SU 12-6; PARKING LOT

ATLANTA—275 E LAKE BLVD (AT MEMORIAL AVE); 404.373.6561; CHECK SCHEDULE ONLINE; FREE PARKING

ATLANTA—3692 ASHFORD-DUNWOODY RD NE (AT JOHNSON FERRY RD NE); 770.451.9622; M-F 5:30-10, SA 8-6, SU 1-8; PARKING LOT

ATLANTA—555 LUCKIE ST NW (AT COCA-COLA PLZ NW); 404.724.9622; M-F 6-9, SA 9-12, SU 12-5; PARKING LOT

Yoga Samadhi ★★★★★

"...low key approach, but Doug is very knowledgeable on most fronts... pregnant students may want to also take yoga from pregnancy instructors unless very experienced..."

Prenatal	✓	$$$	Prices
Mommy & me	✗	❹	Decor
Child care available	✗	❺	Customer service

WWW.YOGAATLANTA.COM

ATLANTA—27 WADDELL ST NE (AT EDGEWOOD AVE NE); 404.584.7616; CHECK SCHEDULE ONLINE

North Fulton

★★★★★

"lila picks"

★Stroller Strides

Alpha Pilates ★★★★★

"...one of the best places to find knowledgeable and reliable fitness information about pilates and yoga... great pre and postpartum classes... non-threatening, studio environment... small classes, all semi-private training..."

Prenatal	✓	$	Prices
Mommy & me	✗	❺	Decor
Child care available	✓	❸	Customer service

WWW.ALPHAPILATES.COM

ALPHARETTA—53 S MAIN (OFF OLD MILTON PKWY); 770.331.4625; CHECK FOR SCHEDULE; PARKING LOT

LA Fitness ★★★☆☆

"...although they don't have any specific pre and postnatal programs I always felt safe and well guided by my aerobics instructor... most facilities have a Kids Klub—only $3 for up to 2 hours... great classes with excellent child care available... they have everything you need to get a great workout... the child care facilities are a lifesaver..."

Prenatal	✗	$$$	Prices
Mommy & me	✗	❸	Decor
Child care available	✓	❸	Customer service

WWW.LAFITNESS.COM

ROSWELL—1475 HOLCOMB BRIDGE RD (AT OLD ALABAMA RD); 770.640.8137; CHECK SCHEDULE ONLINE

ROSWELL—4801 OLD ALABAMA RD NE (OFF SANDY PLAINS RD); 678.494.6464; CHECK SCHEDULE ONLINE; PARKING LOT

Stroller Strides ★★★★★

"...fantastic fun and very effective for losing those post-baby pounds... this is the greatest way to stay in shape as a mom—you have your baby in the stroller with you the whole time... the instructors are very professional, knowledgeable and motivating... beautiful, outdoor locations... classes consist of power walking combined with body toning exercises using exercise tubing and strollers... a great way to bond with my baby and other moms..."

Prenatal	✗	$$$	Prices
Mommy & me	✓	❺	Decor
Child care available	✗	❸	Customer service

WWW.STROLLERSTRIDES.NET

ALPHARETTA—VARIOUS LOCATIONS; 800.494.7918; CHECK SCHEDULE ONLINE

DUNWOODY—VARIOUS LOCATIONS; 888.232.2397; CHECK SCHEDULE ONLINE

ROSWELL—VARIOUS LOCATIONS; 800.494.7918; CHECK SCHEDULE ONLINE

YMCA ★★★★☆

"...the variety of fitness programs offered is astounding... class types and quality vary from facility to facility, but it's a must for new moms to check out... most facilities offer some kind of kids' activities or childcare so you can time your workouts around the classes... aerobics, yoga, pool—our Y even offers Pilates now... my favorite classes are the mom & baby yoga... the best bang for your buck... they have it all—great programs that meet the needs of a diverse range of families..."

Prenatal	✓	$$	Prices
Mommy & me	✓	❺	Decor
Child care available	✓	❺	Customer service

WWW.YMCAATLANTA.ORG

ALPHARETTA—3655 PRESTON RIDGE RD (AT NORTH POINT PKWY); 770.664.1220; M-F 5:30-9:30, SA 8-5, SU 1-5:30; PARKING LOT

South Fulton, Fayette & Clayton

LA Fitness

★★★☆☆

"...although they don't have any specific pre and postnatal programs I always felt safe and well guided by my aerobics instructor... most facilities have a Kids Klub—only $3 for up to 2 hours... great classes with excellent child care available... they have everything you need to get a great workout... the child care facilities are a lifesaver..."

Prenatal	✗	$$$	Prices
Mommy & me	✗	❸	Decor
Child care available	✓	❸	Customer service

WWW.LAFITNESS.COM

MORROW—7057 MT ZION CIR (AT MT ZION RD); 770.960.0393; CHECK SCHEDULE ONLINE; PARKING LOT

YMCA

★★★★☆

"...the variety of fitness programs offered is astounding... class types and quality vary from facility to facility, but it's a must for new moms to check out... most facilities offer some kind of kids' activities or childcare so you can time your workouts around the classes... aerobics, yoga, pool—our Y even offers Pilates now... my favorite classes are the mom & baby yoga... the best bang for your buck... they have it all—great programs that meet the needs of a diverse range of families..."

Prenatal	✓	$$$	Prices
Mommy & me	✓	❸	Decor
Child care available	✓	❸	Customer service

WWW.YMCAATLANTA.ORG

FAYETTEVILLE—215 HUIET RD (AT LESTER RD); 770.719.9622; M-F 9-5:30; PARKING LOT

Dekalb

YMCA ★★★★☆

"...the variety of fitness programs offered is astounding... class types and quality vary from facility to facility, but it's a must for new moms to check out... most facilities offer some kind of kids' activities or childcare so you can time your workouts around the classes... aerobics, yoga, pool—our Y even offers Pilates now... my favorite classes are the mom & baby yoga... the best bang for your buck... they have it all—great programs that meet the needs of a diverse range of families..."

Prenatal ✓ $$$ Prices
Mommy & me ✓ ❸ Decor
Child care available ✓ ❹ Customer service

WWW.YMCAATLANTA.ORG

DECATUR—1100 CLAIREMONT AVE (AT N DECATUR RD); 404.377.0241; CALL FOR SCHEDULE; FREE PARKING

DECATUR—2565 SNAPFINGER RD (AT WESLEY CHAPEL RD); 770.987.3500; M-F 6-9:30, SA 9-6, SU 2-6; PARKING LOT

LITHONIA—1185 ROCK CHAPEL RD (AT STEPHENSON RD); 770.484.9622; M-F 9-5; PARKING LOT

LITHONIA—2924 EVANS MILL RD (AT WOODROW DR); 770.484.1625; CHECK SCHEDULE ONLINE

CUMMING—5920 ODELL ST (AT POST RD); 770.888.2788; M-F 8-5; PARKING LOT

Gwinnett

★★★★★
"lila picks"

★Stroller Strides

LA Fitness ★★★☆☆

"...although they don't have any specific pre and postnatal programs I always felt safe and well guided by my aerobics instructor... most facilities have a Kids Klub—only $3 for up to 2 hours... great classes with excellent child care available... they have everything you need to get a great workout... the child care facilities are a lifesaver..."

Prenatal	✗	$$$	Prices
Mommy & me	✗	❸	Decor
Child care available	✓	❸	Customer service

WWW.LAFITNESS.COM

DULUTH—11720 MEDLOCK BRIDGE RD (AT PEACHTREE PKWY); 770.623.9433; CHECK SCHEDULE ONLINE

NORCROSS—7050 JIMMY CARTER BLVD (OFF PEACHTREE INDUSTRIAL BLVD); 770.797.2661; CHECK SCHEDULE ONLINE; PARKING LOT

SNELLVILLE—2314 HENRY CLOWER BLVD SW (OFF RT 78); 770.982.5000; CHECK SCHEDULE ONLINE; PARKING LOT

Stroller Strides ★★★★★

"...fantastic fun and very effective for losing those post-baby pounds... this is the greatest way to stay in shape as a mom—you have your baby in the stroller with you the whole time... the instructors are very professional, knowledgeable and motivating... beautiful, outdoor locations... classes consist of power walking combined with body toning exercises using exercise tubing and strollers... a great way to bond with my baby and other moms..."

Prenatal	✗	$$	Prices
Mommy & me	✓	❺	Decor
Child care available	✗	❸	Customer service

WWW.STROLLERSTRIDES.NET

BUFORD—VARIOUS LOCATIONS; 678.858.2886; CHECK SCHEDULE ONLINE

DACULA—VARIOUS LOCATIONS; 678.858.2886; CHECK SCHEDULE ONLINE

DULUTH—VARIOUS LOCATIONS; 800.494.7918; CHECK SCHEDULE ONLINE

YMCA ★★★★☆

"...the variety of fitness programs offered is astounding... class types and quality vary from facility to facility, but it's a must for new moms to check out... most facilities offer some kind of kids' activities or childcare so you can time your workouts around the classes... aerobics, yoga, pool—our Y even offers Pilates now... my favorite classes are the mom & baby yoga... the best bang for your buck... they have it all—great programs that meet the needs of a diverse range of families..."

Prenatal	✓	$$$	Prices

Mommy & me .... ✓ ❸ .... Decor
Child care available...................... ✓ ❸ .... Customer service

WWW.YMCAATLANTA.ORG

LAWRENCEVILLE—2985 SUGARLOAF PKWY (AT SCENIC HWY SW); 770.963.1313; M-TH 5:45-7:45, F 5:45-8:45, SA 8-5:45,SU 1-7:45; PARKING LOT

NORCROSS—5600 W JONES BRIDGE RD; 770.246.9622; CALL FOR SCHEDULE; FREE PARKING

Cobb & Douglas

★★★★★

"lila picks"

★Fit For 2 ★Stroller Strides

Fit For 2 ★★★★★

"...a great step aerobics class for expectant and new moms... you can bring your baby to class and use him in your workout or simply let them hang out in the stroller... pretty casual and you can make the workouts as light or hard as you want... the best program for new and expecting moms in the area... the instructors are knowledgeable, committed, energetic and caring..."

Prenatal	✓	$$	Prices
Mommy & me	✓	❹	Decor
Child care available	✓	❺	Customer service

WWW.FITFOR2.COM

MARIETTA—770.509.8078; CHECK SCHEDULE ONLINE

LA Fitness ★★★☆☆

"...although they don't have any specific pre and postnatal programs I always felt safe and well guided by my aerobics instructor... most facilities have a Kids Klub—only $3 for up to 2 hours... great classes with excellent child care available... they have everything you need to get a great workout... the child care facilities are a lifesaver..."

Prenatal	×	$$$	Prices
Mommy & me	×	❸	Decor
Child care available	✓	❸	Customer service

WWW.LAFITNESS.COM

KENNESAW—2801 GEORGE BUSBEE PKWY NW (AT TOWN CTR AT COBB); 770.427.9668; CHECK SCHEDULE ONLINE

MARIETTA—4400 ROSWELL RD NE (AT HERITAGE GLEN DR NE); 770.321.4774; CHECK SCHEDULE ONLINE

Stroller Strides ★★★★★

"...fantastic fun and very effective for losing those post-baby pounds... this is the greatest way to stay in shape as a mom—you have your baby in the stroller with you the whole time... the instructors are very professional, knowledgeable and motivating... beautiful, outdoor locations... classes consist of power walking combined with body toning exercises using exercise tubing and strollers... a great way to bond with my baby and other moms..."

Prenatal	×	$$$	Prices
Mommy & me	✓	❸	Decor
Child care available	×	❸	Customer service

WWW.STROLLERSTRIDES.NET

KENNESAW—VARIOUS LOCATIONS; 404.374.9919; CHECK SCHEDULE ONLINE

MARIETTA—VARIOUS LOCATIONS; 404.374.9919; CHECK SCHEDULE ONLINE

SMYRNA—VARIOUS LOCATIONS; 770.843.2831; CHECK SCHEDULE ONLINE

parent education & support

Greater Atlanta Area

★★★★★

"lila picks"

- ★Better Birth Foundation
- ★Northside Hospital (Women's Place)

Better Birth Foundation (Dekalb Medical Center) ★★★★★

"...lots of informative classes... this was an amazing experience for my husband and me... very helpful, especially for first time parents... let me realize what my options were and that I had a choice in how the delivery was handled... free parenting group where you can exchange stories and experiences with other parents... the leader is informative and the camaraderie is great..."

Childbirth classes	✓	$$	Prices
Parent group/club	✓	❺	Class selection
Breastfeeding support	✗	❺	Staff knowledge
Child care info	✗	❺	Customer service

WWW.BETTERBIRTHFOUNDATION.COM

DECATUR—2701 N DECATUR RD (AT CHURCH ST); 770.297.2880; CALL FOR SCHEDULE

SNELLVILLE—1700 MEDICAL WY (AT NEW HAMPTON DR SW); 770.297.2880; CALL FOR SCHEDULE

ROSWELL—3000 HOSPITAL BLVD (AT HAMBREE RD); 770.751.2687; CHECK SCHEDULE ONLINE

Birth of a Family

Childbirth classes	✗	✗	Breastfeeding support
Parent group/club	✗	✗	Child care info

WWW.BIRTHOFAFAMILY.COM

MARIETTA—VARIOUS LOCATIONS; 770.794.6861

Bradley Method, The ★★★½☆

"...12 week classes that cover all of the basics of giving birth... run by individual instructors nationwide... classes differ based on the quality and experience of the instructor... they cover everything from nutrition and physical conditioning to spousal support and medication... wonderful series that can be very educational... their web site has listings of instructors on a regional basis..."

Childbirth classes	✓	$$$	Prices
Parent group/club	✗	❺	Class selection
Breastfeeding support	✗	❺	Staff knowledge
Child care info	✗	❺	Customer service

WWW.BRADLEYBIRTH.COM

ATLANTA—VARIOUS LOCATIONS; 800.422.4784; CHECK SCHEDULE & LOCATIONS ONLINE

Choices In Childbirth

Childbirth classes .... ✗ ✓ .... Breastfeeding support
Parent group/club .... ✗ ✓ .... Child care info

WWW.CHOICESINCHILDBIRTH.COM

MARIETTA—3105 INDIAN HILL DR (AT OLD CANTON RD NE); 770.509.7699

Emory Crawford Long Hospital (Perinatal Education) ★★★★☆

"...the classes were fun and the facility is clean and well maintained... informative presenters provide very good information in a very organized fashion... very educational for parents-to-be—I highly recommend it... the instructors were generally available to answer questions, even outside of class..."

Childbirth classes .... ✓ $$ .... Prices
Parent group/club .... ✗ ❹ .... Class selection
Breastfeeding support .... ✓ ❹ .... Staff knowledge
Child care info .... ✗ ❹ .... Customer service

WWW.EMORYHEALTHCARE.ORG

ATLANTA—550 PEACHTREE ST NE (AT NORTH AVE NE); 770.297.2880; CALL FOR SCHEDULE; GARAGE AT PEACHTREE ST ENTRANCE

Emory Dunwoody Medical Center (Perinatal Education)

Childbirth classes .... ✗ ✓ .... Breastfeeding support
Parent group/club .... ✗ ✗ .... Child care info

WWW.EMORYHEALTHCARE.ORG

ATLANTA—4575 N SHALLOWFORD RD (AT PEELER RD); 770.297.2880; CALL FOR SCHEDULE

Grady Memorial Hospital

Childbirth classes .... ✗ ✓ .... Breastfeeding support
Parent group/club .... ✓ ✓ .... Child care info

WWW.GRADYHEALTHSYSTEM.ORG

ATLANTA—80 JESSE HILL JR DR NE (AT AUBURN AVE NE); 404.616.3837; CALL FOR HOURS

Gwinnett Women's Pavilion ★★★★☆

"...prices are very affordable and instructors are very knowledgeable... they will answer any and all questions... very pro-breastfeeding... classes are located on-site so you feel more comfortable with the hospital by the time you deliver... classes taught by staff nurses..."

Childbirth classes .... ✓ $$ .... Prices
Parent group/club .... ✗ ❹ .... Class selection
Breastfeeding support .... ✓ ❺ .... Staff knowledge
Child care info .... ✗ ❹ .... Customer service

WWW.GWINNETTHEALTH.ORG

LAWRENCEVILLE—550 MEDICAL CTR BLVD (AT PROFESSIONAL DR NW); 770.541.4743; CALL FOR SCHEDULE

Home Safety Solutions ★★★☆☆

"...all sorts of safety solutions for your home... a consultant will even come out to your home... can get expensive, but having peace-of-mind is worth it..."

Childbirth classes .... ✗ $$$ .... Prices
Parent group/club .... ✗ ❸ .... Class selection
Breastfeeding support .... ✗ ❸ .... Staff knowledge
Child care info .... ✗ ❸ .... Customer service

WWW.HOMESAFETYSOLUTIONS.COM

ATLANTA—181 14TH ST NE (AT JUNIPER ST NE); 404.601.3100; CALL FOR APPT

Lactation Consultants of Atlanta

Childbirth classes ✗	✓ Breastfeeding support
Parent group/club ✗	✗ Child care info

WWW.BREASTFEEDINGATLANTA.COM

ACWORTH—404.610.5544; CALL FOR APPT

MARIETTA—1950 SPECTRUM CIR (AT WINDY HILL RD SE); 678.921.2838; M-F 9-4 BY APPT; FREE PARKING AT BLDG

Lamaze International ★★★★☆

"...thousands of women each year are educated about the birth process by Lamaze educators... their web site offers a list of local instructors... they follow a basic curriculum, but invariably class quality will depend on the individual instructor... in many ways they've set the standard for birth education classes..."

Childbirth classes ✓	$$$ Prices
Parent group/club ✓	❸ Class selection
Breastfeeding support ✓	❸ Staff knowledge
Child care info ✓	❸ Customer service

WWW.LAMAZE.ORG

ATLANTA—VARIOUS LOCATIONS; 800.368.4404; CHECK SCHEDULE AND LOCATIONS ONLINE

Mocha Moms ★★★★½

"...a wonderfully supportive group of women—the kind of place you'll make lifelong friends for both mother and child... a comfortable forum for bouncing ideas off of other moms with same-age children... easy to get involved and not too demanding... the annual membership dues seem a small price to pay for the many activities, play groups, field trips, Moms Nights Out and book club meetings... local chapters in cities nationwide..."

Childbirth classes ✗	$$$ Prices
Parent group/club ✓	❸ Class selection
Breastfeeding support ✗	❸ Staff knowledge
Child care info ✗	❸ Customer service

WWW.MOCHAMOMS.ORG

ATLANTA—VARIOUS LOCATIONS

MOMS Club ★★★★☆

"...an international nonprofit with lots of local chapters and literally tens of thousands of members... designed to introduce you to new mothers with same-age kids wherever you live... they organize all sorts of activities and provide support for new mothers with babies... very inexpensive for all the activities you get... book clubs, moms night out, play group connections... generally a very diverse group of women..."

Childbirth classes ✗	$$ Prices
Parent group/club ✓	❹ Class selection
Breastfeeding support ✗	❹ Staff knowledge
Child care info ✗	❹ Customer service

WWW.MOMSCLUB.ORG

CITY OF ATLANTA—VARIOUS LOCATIONS

Mothers and More ★★★½☆

"...a very neat support system for moms who are deciding to stay at home... a great way to get together with other moms in your area for organized activities... book clubs, play groups, even a 'mom's only'

night out... local chapters offer more or less activities depending on the involvement of local moms... ❞

Childbirth classes .... ✗ | $ .... Prices
Parent group/club .... ✓ | ❹ .... Class selection
Breastfeeding support .... ✗ | ❹ .... Staff knowledge
Child care info .... ✗ | ❹ .... Customer service

WWW.MOTHERSANDMORE.COM

ATLANTA—VARIOUS LOCATIONS; CHECK SCHEDULE & LOCATIONS ONLINE

Northside Hospital (Women's Place) ★★★★★

❝*...incredible array of classes from birthing and breastfeeding to baby CPR... the classes were invaluable to me... very happy and satisfied... quelled my fear... they also have classes at the Northside satellites... there is some variability in the instructors... don't miss the classes for Daddy and Big Sister... I felt well prepared and supported...* ❞

Childbirth classes .... ✓ | $$ .... Prices
Parent group/club .... ✗ | ❹ .... Class selection
Breastfeeding support .... ✓ | ❹ .... Staff knowledge
Child care info .... ✓ | ❹ .... Customer service

WWW.NORTHSIDE.COM/AWOMANSPLACE/MAIN.HTM

ATLANTA—1000 JOHNSON FERRY RD NE (AT MERIDIAN MARK RD NE); 404.845.5555; M-F 9-5; PARKING LOT AT HOSPITAL

Piedmont Hospital ★★★★☆

❝*...lots of informative classes... this was an amazing experience for my husband and me... very helpful, especially for first time parents... let me realize what my options were and that I had a choice in how the delivery was handled... free parenting group where you can exchange stories and experiences with other parents... the leader is informative and the camaraderie is great...* ❞

Childbirth classes .... ✓ | $$ .... Prices
Parent group/club .... ✓ | ❶ .... Class selection
Breastfeeding support .... ✓ | ❹ .... Staff knowledge
Child care info .... ✗ | ❹ .... Customer service

WWW.PIEDMONTHOSPITAL.ORG

ATLANTA—1968 PEACHTREE RD NW (AT PEACHTREE HILLS AVE NE); 866.900.4321; CHECK SCHEDULE ONLINE

South Fulton Medical Center (Maternity Services)

Childbirth classes .... ✗ | ✓ .... Breastfeeding support
Parent group/club .... ✗ | ✓ .... Child care info

EAST POINT—1170 CLEVELAND AVE (OFF NORMAN BERRY DR); 770.297.2880

Southern Regional Medical Center (Women's Life Center) ★★★★☆

❝*...our instructor was a nurse and a mom, she was able to condense the medical information and deliver it in an understandable way... three week childbirth series focuses on relaxation and breathing techniques...* ❞

Childbirth classes .... ✓ | $$$ .... Prices
Parent group/club .... ✗ | ❹ .... Class selection
Breastfeeding support .... ✓ | ❹ .... Staff knowledge
Child care info .... ✓ | ❹ .... Customer service

WWW.SOUTHERNREGIONAL.ORG

RIVERDALE—11 UPPER RIVERDALE RD SW (AT DON HASTINGS DR); 770.991.8246; CHECK SCHEDULE ONLINE

Wellstar Health System Breastfeeding Center

Childbirth classes .... ✗ ✓ .... Breastfeeding support
Parent group/club .... ✗ ✗ .... Child care info

WWW.WELLSTAR.ORG

AUSTELL—VARIOUS LOCATIONS; 770.956.7827; M-F 8:15-4:15

WellStar Kennestone Hospital (Women's Resource Center)

Childbirth classes .... ✗ ✓ .... Breastfeeding support
Parent group/club .... ✗ ✗ .... Child care info

WWW.WELLSTAR.ORG

MARIETTA—677 CHURCH ST NE (AT WITCHER ST); 770.793.8075; M-F 9-5

Women's Resource Center At Wellstar Cobb Hospital ★★★★★

"...worth every penny... I thoroughly enjoyed the breastfeeding class and felt well prepared... the teachers stress that they are available even after the class session... the newborn care class was outstanding... I was surprised at how fun these classes turned out to be... outstanding staff..."

Childbirth classes .... ✗ $ .... Prices
Parent group/club .... ✗ ❺ .... Class selection
Breastfeeding support .... ✓ ❺ .... Staff knowledge
Child care info .... ✗ ❺ .... Customer service

WWW.WELLSTAR.ORG

AUSTELL—3950 AUSTELL RD (AT ROCK HILL DR); 770.793.8068

pediatricians

Editor's Note: Pediatricians provide a tremendous breadth of services and are very difficult to classify and rate in a brief guide. For this reason we list only those practices for which we received overwhelmingly positive reviews. We hope this list of pediatricians will help you in your search.

City of Atlanta

Children's Medical Group

WWW.CMG-PC.COM

ATLANTA—1875 CENTURY BLVD NE (AT CLAIRMONT WAY NE); 404.633.4595; M-F 8:30-5

Kenmar Pediatrics

WWW.WELLSTAR.ORG/

ATLANTA—760 KENNESAW AVE NE (AT PONCE DE LEON AVE NE); 770.427.0183; M-F 7:30-12 & 1-5

North Atlanta Pediatrics

WWW.BEANSPROUT.COM

ATLANTA—1100 LAKE HEARN DR NE (AT PEACHTREE DUNWOODY RD NE); 404.256.3178; M-F 8:30-5; PARKING AT 1100 LAKE HEARN

Northside Pediatrics

WWW.NORTHSIDEPEDIATRICS.COM

ATLANTA—1140 HAMMOND DR NE (AT PERIMETER MALL); 404.256.2688; M-F 8:30-5

ATLANTA—333 SANDY SPRINGS CIR NW (AT ROSEWELL DR NE); 404.705.8990; M-F 8-5

Piedmont Pediatrics

ATLANTA—105 COLLIER RD NW (AT ANJACO RD NW); 404.351.6662; M-F 9-5, SA 9-12

We Care Pediatrics & Adolescent Group

ATLANTA—777 CLEVELAND AVE SW (AT ST SYLVAN RD); 404.766.3337; M-T 8:30-5, W 8:30-3, TH 8:30-6, F 8:30-3

North Fulton

Benaroch, Roy MD

WWW.PEDIATRICPHYSICIANSPC.COM

ROSWELL—11050 CRABAPPLE RD (AT PARKER PL); 770.518.9277; CALL FOR APPT

Dunwoody Pediatrics

ALPHARETTA—5075 ABBOTTS BRIDGE RD (AT ADDISON LN); 770.664.9299; M-F 8-5 SA 9-12

DUNWOODY—5501 CHAMBLEE DUNWOODY RD (AT DUNWOODY VILLAGE PKWY); 770.394.2358; M-F 8-5, SA 9-12

Georgetown Pediatrics

ALPHARETTA—3400-A OLD MILTON PKWY (AT MORRIS RD); 770.475.2233; M-F 8-5

North Fulton Pediatrics

WWW.NORTHFULTONPEDIATRICS.COM

ROSWELL—1285 HEMBREE RD (AT ALPHARETTA HWY); 770.442.1050; M-F 8:30-5 SA 8:30-11; FREE PARKING

North Point Pediatrics

WWW.NORTHPOINTPEDIATRICS.YOURMD.COM/

ALPHARETTA—11975 MORRIS RD (AT WEBB BRIDGE RD); 770.664.0088; M-F 9-5

Preston Ridge Pediatrics

ALPHARETTA—3400 OLD MILTON PKWY (AT N POINT PKWY); 770.751.6111; M-F 8-5

Roswell Pediatric Center

WWW.ROSWELLPEDIATRICS.COM

ALPHARETTA—12385 CRABAPPLE RD (AT ARNOLD MILL RD); 770.343.9900; M-F 8:30-5:30

South Fulton, Fayette & Clayton

Children's Clinic, The

MORROW—1000 CORPORATE CTR DR (AT N LAKE DR); 770.960.9999; M-F 8:45-4:30, SA 8:45-11; PARKING IN FRONT OF BLDG

Fayette Medical Clinic

PEACHTREE CITY—4000 SHAKERAG HL (AT ROBINSON RD); 770.486.7111; M-F 8-5

Kids Avenue Pediatrics

COLLEGE PARK—1720 PHOENIX BLVD (AT PHOENIX PKWY); 770.909.8007; M-F 8:30-5, EXCEPT TH11-7:30; STREET PARKING

Potts & Smith Pediatrics

FAYETTEVILLE—365 N JEFF DAVIS DR (AT FENWYCK COMMONS); 770.461.5003; M-TH 9-11:30 & 1:45-7:30, F 9-11:30 & 1:45-4:30, SA 9-11:30; PARKING LOT

Dekalb

Dekalb Medical Center

WWW.DEKALBMEDICALCENTER.ORG/

DECATUR—440 WINN WAY (AT IRVIN WAY); 404.508.7899

Dekalb Pediatric Center

WWW.DEKALBPEDS.COM

DECATUR—484 IRVIN CT (AT IRVIN WAY); 404.508.1177

Foster, Harry MD

LITHONIA—7660 COVINGTON HWY (AT KLONDIKE RD); 770.482.8887; M-F 8:30-5 TH 8:30-12; PARKING LOT

Milestone Pediatrics

DECATUR—1438 MCLENDON DR (OFF RT 29); 770.414.0337; M-F 8-5

Sulton Pediatric Group

DECATUR—5910 HILLANDALE DR (AT PANOLA); 404.501.8300; M 8:30-5:30, T-F 8:30-4:30; PARKING LOT

Verras Pediatrics

TUCKER—2181 NORTHLAKE PKWY (AT LAVISTA RD); 770.491.1285; M TH 9-7, T-W F 9-5, SA 9-12

Gwinnett

Children's Medical Group

WWW.CMG-PC.COM

SUWANEE—3895 JOHNS CREEK PKWY (AT JOHNS CREEK CT); 770.622.5758; M-F 8:45-11:50 & 1:50-5; PARKING IN FRONT OF BLDG

Children's Medicine

WWW.CHILDRENSMEDICINE.YOURMD.COM

BUFORD—2050 BUFORD HWY (AT SOUTH LEE ST); 770.614.7366

Cooper Pediatrics

WWW.COOPERPEDIATRICS.COM

DULUTH—3645 HOWELL FERRY RD NW (AT INDUSTRIAL BLVD NW); 678.473.4738; M-TH 8-7 F 8-5

Gwinnett Pediatrics

WWW.GWINNETTPEDS.COM

LAWRENCEVILLE—601 A PROFESSIONAL DR (AT HWY 120); 770.995.0823; M-F 9-5

Longstreet Clinic Pediatrics

WWW.LONGSTREETCLINIC.COM

BUFORD—4445 S LEE ST NE (AT BUFORD DR NE); 770.932.8519; M-F 8-5

Pediatric Associates Of North Atlanta

DULUTH—10700 MEDLOCK BRIDGE RD (AT PARSONS RD); 770.476.9885; M-F 9-4:30

Pohl, Joseph MD

LAWRENCEVILLE—500 MEDICAL CTR BLVD NW (AT W PIKE ST); 770.962.2051; M-F 8:30-5

Snellville Pediatrics

SNELLVILLE—1700 TREE LN (AT MEDICAL WAY SW); 770.972.0860; M-F 8:30-5

Suwanee Pediatrics PC

WWW.SUWANEEPEDIATRICS.COM

LAWRENCEVILLE—1885 LAWRENCEVILLE SUWANEE RD (AT SUWANEE EAST DR NW); 678.442.0205; M 7-5, T-TH 9-7, F 9-5, SA 9-12; PARKING IN FRONT OF BLDG

United Pediatrics

NORCROSS—4775 JIMMY CARTER BLVD (AT QUEEN ANNE CT NW); 770.717.0033; M-F 10-4:30

Zaman Pediatric Center

SNELLVILLE—2800 MAIN ST WEST (AT VALLEY DR SW); 770.979.2600; M-F 8:30-5, SA 10-12; PARKING LOT

Cobb & Douglas

Cobb Pediatric Associates

AUSTELL—1664 MULKEY RD (AT AUSTELL RD SW); 770.941.7709; M-F 8-5

Creekside Pediatrics

WWW.WELLSTAR.ORG

DOUGLASVILLE—6095 PROFESSIONAL PKWY (AT HOSPITAL DR); 770.920.2255; M-F 8:30-5

East Cobb Pediatrics

MARIETTA—1121 JOHNSON FERRY RD NE (AT WOODLAWN DR); 770.977.0094; M-F 8:30-5

Kenmar Pediatrics

WWW.WELLSTAR.ORG

MARIETTA—760 KENNESAW AVE NW (AT DICKSON AVE NW); 770.427.0183; M-F 7:30-5, LUNCH 12-1

Kennesaw Pediatrics

WWW.KENNESAWPEDIATRICS.COM

KENNESAW—3745 CHEROKEE ST NW (OFF JILES RD); 770.429.1005; M-F 8-5; PARKING LOT

Pediatrics & Adolescent Medicine

MARIETTA—2155 POST OAK TRITT RD NE (AT SHADY PLAINS RD NE); 770.973.4700; M-F 8-5 SA 8:30-11

Wellstar-Smyrna Pediatrics

SMYRNA—562 CONCORD RD SE (AT OLD CONCORD RD); 770.384.9830; M-F 9-5; PARKING LOT

West Cobb Pediatrics

POWDER SPRINGS—5041 DALLAS RD SW (AT SCHOFIELD DR SW); 770.425.5331; M-F 9-4:30

breast pump sales & rentals

Greater Atlanta Area

★★★★★

"lila picks"

- ★Lactation Consultants of Atlanta
- ★New Baby Products
- ★Northside Hospital (Women's Place)

Atlanta's Lactation Station

WWW.MISSJAMIESHOUSE.COM

TUCKER—2273 BROCKETT RD (AT LAVISTA RD); 770.938.5108

Babies R Us ★★★½☆

"...Medela pumps, Boppy pillows and lots of other breastfeeding supplies... staff knowledge varies from store to store, but everyone was friendly and helpful... clean and well-stocked... not a huge selection, but what they've got is great and very competitively priced..."

Customer Service .... ❹ $$.. Prices

WWW.BABIESRUS.COM

ALPHARETTA—6380 NORTH POINT PKWY (AT NORTH POINT MALL); 770.752.9000; M-SA 9:30-9:30, SU 11-7; PARKING IN FRONT OF BLDG

ATLANTA—1155 MOUNT VERNON HWY (AT PERIMETER MALL); 770.913.0222; M-SA 9:30-9:30, SU 11-7; PARKING IN FRONT OF BLDG

DOUGLASVILLE—6875 DOUGLAS BLVD (AT ARBOR PL); 770.949.2209; M-SA 9:30-9:30, SU 11-7; PARKING IN FRONT OF BLDG

DULUTH—3925 VENTURA DR (AT STEVE REYNOLDS BLVD NW); 770.622.8888; M-SA 9:30-9:30, SU 11-7; PARKING IN FRONT OF BLDG

KENNESAW—1875 GREERS CHAPEL RD (AT BARRETT PKWY); 770.919.2229; M-SA 9:30-9:30, SU 11-7; PARKING IN FRONT OF BLDG

LITHONIA—8160 MALL PKWY (AT THE MALL AT STONECREST); 770.484.9697; M-SA 9:30-9:30, SU 11-7; PARKING IN FRONT OF BLDG

MORROW—1960 MT ZION RD (AT MT ZION BLVD); 770.477.5111; M-SA 9:30-9:30, SU 11-7; PARKING IN FRONT OF BLDG

Better Birth Foundation (Dekalb Medical Center) ★★★★½

"...this is the place to rent or buy pumps in the Decatur area... excellent selection of Medela pumps and bras... the lactation consultants are very helpful... they rent baby scales... will help fit a nursing bra!.. prices comparable to retail stores, but you get the bonus of a lactation consultant's advice..."

Customer Service .... ❺ $$.. Prices

WWW.DEKALBMEDICALCENTER.ORG

DECATUR—2701 N DECATUR RD (AT CHURCH ST); 770.297.2880; CALL FOR SCHEDULE

Bloom Maternity

ATLANTA—2140 PEACHTREE RD (AT PEACHTREE PARK DR NE); 404.351.6262; M-F 10-6, SA 10-5

East Marietta Drugs

MARIETTA—1486 ROSWELL RD NE (AT LOWER ROSWELL RD NE); 770.973.7600; M-F 9-6, SA 9:30-1:30

Gwinnett Medical Center (Women's Pavilion) ★★★★½

"...fantastic lactation specialists... really good selection of pumps, and they explain them so you understand it all... lactation consultant came to my room after I had my son and helped me begin to nurse him... really helpful when I didn't have a clue as to what I needed... best to call ahead, as hours are limited... Medela products for rental or purchase... very reasonable prices..."

Customer Service........................ ❺ $$.. Prices

WWW.GWINNETTHEALTH.ORG

LAWRENCEVILLE—1000 MEDICAL CTR BLVD (AT PROFESSIONAL DR NW); 678.442.4743; M-F 9-5; FREE PARKING

Lactation Consultants of Atlanta ★★★★★

"...rental and professional grade pumps for sale... also spare parts and accessories... available for consultation, teaching and support of pumping/breastfeeding mothers... friendly and knowledgeable... they can provide a massive amount of information, and will help solve any problem..."

Customer Service........................ ❺ $$.. Prices

WWW.BREASTFEEDINGATLANTA.COM

ACWORTH—404.610.5544; CALL FOR APPT

MARIETTA—1950 SPECTRUM CIR (AT WINDY HILL RD SE); 678.921.2838; M-F 9-4 BY APPT; FREE PARKING AT BLDG

Medicine Shoppe

DUNWOODY—4675 N SHALLOWFORD RD (AT PEELER RD); 770.455.1144

New Baby Products ★★★★★

"...if you're going to rent a pump, then rent it here... they are friendly, knowledgeable and more importantly, carry the best Medela pumps... prices are competitive... they'll show you how to use the pumps... very easy and reassuring..."

Customer Service........................ ❺ $$$.. Prices

WWW.NEWBABYPRODUCTS.COM

ATLANTA—2200 CHESHIRE BRIDGE RD NE (AT WOODLAND AVE NE); 404.321.3874; M 10-8, T-SA 10-6; PARKING LOT

SNELLVILLE—2334 HENRY CLOWER BLVD (AT KNOLLWOOD DR SW); 770.978.9810; M F 10-8, T-TH SA 10-6; PARKING LOT

North Fulton Regional Hospital (Lactation Department) ★★★★½

"...breast pump rentals at decent prices... assistance and training provided by knowledgeable staff... they carry the Hollister line of

pumps... for outpatient rentals, you pay $40 for the personal kit and either $20 for a 10 day rental or $45 per month..."

Customer Service .... ❺ $$$....................................... Prices

WWW.NORTHFULTONREGIONAL.COM

ROSWELL—3000 HOSPITAL BLVD (AT HAMBREE RD); 770.751.2686; CALL FOR HOURS

Northside Hospital (Women's Place) ★★★★★

"*...the rental process was easy and made it convenient to renew... they returned my calls right away... the lactation consultant came to visit three times in a 48 hour period and gave great advice... they go above and beyond the call every time I visit... reasonable prices... first-rate support group...*"

Customer Service .... ❺ $$$....................................... Prices

WWW.NORTHSIDE.COM/AWOMANSPLACE/MAIN.HTM

ATLANTA—1000 JOHNSON FERRY RD NE (AT MERIDIAN MARK RD NE); 404.845.5555; M-F 9-5; PARKING LOT AT HOSPITAL

Peachcare Drugs ★★★★★

"*...pharmacist gives you her personal knowledge of the pumps and pumping... rentals and pumps for sale... accessories and spare parts, too... the process is easy, quick and competitvely priced (around $50 per month)...*"

Customer Service .... ❺ $$... Prices

WWW.PEACHCAREDRUGS.COM

MARIETTA—585 FRANKLIN RD SE (AT S MARIETTA PKWY SE); 678.581.1223

Piedmont Hospital (Women's Center) ★★★★☆

"*...a wonderful experience overall... the best place to have a baby, learn how to nurse, and get the equipment...*"

Customer Service .... ❹ $$$....................................... Prices

WWW.PIEDMONTHOSPITAL.ORG

ATLANTA—1968 PEACHTREE RD NE (AT COLLIER RD NW); 404.605.3242; CALL FOR APPT; FREE PARKING

Pretty Please

DECATUR—3920 N DRUID HILLS RD (AT N DEKALB SQ SHOPPING CTR); 404.634.6309; M-F 10-5, SA 10-2; FREE PARKING

Online

amazon.com ★★★★☆

“...I'm always amazed by the amount of stuff Amazon sells—including a pretty good selection of pumps... Medela, Avent, Isis, Ameda... prices range from great to average... pretty easy shopping experience... free shipping on bigger orders...”

babycenter.com ★★★★½

“...they carry all the major brands... prices are competitive, but keep in mind you'll need to pay for shipping too... the comments from parents are incredibly helpful... excellent customer service... easy shopping experience...”

birthexperience.com ★★★½☆

“...Medela and Avent products... great deal with the Canadian currency conversion... get free shipping with big orders... easy site to navigate...”

breast-pumps.com

breastmilk.com

ebay.com ★★★★½

“...you can get Medela pumps brand new in packaging with the warranty for $100 less than retail... able to buy immediately instead of having to bid and wait... wide variety... be sure to check for shipping price... great place to find deals, but research the seller before you bid...”

express-yourself.net

healthchecksystems.com

lactationconnection.com ★★★½☆

“...Ameda and Whisper Wear products... nice selection and competitive prices... quick delivery of any nursing or lactation product you can imagine... the selection of mom and baby related items is fantastic...”

medela.com ★★★★☆

“...well worth the money... fast, courteous and responsive... great site for a full listing of Medela products and links to purchase online... quality of customer service by phone varies... licensed lactation specialist answers e-mail via email at no charge and with quick turnaround...”

mybreastpump.com ★★★☆☆

“...a great online one-stop-shop for all things breast feeding... you can purchase hospital grade pumps from them... fast service for all you breastfeeding needs...”

diaper delivery services

Greater Atlanta Area

Atlantex Linen Service

Service Area ....greater Atlanta area

WWW.ATLANTALINENS.COM

ATLANTA—5616 NEW PEACHTREE RD (AT BROGDON CT); 770.455.8362

Belvedere Diaper Outlet

Service Area ....call for delivery

DECATUR—1203 COLUMBIA DR (AT BELVEDERE PLZ SHOPPING CTR); 404.289.8003

Diapers King

Service Area ....call for delivery

HTTP://ATLANTAMOMS.COM/HTML/DIAPER.HTML

DECATUR—1203 COLUMBIA DR (AT MEMORIAL DR); 404.289.8003; M-SA:11-7

Diapers Outlet

Service Area ... pick-up diaper service

CHAMBLEE—5241 NEW PEACHTREE RD (AT CHAMBLEE RD); 770.216.9938

DOUGLASVILLE—3311-C HWY 5 (AT WENONA ST); 770.577.3777

LAWRENCEVILLE—3870 LAWRENCEVILLE HWY NW (AT LESTER RD NW); 770.923.2400

Lullaby Changing Time Diaper Services

ATLANTA—5616 NEW PEACHTREE RD (AT BROGDAN CT); 770.455.8362

Mc Diapers

Service Area ....call for delivery info

DECATUR—5235 SNAPFINGER WOODS DR (AT LANTRAC CT); 770.359.2020

haircuts

Greater Atlanta Area

★★★★★

"lila picks"

- ★Cartoon Cuts
- ★Hairy's Hair Salon
- ★Little Scissors Hair Styling Shop
- ★Pigtails & Crewcuts
- ★Snip-its Haircuts For Kids

Cartoon Cuts ★★★★★

"...if your tot squirms at the thought of getting his hair cut, then you might want to try Cartoon Cuts... cartoons and toys catch your kid's attention while the cutters do their job... the staff is patient and friendly... cuts vary depending on the staff, so once you've found someone good I'd suggest coming back to her... lollipops are an extra added bonus... a fun waiting area and TV's at each station to keep the little ones happy... kids seem to love it..."

Customer Service .... ❸ $$.. Prices

WWW.CARTOONCUTS.COM

KENNESAW—400 ERNEST W BARRETT PKWY NW (AT MALL BLVD NW); 770.795.0014; M-SA 10-9, SU 12:30-6; MALL PARKING

Circus Cuts ★★★½☆

"...I've tried the other places, but I keep coming back here... a great place for a screamer—the stylists are incredibly patient... waiting room full of toys helps ease the pain... if you are a working parent, plan on a weekend trip... great rides and a locket of hair and a certificate for the baby book... this place is always busy, expect a wait... warm, friendly atmosphere... quality of cut definitely depends on the stylist..."

Customer Service .... ❹ $$$...................................... Prices

WWW.CIRCUSCUTS.COM

DULUTH—9700 MEDLOCK BRIDGE RD (AT STATE BRIDGE RD); 678.417.9707; M-F 10-6, SA 9-5, SU 12-4

Dass ★★★★½

"...it looks like it's really high-end, but it really is a salon for all ages... a real, quality haircut by family-friendly stylists... discount designer cuts for kids... my wife's stylist at DASS also cuts our kids' hair for less than $15 and the quality of the cut is so much better than at other places..."

Customer Service .... ❹ $$$...................................... Prices

WWW.DASS.TV

ATLANTA—4400 ASHFORD DUNWOODY RD NE (AT PERIMETER MALL); 770.393.8303; M-SA 9-9, SU 12-6; MALL PARKING

Floyd's Barber Shop ★★★☆☆

"...fast and friendly service... great, old-school barber shop feel... they don't have cartoons playing and fancy race car chairs, but they'll turn on the old-time charm... my kids love coming here..."

Customer Service .... ❸ $$$ .... Prices

KENNESAW—2500 COBB PKWY NW (AT KENNESAW DUE WEST RD NW); 770.427.4316; M-F 8-5, SA 7-12

Great Clips ★★★★☆

"...cheap, decent cuts... not specifically tailored around children so there aren't any horses or cars to sit in... stylists' experience with kids vary, but we generally walk away satisfied... you can't beat the price and you don't have to make an appointment... the balloon at the end makes it all worthwhile..."

Customer Service .... ❹ $$ .... Prices

WWW.GREATCLIPS.COM

ALPHARETTA—12850 HWY 9 N (AT WINDWARD PKWY W); 770.664.6221; M-F 9-5, SA 9-6, SU 11-6

Hair Cuttery ★★★½☆

"...much easier on the wallet than the gimmicky salons... usually a positive experience...best to find a stylist you like and stick with him or her... you lose the fluff of the kid-friendly salon, but you get a shampoo and haircut for under $10... with so many locations, you won't lose half a day driving to get a trim..."

Customer Service .... ❸ $$ .... Prices

WWW.HAIRCUTTERY.COM

ACWORTH—1727 MARS HILL RD; 770.420.9007

ACWORTH—3505 BAKER RD (AT CHEROKEE RD); 770.529.9630

ATLANTA—1715 HOWELL MILL RD (AT CHATTAHOOCHEE AVE); 404.355.2401

ATLANTA—2341 PEACKTREE RD NE (AT PEACHTREE BATTLE AVE); 404.364.9648

ATLANTA—2460 CUMBERLAND PKWY (AT PACES FERRY RD); 770.803.9598

ATLANTA—3441 ASHFORD DUNWOODY RD NE (AT JOHNSON FERRY RD); 770.234.9785

ATLANTA—350 FERST DR NW (AT TECH PKY); 404.894.2813

ATLANTA—3974 PEACHTREE RD NE (AT DRUID HILLS RD); 404.231.9019

ATLANTA—6309 ROSWELL RD NE (AT MT VERNON HWY); 404.843.3678

ATLANTA—8725 ROSWELL RD (AT DUNWOODY PL); 770.992.9806

KENNESAW—3895 CHEROKEE ST NW (AT JILES RD NW); 770.420.9988; M-F 8-8, SA 8-5, SU 11-5

Hairy's Hair Salon ★★★★★

"...a fun atmosphere with true professionals—I've never been able to get my son to sit still the way they did... kids watch videos while driving a car and get their hair cut too... they get a sucker during the cut and a prize afterwards... fun and quick..."

Customer Service .... ❸ $ .... Prices

MARIETTA—3420 CANTON RD NE (AT PINE CIRCLE NE); 678.797.5303; T-W F 10-5, TH 1-6, SA 9-5

Kids Kuts Salon ★★★★☆

"...a cape, a car and a movie—what could be better... pleases even the trickiest of tots..."

Customer Service .... ❸ $$ .... Prices

WWW.KIDS-KUTS-SALON.COM

ACWORTH—4614 S MAIN ST (AT PARK ST NW); 678.574.5008; M-TH 10-6, F-SA 9-5

MARIETTA—2323 SHALLOWFORD RD (AT TRICKUM RD NE); 770.924.4950; M BY APPT, T-TH 10-7, F-SA 9-5

Klassic Kuts ★★★½☆

"...they are amazingly understanding and unphased about screaming kids... the movies are a good distraction... we've been going here for five years... reasonable... the first cut gets a photograph and a lock of hair... friendly staff... go during the week for the fastest service... even wiggly kids get a decent cut... cute certificate for the first cut... hours seem somewhat informal..."

Customer Service ❹ $$ Prices

ALPHARETTA—3000 OLD ALABAMA RD (AT HAYNES BRIDGE RD); 770.664.9506; T-F 9-7, SA 9-5

Kuts 4 Kids ★★★½☆

"...my son loves to sit in the airplane to get his hair cut... they work well with difficult kids... satisfaction really depends on the stylist you get... best to make an appointment... the new management equals better customer service... I like the boat seats for babies—it's a great photo op..."

Customer Service ❸ $$ Prices

ALPHARETTA—5075 ABBOTTS BRIDGE RD (AT JONES BRIDGE RD); 770.663.0606; M-F 10-5, SA 9-5

LAWRENCEVILLE—4850 SUGARLOAF PKWY NW (AT CRUSE RD NW); 770.822.6944; CALL FOR APPT

Little Scissors Hair Styling Shop ★★★★★

"...exactly what you need in a kid's shop... fast and easy... these women do a fabulous job in an amazingly short time frame... crying—actually screaming—children don't bother them in the least... the haircuts look great, too... also have a little play area..."

Customer Service ❹ $$ Prices

ATLANTA—3125 BRIARCLIFF RD NE (AT WILLIAMSBURG VILLAGE SHOPPING CTR); 404.325.1325; M-F 9-6:30, SA 8:30-5

Pigtails & Crewcuts ★★★★★

"...the styling chairs are cars, airplanes or a fire truck, which are fun and provide distraction for a 'little one' that may be apprehensive... my kids love the special pedal chairs and movies... drop-ins only... best to go in the morning when the wait is short... pricey, but worth it... staff really knows how to distract kids in order to give a good hair cut..."

Customer Service ❹ $$$ Prices

WWW.PIGTAILSANDCREWCUTS.COM

ATLANTA—3208 PACES FERRY PL NW (AT W PACES FERRY RD NW); 404.842.0383; T-SA 9:30-5:30

MARIETTA—4724 LOWER ROSWELL RD (AT JOHNSON FERRY RD NE); 770.565.8765; T-SA 9:30-5:30

Salon Red Kids ★★★★☆

Customer Service ❹ $$$ Prices

WWW.SALONRED.COM

DECATUR—123 E PONCE DE LEON AVE (AT CHURCH ST); 404.377.6230

Snip-its Haircuts For Kids ★★★★★

"...the entertainment is unbeatable... kids' haircuts without all the stress... the only place we ever go... quick, painless and relatively *cheap... they really know kids and how to keep them entertained while snipping away... they do a fabulous job... long waits (can be an hour or more) and they don't take appointments unless you join a VIP club... bubbles, videos, games and lollipops kept my daughter busy throughout the cut... patient stylists who know all the tricks to put your little one at ease... pricey, but worth it for a stylist used to squirming kids...* ”

Customer Service........................ ❹ $$$ .... Prices

WWW.SNIPITS.COM

MARIETTA—4475 ROSWELL RD (AT THE AVENUE AT EAST COBB); 770.578.4574; M-F 10-8, SA 9-8, SU 11-6; MALL PARKING

NORCROSS—4880 PEACHTREE CORNERS CIR (AT MEDLOCK BRIDGE RD NW); 770.246.0450; M-F 10-6, SA 9-6, SU 11-5; MALL PARKING

Spalding Haircutters ★★★☆☆

“*...baby got his first haircut at 11 months by the same barber who cuts Daddy's, Grandpa's, and Uncle's hair... I was a little worried, but out came the booster seat and some toys to distract him... good haircuts for all ages—even little kids...* ”

Customer Service........................ ❹ $... Prices

NORCROSS—7708 SPALDING DR (AT IVY CHASE LN); 770.447.4666

Sport Clips ★★★☆☆

“*...a sports-themed haircutter with TVs at every station... staff is friendly and they do a good job... the price is reasonable at about $12 per cut... it's not a specialty kids' salon, but it's fun coming here and the cuts generally turn out pretty good...* ”

Customer Service........................ ❹ $$ .... Prices

WWW.SPORTCLIPS.COM

ALPHARETTA—5250 WINDWARD PKWY (AT CINGULAR WY); 770.751.9665

Stylin Kids ★★★☆☆

“*...they have flat screen TVs at each station for the kids to watch movies while getting their hair cut... supervised play room for children to play in while waiting... they're the best—my son feels so at ease here... I also like that my child can play while I get a pedicure or haircut myself... free babysitting, but check the times before making an appointment... good cuts and make kids feel special...* ”

Customer Service........................ ❹ $$$ .... Prices

WWW.STYLIN-KIDS.COM

ALPHARETTA—10595 OLD ALABAMA RD CONNECTOR (AT MANSELL RD); 770.645.5779; M-F 10-6, SA 9-6

ATLANTA—4920 ROSWELL RD NE (AT LONG ISLAND DR NW); 404.303.1351; M-F 10-6, SA 9-6

nanny & babysitter referrals

Greater Atlanta Area

★★★★★

"lila picks"

★A Friend Of The Family

★Nannies And More

A Friend Of The Family ★★★★★

"...very efficient and professional... they helped me out in an emergency—a staff member stayed late to find someone to stay with my sick child... all the caregivers have been great—we've never had a problem... they only refer adults with experience..."

Baby nurses ✓	$$$ Prices
Nannies ✓	❸ Candidate selection
Au pairs ✕	❹ Staff knowledge
Babysitters ✓	❹ Customer service

Service Area ...... Greater Atlanta area

WWW.AFRIEND.COM

SMYRNA—1262 CONCORD RD SE (AT MEDLIN ST SE); 770.725.2748; CALL FOR APPT

Georgia Babysitters

Baby nurses ✕	✕ Nannies
Au pairs ✕	✓ Babysitters

Service Area ...... Georgia

WWW.GEORGIABABABYSITTERS.COM

ALPHARETTA—11770 HAYNES BRIDGE RD (AT OLD MILTON PKWY)

Homestaff ★★☆☆☆

"...professional... pleasant... prompt... quality of the sitters is variable... $12 booking fee... can always find a sitter on short notice, but I've never been overwhelmed with the sitters the service sends... service has twice sent sitters who are deathly afraid of cats to my home (and we have a cat!)..."

Baby nurses ✕	$$$ Prices
Nannies ✓	❸ Candidate selection
Au pairs ✕	❹ Staff knowledge
Babysitters ✓	❹ Customer service

Service Area ...... Greater Atlanta Area

ATLANTA—3133 MAPLE DR NE (AT E PACES FERRY RD NE); 404.364.0953; M-F 8-5, SA-SU ON CALL

Nannies And More ★★★★★

"...they'll get the job done... even though it didn't work out the first time around, they were great about working with us to find a replacement quickly... good, but pricey... if your budget will allow, I wouldn't hesitate to use them..."

Baby nurses ✓	$$$$ Prices

Nannies	✓	❹	Candidate selection
Au pairs	✗	❹	Staff knowledge
Babysitters	✗	❹	Customer service

Service AreaNationwide (focus on East Coast)

WWW.NANNIESANDMORE.COM

ATLANTA—3475 LENOX RD NE (AT PEACHTREE RD NE); 404.467.0678; CALL FOR APPT

Nanny On The Net, A ★★★½☆

"...a national agency that places experienced (at least three years) nannies... easy to use and efficient... detailed background checks... all prospects are trained in CPR... legal, financial, and practical help for first-time 'employer' families... about $75 for the application fee and then additional placement fees when you succeed in finding a nanny..."

Baby nurses	✓	$$$	Prices
Nannies	✓	❷	Candidate selection
Au pairs	✗	❸	Staff knowledge
Babysitters	✗	❷	Customer service

Service Area....... Greater Atlanta area

WWW.ANANNYONTHENET.COM

ATLANTA—404.816.2337; M-F 9-5

Nanny Solutions ★★★☆☆

"...they place nannies on a live-out basis for full- or part-time positions with a one-year contract... dependable... reasonably priced..."

Baby nurses	✓	$$$	Prices
Nannies	✓	❸	Candidate selection
Au pairs	✗	❸	Staff knowledge
Babysitters	✗	❸	Customer service

ATLANTA—356 5TH ST NE (AT DURANT PL NE); 404.607.7709; M-F 10-4

Premier Domestic Staffing ★★★☆☆

"...not as pricey as the other agencies and had a lot of good CVs to review..."

Baby nurses	✓	$$	Prices
Nannies	✓	❹	Candidate selection
Au pairs	✗	❹	Staff knowledge
Babysitters	✗	❹	Customer service

WWW.PREMIERDOMESTICSTAFFING.COM

ROSWELL—300 COLONIAL CENTER PKWY (AT MANSELL RD); 770.704.9515; M-F 8:30-5:30

TLC Sitters Of Atlanta ★★★½☆

"...pricier than finding a babysitter yourself, but the service is hassle-free and caregivers are experienced and very friendly... membership fee plus an annual fee... great availability of sitters 7 days a week, 24 hours a day... worth every penny to know that you are covered in a pinch..."

Baby nurses	✓	$$$$	Prices
Nannies	✓	❸	Candidate selection
Au pairs	✗	❹	Staff knowledge
Babysitters	✓	❹	Customer service

Service Area........ all of Atlanta Metro

WWW.TLCSITTERSOFATLANTA.COM

SMYRNA—1258 CONCORD RD SE (BTWN CONCORD & ATLANTA); 770.435.6250; M-F 9-5:30

Online

★★★★★

"lila picks"

★craigslist.org

4nannies.com

Baby nurses .... ✗ ✓ .... Nannies
Au pairs .... ✗ ✗ .... Babysitters
Service Area .... nationwide
WWW.4NANNIES.COM

aupaircare.com

Baby nurses .... ✗ ✗ .... Nannies
Au pairs .... ✓ ✗ .... Babysitters
Service Area .... International
WWW.AUPAIRCARE.COM

aupairinamerica.com

Baby nurses .... ✗ ✗ .... Nannies
Au pairs .... ✓ ✗ .... Babysitters
Service Area .... International
WWW.AUPAIRINAMERICA.COM

babysitters.com

Baby nurses .... ✗ ✗ .... Nannies
Au pairs .... ✗ ✓ .... Babysitters
Service Area .... nationwide
WWW.BABYSITTERS.COM

craigslist.org ★★★★★

"...you can find just about anything on craigslist... good starting point, especially if you don't want to spend a lot of money and are willing to do your own screening... we received at least 50 responses to our 'nanny wanted' ad... helped me find very qualified baby-sitters... includes all major cities in the US..."

Baby nurses .... ✓ ✓ .... Nannies
Au pairs .... ✗ ✓ .... Babysitters
WWW.CRAIGSLIST.ORG

enannysource.com

Baby nurses .... ✗ ✓ .... Nannies
Au pairs .... ✗ ✗ .... Babysitters
Service Area .... nationwide
WWW.ENANNYSOURCE.COM

findcarenow.com

Baby nurses .... ✗ ✗ .... Nannies
Au pairs .... ✗ ✓ .... Babysitters
Service Area .... nationwide

WWW.FINDCARENOW.COM

get-a-sitter.com

Baby nurses	×	×	Nannies
Au pairs	×	✓	Babysitters

Service Area .... nationwide

WWW.GET-A-SITTER.COM

householdstaffing.com

Baby nurses	✓	✓	Nannies
Au pairs	×	×	Babysitters

WWW.HOUSEHOLDSTAFFING.COM

interexchange.org

Baby nurses	×	×	Nannies
Au pairs	✓	×	Babysitters

Service Area .... International

WWW.INTEREXCHANGE.ORG

nannies4hire.com

Baby nurses	×	✓	Nannies
Au pairs	×	×	Babysitters

WWW.NANNIES4HIRE.COM

nannylocators.com

★★★½☆

"...many listings of local nannies available... I have found that the listings are not always up to date... $100 subscriber fee to respond and contact nannies that have posted... different regions have varying amounts of listings available..."

Baby nurses	×	✓	Nannies
Au pairs	×	×	Babysitters

Service Area .... Nationwide

WWW.NANNYLOCATORS.COM

sittercity.com

★★★★☆

"...Wonderful online resource... an online baby-sitter database filled with mostly college and graduate students looking for baby-sitting and nanny jobs... candidates are not prescreened so you must check references... Fee to access the database is $35 plus $5 per month... tends to be be more useful for baby-sitters than regular daytime nannies..."

Baby nurses	×	×	Nannies
Au pairs	×	✓	Babysitters

Service Area .... nationwide

WWW.SITTERCITY.COM

student-sitters.com

Baby nurses	×	×	Nannies
Au pairs	×	✓	Babysitters

WWW.STUDENT-SITTERS.COM

photographers

Greater Atlanta Area

★★★★★

"lila picks"

- ★Ann Erdenberger Photographer
- ★Celebrity Kids Portrait Studio
- ★Curt Davis Photography
- ★Ellen Koransky Photography
- ★Kiddie Kandids
- ★Potraits By Wendy

Ann Erdenberger Photographer ★★★★★

"...she is great with children and her work is phenomenal... she takes beautiful pictures without resorting to the cheesy props that other studios use... the pictures are very classy and we look at our 'first year' album frequently..."

Customer service........................❺ $$$$.................................... Prices

Service Area ...... Greater Atlanta area

WWW.ANNERDENBERGER.COM

ATLANTA—404.358.1826; CALL FOR APPT

Celebrity Kids Portrait Studio ★★★★★

"...fast and fabulous kid shots... computerized photos means you get to see and choose your pictures immediately... no negatives so make plenty of copies... they are willing to incorporate your ideas and props to personalize the portrait... the session can feel rushed, but the photos still come out great..."

Customer service........................❹ $$$$.................................... Prices

WWW.CELEBRITYKIDS.COM

MARIETTA—50 BARRETT PKWY (AT BELLS FERRY RD NE); 770.428.5437; CALL FOR APPT

Curt Davis Photography ★★★★★

"...Curt is a photographer without bounds... his black and whites are magic and his color shots are simple, direct and powerful... you won't get a picture, you will get a work of art... pricey, but absolutely fantastic..."

Customer service........................❸ $$$...................................... Prices

Service Area ...... Greater Atlanta area

WWW.CURTISDAVISPHOTO.COM

ATLANTA—659 AUBURN AVE (AT IRWIN AVE); 404.521.2312; CALL FOR APPT

DayC Photography ★★★★½

"...they have done all our family photography—engagement, wedding, pregnancy, and christening... Debbie will go to the location of your choice or work with you in her studio... if your kid needs to eat or calm down from a tantrum or get cleaned up after a messy diaper she'll wait... her goal is beautiful photos for happy clients and that's what you get... rates are per session and they aren't adjusted upward for certain occasions or multiple subjects like many other photographers... they're not the cheapest photographers out there, but they are worth every penny..."

Customer service .... ❺ $$$ .... Prices

Service Area....... Greater Atlanta area

WWW.DAYCPHOTOGRAPHY.COM

ATLANTA—5125 FOXWOOD CRT (AT KINGSLAND DR); 678.265.4030; CALL FOR APPT

Diane Douglass Photography ★★★★☆

"...great with kids... she has a talent for capturing their personalities... very reasonable pricing... Diane works with the child on the child's terms... she is patient and really captures the most expressive photos... she also came to our house to make sure our daughter was as comfortable as possible..."

Customer service .... ❺ $$ .... Prices

Service Area....... Greater Atlanta area

ATLANTA—966 EULALIA RD (AT ROXBORO RD NE); 404.816.6478; CALL FOR APPT

Ellen Koransky Photography ★★★★★

"...Ellen portrays each child's personality... fun props for hilarious Ann Geddes-type pictures... black and white and color, indoor or beautiful outside garden settings... not rushed or hurried... flexible enough to accommodate my working mom's schedule... kids love her and cooperate with her... produces beautiful photos, from playful to formal... patient, creative and professional..."

Customer service .... ❹ $$$ .... Prices

Service Area....... Greater Atlanta area

WWW.KORANSKY.COM/ELLEN

ATLANTA—6235 RIVER CHASE CIR NW (AT FERRY LANDING NW); 770.952.9652; CALL FOR APPT

Haigwood Studios Photography

WWW.HAIGWOODSTUDIOS.COM

ROSWELL—565 S ATLANTA ST (AT MARIETTA HWY); 770.594.7845

Harry's Photography Studio

ATLANTA—42 FORSYTH ST NW (AT LUCKIE ST NW); 404.688.2815; M-SA 11-5

Hollywood Shot ★★★★☆

"...great shots... my daughter likes to laugh with this guy... some kids act like they do not want to smile when they get in front of a camera, but when the camera guy got behind the camera and did that little baby thing, my daughter went crazy... photos came out great..."

Customer service .... ❺ $$ .... Prices

ATLANTA—2841 GREENBRIAR PKWY SW (AT HEADLAND DR); 404.344.2449; M-SA 10-9, SU 12-6

JCPenney Portrait Studio ★★★½☆

"...don't expect works of art, but they are great for a quick wallet photo... photographers and staff range from great to not so good... a quick portrait with standard props and backdrops... definitely join the portrait club and use coupons... waits are especially long around the holidays, so consider taking your Christmas pictures early... the e-picture option is a time saver... wait time for prints can be up to a month... look for coupons and you'll never have to pay full price..."

Customer service........................❹ $$..Prices

WWW.JCPENNEYPORTRAITS.COM

ALPHARETTA—2000 NORTH POINT CIR (AT NORTH POINT MALL); 770.475.9850; M-SA 10-9, SU 12-6; MALL PARKING

ATLANTA—1400 CUMBERLAND MALL (AT COBB PKWY); 770.434.2561; M-SA 10-9, SU 12-6; MALL PARKING

ATLANTA—4840 BRIARCLIFF RD NE (AT NORTHLAKE SHOPPING CTR); 770.934.8111; M-SA 10-9, SU 11-7; MALL PARKING

LITHONIA—8040 MALL PKWY (AT TURNER HILL RD); 770.484.5604; M-SA 10-9, SU 12-6; MALL PARKING

MORROW—1400 SOUTHLAKE MALL (AT MORROW INDUSTRIAL BLVD); 770.961.8381; M-T SA 10-7, W-F 12-8, SU 12-5; MALL PARKING

Judith Ann Photography ★★★☆☆

"...Judith Ann specializes in pregnancy, newborn, child, and family portraits, along with others... very professional, elegant, and spends a lot of time planning on the way it will look with you... wonderful results—breathtaking photos..."

Customer service........................❸ $$$......................................Prices

Service Area ...... Greater Atlanta area

WWW.JUDITHANNPHOTOGRAPHY.COM

POWDER SPRINGS—4217 MARIETTA ST (AT NEW MACLAND RD SW); 770.222.1577; CALL FOR APPT

Kiddie Kandids ★★★★★

"...good quality photos for all occasions... they made a big effort to get a smile out of my grumpy son... you don't need to make a reservation, just pop in and have the pictures taken... no sitting fee... photographers take the extra time necessary to get a great shot and they have the cutest props... lots of items to buy with your pictures on them—cups, bags, mouse pads... buy the CD of pictures rather than buying the prints... pictures are available right after the sitting..."

Customer service........................❹ $$$......................................Prices

WWW.KIDDIEKANDIDS.COM

ALPHARETTA—6380 NORTH POINT PKWY (AT NORTH POINT CT); 678.762.0094; M-SA 9:30-8:30, SU 11-6

DULUTH—3925 VENTURE DR (AT STEVE REYNOLDS BLVD NW); 678.584.1200; M-SA 9:30-8, SU 11-6

DUNWOODY—1155 MT VERNON HWY (AT NORTHSIDE DR NW); 770.394.1747; M-SA 9:30-8:30, SU 11-6

KENNESAW—1875 GREERS CHAPEL RD (AT LAKES BLVD NW); 770.426.0560; M-SA 9:30-8:30, SU 11-6

Kristen Alexander Photography ★★★★★

"...takes pictures on location, not in a studio... she took excellent pictures—very high quality and very charming... she was very good at working with my difficult family... she met us on the location we chose... kind of expensive though..."

Customer service........................❺ $$$$....................................Prices

WWW.KRISTENPHOTO.COM

DECATUR—404.296.9161

Lightscapes Photographic Artwork ★★★☆☆

"...good prices and lots of options for baby photos... cute, creative displays for taking baby photos... very nice and natural looking, with a timeless look..."

Customer service .... ❸ $$$ .... Prices

WWW.LIGHTSCAPESPHOTO.COM

DULUTH—3883 ROGERS BRIDGE RD NW (AT HIGHBROOKE TRL NW); 770.623.1040; CALL FOR APPT

Markle Studio

Service Area....... Greater Atlanta area

WWW.MARKLEPORTRAITS.COM

ACWORTH—1280 ROLLING GREEN DR NW (AT WILLOW TARN); 770.928.1256; CALL FOR APPT

Memory Cottage Portrait Studio, The ★★★★½

"...sweet portraits... either in their cool studio, or at a location of your choice... natural pictures and backgrounds... unique and precious images... very professional and the results are spectacular..."

Customer service .... ❹ $$$ .... Prices

Service Area....... Greater Atlanta area

WWW.THEMEMORYCOTTAGE.COM

FAYETTEVILLE—110 GENEVIEVE CT (AT HIGHWAY 54); 770.631.7676; M-F 9-5, SA BY APPT ONLY

Olan Mills Portrait Studio ★★★☆☆

"...cheap packages and lots of specials—check their web site often... located in most K-mart and Big K stores... you can choose various finishes, from matte to glossy or antique... great props... most photographers are accommodating and will set up a variety of backgrounds for you... you pay extra if you want more than one pose..."

Customer service .... ❹ $$$ .... Prices

WWW.OLANMILLS.COM

KENNESAW—425 ERNEST BARRETT PKWY (AT TOWN CENTER AT COBB); 770.424.2238; W-SA 10-6:30, SU 1-4:30

SNELLVILLE—2400 WISTERIA DR SW (AT MAIN ST EAST SW); 770.978.2433

Photographic Concepts ★★★★½

"...excellent service... complimentary newborn session within first eight weeks of birth... baby footsteps program reasonably priced... specialty is black and white, but color is exquisite as well... completely focused on my son, allowed plenty of time and were very flexible... expensive, but truly outstanding work..."

Customer service .... ❺ $$$$ .... Prices

Service Area....... Greater Atlanta area

WWW.LIFELOVEIMAGES.COM

PEACHTREE CITY—101 CROSSINGS E (AT HWY 54 AND PEACHTREE PKWY); 770.486.5407; CALL FOR APPT

Picture People ★★★½☆

"...this well-known photography chain offers good package deals that get even better with coupons... generally friendly staff despite the often 'uncooperative' little customers... they don't produce super fancy,

artistic shots, but you get your pictures in under an hour... reasonable quality for a fast portrait... kind of hit-or-miss quality and customer service... ❞

Customer service........................❹ $$$....................................Prices

WWW.PICTUREPEOPLE.COM

ALPHARETTA—1094 NORTH POINT CIR (AT NORTH POINT MALL); 770.754.9304; M-SA 10-9, SU 12-6; MALL PARKING

ATLANTA—3333 BUFORD DR NE (AT MALL OF GEORGIA); 770.831.1211; M-SA 10-9, SU 12-6

BUFORD—MALL OF GEORGIA (AT NORTHEAST PLAZA FASHION SQUARE); 770.831.1211; M-SA 10-9, SU 12-6

DOUGLASVILLE—6700 DOUGLAS BLVD (AT ARBOR PLACE MALL); 770.920.1319; M-SA 10-9, SU 12-6

DULUTH—2100 PLEASANT HILL RD (AT GWINNETT PLACE MALL); 770.232.8660; M-SA 10-9, SU 12-6; MALL PARKING

KENNESAW—400 ERNEST BARRETT PKWY NW (AT TOWN CENTER AT COBB); 770.421.1482; MALL PARKING

LITHONIA—2929 TURNER HILL RD (AT STONECREST PKWY); 770.482.1438; M-SA 10-9, SU 12-6

Picture Perfect Photography ★★★★★

❝*...the option of studio or outdoor shots... we will keep going back for years to come... the pictures of our 3-month-old are a treasure... their photo tips really made the portraits wonderful...* ❞

Customer service........................❺ $$$$...................................Prices

WWW.ATLANTA-PHOTOGRAPHY.COM

ROSWELL—875 OLD ROSWELL RD (AT OLD FORGE DR); 770.993.7129; CALL FOR APPT

Portraits By Wendy ★★★★★

❝*...wonderful portraits... beach, snow or studio shots... subtle, delicate color... Wendy worked beautifully with our active kids, and was so patient... we loved being able to view our pictures online... the best pictures I've ever had...* ❞

Customer service........................❺ $$$....................................Prices

Service Area ...... Greater Atlanta area

WWW.PORTRAITSBYWENDY.COM

BUFORD—37 E MAIN ST (AT GARNETT ST); 770.831.0922; CALL FOR APPT

Sears Portrait Studio ★★★☆☆

❝*...the price is right, but the service and quality are variable... make an appointment to cut down on the wait time... bring your coupons for even better prices... perfect for getting a nice wallet size portrait without spending a fortune... I wish the wait time for prints wasn't so long (2 weeks)... the quality and service-orientation of the photographers really vary a lot—some are great, some aren't...* ❞

Customer service........................❸ $$.......................................Prices

WWW.SEARSPORTRAIT.COM

ALPHARETTA—1000 NORTH POINT CIR (AT NORTH POINT MALL); 770.667.6736; MALL PARKING

ATLANTA—1850 S W AVE (AT KASIA); 770.433.7420; M W TH-F 10-8, T 10-6, SA 9-6, SU 11-6

ATLANTA—2201 HENDERSON MILL RD NE (AT NORTHLAKE SHOPPING MALL); 770.939.8254

DOUGLASVILLE—6580 DOUGLAS BLVD (AT ARBOR PLACE MALL); 770.577.5269; M-T 10-6, W-SA 10-8, SU 11-6; MALL PARKING

DULUTH—2100 PLEASANT HILL RD (AT GWINNETT PLACE MALL); 770.476.6636; M-F 10-8, SA 9-8, SU 11-7; MALL PARKING

KENNESAW—400 EARNEST BARRETT PKWY (AT TOWN CENTER AT COBB); 770.429.4136; M-F 10-8, SA 9-8, SU 11-6

LITHONIA—8020 MALL PKWY (AT TURTLEHILL RD); 678.629.5069; M-SA 9-8, SU 11-6; MALL PARKING

MORROW—1300 SOUTHLAKE MALL (AT MORROW INDUSTRIAL BLVD); 770.968.2235; M W TH-F 10-8, T 10-6, SA 10-6, SU 11-6; MALL PARKING

UNION CITY—600 SHANNON MALL (AT JONESBORO RD); 770.969.3346; M-F 10-8, T 10-6, SA 9-6, SU 12-6; MALL PARKING

Sutherland Photography

WWW.SUTHERLANDPHOTO.COM

MARIETTA—770.517.2363; CALL FOR APPT

Target Portrait Studio ★★★☆☆

“...no sitting fee, reasonable prices (especially with the frequent buyers club), a shopping trip for me and the digital preview system for immediate gratification... pretty hit or miss with the photographer—some are patient and others are not... lots of backgrounds to choose from... even with an appointment we often have to wait... we've gotten some great pictures, enough to share with the entire extended family...”

Customer service .... ❹ $$ .... Prices

WWW.TARGET.COM

DULUTH—3935 VENTURE DR (AT STEVE REYNOLDS BLVD NW); 770.232.1929; M-SA 8-10, SU 8-9; PARKING IN FRONT OF BLDG

STONE MOUNTAIN—2055 W PARK PLACE BLVD (AT BERMUDA RD); 770.465.7873; M 10-2, T 10-7, F 10-6, SA 10-4, SU 12-4

Wittmayer Photographers ★★★☆☆

“...I liked some of what they did for us... our mother/son portrait was done with kind of a strange background... my son's best picture was one taken while I was changing his outfit and he found the little piano...”

Customer service .... ❹ $$$$ .... Prices

Service Area....... Greater Atlanta area

WWW.WITTMAYER.COM

ATLANTA—4360 GEORGETOWN SQ (AT OLD SPRINGHOUSE LN); 770.936.8730; T-F 10-6, SA BY APPT ONY

Wolf Camera ★★★★☆

“...this portrait studio is great!.. the photographers are very talented and friendly... they are very good at getting those wonderful smiles that all parents look for... I love the way they do their portraits; you get that expensive look without having to pay too much... you feel like you are in control and you don't feel pressured to buy more then you can afford...”

Customer service .... ❹ $$$ .... Prices

WWW.WOLFCAMERA.COM

ATLANTA—8725 ROSWELL RD (AT DUNWOODY PLACE); 770.518.6527

Online

clubphoto.com

WWW.CLUBPHOTO.COM

dotphoto.com

WWW.DOTPHOTO.COM

flickr.com

WWW.FLICKR.COM

kodakgallery.com ★★★★½

“...the popular ofoto.com is now under it's wings... very easy to use desktop software to upload your pictures on their site... prints, books, mugs and other photo gifts are reasonably priced and are always shipped promptly... I like that there is no limit to how many pictures and albums you can have their site...”

WWW.KODAKGALLERY.COM

photoworks.com

WWW.PHOTOWORKS.COM

shutterfly.com ★★★★½

“...I've spent hundreds of dollars with them—it's so easy and the quality of the pictures is great... they use really nice quality photo paper... what a lifesaver—since I store all of my pictures with them I didn't lose any when my computer crashed... most special occasions are take care of with a personal photo calendar, book or other item with the cutest pictures of our kids... reasonable prices...”

WWW.SHUTTERFLY.COM

snapfish.com ★★★★☆

“...great photo quality and never a problem with storage limits... we love their photo books and flip books—easy to make and fun to give... good service and a good price... we have family that lives all over the country and yet everyone still gets to see and order pictures of our new baby...”

WWW.SNAPFISH.COM

indexes

alphabetical

by city/neighborhood

alphabetical

participate in our survey at

by city/neighborhood

Austell

Avondale Estates

Buford

Lilburn

Lithia Springs

Lithonia

Loganville

Marietta

Notes

YOUR RECOMMENDATIONS MAKE THE LILAGUIDE BETTER!
PLEASE SHARE YOUR NOTES WITH US AT WWW.LILAGUIDE.COM

Notes

YOUR RECOMMENDATIONS MAKE THE LILAGUIDE BETTER!
PLEASE SHARE YOUR NOTES WITH US AT WWW.LILAGUIDE.COM

Notes

YOUR RECOMMENDATIONS MAKE THE LILAGUIDE BETTER!
PLEASE SHARE YOUR NOTES WITH US AT WWW.LILAGUIDE.COM

Notes

YOUR RECOMMENDATIONS MAKE THE LILAGUIDE BETTER!
PLEASE SHARE YOUR NOTES WITH US AT WWW.LILAGUIDE.COM

Notes

YOUR RECOMMENDATIONS MAKE THE LILAGUIDE BETTER!
PLEASE SHARE YOUR NOTES WITH US AT WWW.LILAGUIDE.COM

Notes

YOUR RECOMMENDATIONS MAKE THE LILAGUIDE BETTER!
PLEASE SHARE YOUR NOTES WITH US AT WWW.LILAGUIDE.COM

Notes

YOUR RECOMMENDATIONS MAKE THE LILAGUIDE BETTER!
PLEASE SHARE YOUR NOTES WITH US AT WWW.LILAGUIDE.COM

Notes

YOUR RECOMMENDATIONS MAKE THE LILAGUIDE BETTER!
PLEASE SHARE YOUR NOTES WITH US AT WWW.LILAGUIDE.COM